UNDERSTANDING A/S ACCOUNTING FOR AQA

MANCHESTER 1824
Manchester University Press

UNDERSTANDINGS

Series editor **DUNCAN WATTS**

Following the review of the national curriculum for 16–19-year-olds, UK examining boards introduced new specifications, first used in 2001 and 2002. A-level courses are now divided into A/S level for the first year of sixth form studies, and the more difficult A2 level thereafter. The **Understandings** series comprehensively covers the syllabuses of all the major examination boards, featuring dedicated A/S- and A2 level textbooks. The books are written in an accessible, user-friendly and jargon-free manner and will be essential to students sitting these examinations.

Already published

Understanding political ideas and movements
Kevin Harrison and Tony Boyd

Understanding British and European political issues
Neil McNaughton

Understanding American government and politics
Duncan Watts

Understanding US/UK government and politics
Duncan Watts

Understanding A/S level government and politics
Chris Wilson

Understanding A/S Accounting for AQA

JEREMY RENALS

Manchester University Press
Manchester and New York

distributed exclusively in the USA by Palgrave

Published by Manchester University Press
Oxford Road, Manchester M13 9NR, UK
and Room 400, 175 Fifth Avenue, New York, NY 10010, USA
www.manchesteruniversitypress.co.uk

Distributed exclusively in the USA by
Palgrave, 175 Fifth Avenue, New York,
NY 10010, USA

Distribued exclusively in Canada by
UBC Press, University of British Columbia, 2029 West Mall,
Vancouver, BC, Canada V6T 1Z2

British Library Cataloguing-in-Publication Data
A catalogue record for this book is available from the British Library

Library of Congress Cataloging-in-Publication Data applied for

ISBN 0 7190 7419 3 *paperback*
EAN 978 0 7190 7419 6

First published 2006

15 14 13 12 11 10 09 08 07 06 10 9 8 7 6 5 4 3 2 1

Typeset
by Northern Phototypesetting Co. Ltd, Bolton
Printed in Great Britain
by CPI, Bath

Account (often in pl.): 'a record or statement of money, goods or services received or expended, with the balance'. (*Oxford Compact English Dictionary*)

All companies used in examples and questions in this book are fictitious. Every care has been taken to ensure that names of real companies have not been used, and any similarity between names of businesses in this book and any real business or entity is accidental and entirely coincidental.

Questions marked (E) are taken from past AQA examinations and are reproduced by permission of the Assessment and Qualifications Alliance.

For my friend Jenny

Contents

Introduction

MATHEMATICS, AND DOING THE WASHING UP

Maths is quite useful in accounting, but it's better if you can do the washing up. Why is this?

Well, in Unit 1 you should be able to add up accurately, but skill with the + button on a calculator is mostly sufficient. In Unit 3 there are some simple processes like dividing by 3 or calculating a percentage. Unit 4 requires you to learn some formulae for calculating profits and so on, and can demand logic and reason.

What's more important, however, is being able to look at the information, and put the right number in the right place.

If your mother does the drying up and hands you some wine glasses, where do they go? Do they go in a different place from tumblers? And what about plates? How about the plates you only use on special occasions – do they go somewhere different? And your father is very fussy about cutlery handles pointing away from you, except for knives when they should point towards you.

Any accountant reading this section should be nodding with recognition. Organisation like this is more important than learning vectors and differential equations. Equally important is to have as much relevant practice as possible at the processes and calculations that you're likely to use.

HOW TO TACKLE THE EXAM

Really learn the most predictable topics (i.e. documents and VAT), and the topics that get you lots of marks (i.e. Trading and Profit and Loss Accounts).

Do the easy questions first. If you like adding numbers, do the adding numbers questions. If you prefer writing facts, do the question on computers in accounting.

Read the question carefully, be clear, and don't spend ages on Question 2 if it's a pig worth 8%, when Question 5 might be a walk in the park worth 18%. For example, there's a question right at the end of the Unit 3 paper for Summer 2003 offering 16% for an 8-minute calculation. For sure you have to learn how to pick out the relevant information from the snow-storm on offer, but if you've learned all the rules it's not too hard.

Most importantly of all, practise, practise, practise. This book isn't a cheat for avoiding work. No such cheat exists. What it does is show you how to focus your effort on getting the best score possible. The more you repeat your work, the better your score will be.

Download every paper available from www.aqa.org.uk and get good at all of them. See p. 24 for the full address.

What does ^{A} mean on the titles in this book?

On some sections of this book there's an ^{A} in the title. This means 'don't go for an A grade yet if you're not sure you've got a C or a B nailed right down'.

These are trickier sections. If you're struggling with what you've already done then go back and try again; this bit isn't any easier. I know it's heresy to say it, but some of you just want a pass so you can get on to another course. To save your energy, don't attempt the sections with ^{A} in the title, and sacrifice those marks in the exam.

HOW EXAMINERS MARK

When I did my degree course, I started each module by copying all of the exam papers from the library so I could see what I was aiming at. If they'd been available, I'd have copied the marking guides as well.

Well, lucky you. Both papers and marking guides for the last few years are available to download from the AQA site:
www.aqa.org.uk/qual/gceasa/acc_assess.html

If you can't remember the whole web address, go to www.aqa.org.uk, and follow Qualifications > GCE AS/A > Accounting, and click on the Assessment Material link at the top of the page.

I suggest that when you complete a paper you mark it as an examiner would before trying the next one.

Get the facts right first and you'll be on to a good start. Make sure you're solid on the:

- Formulae
- Vocabulary
- Definitions
- Layouts
- Calculations

and you'll be on the way. And don't forget to get everything the right way round in the Hall of Mirrors, and to get the system right for any adjustments.

Do learn the material. Waffle and bodgery don't fool anyone. Show what you know, and the examiner will give you credit for what's there. You can still score well even if it's not perfect. You won't lose marks for extra incorrect work, although you won't be doing yourself any favours either.

Try to follow the layouts in the book, although there will be variations in some cases. For example, there's more than one way to use the three columns in a Balance Sheet. The examiner can tell if you've used a meaningful system of presentation (so don't just make up your own), and make your totals and subtotals especially clear.

Own figure rule

Don't worry if you think your bottom line result is wrong. Yes, in business you should get it perfect. However, in the exam you may just have made one error somewhere in the calculation, and you'll only lose a mark for that error. Still, you should present your calculations clearly throughout, with labels where appropriate, to make it easy for the examiner to find the mistake, and to award you marks for the correct work you have done before and after it.

Quality of written communication

While we're on the subject, there are extra marks available for written communication. Clarity is worth up to 5%, which could bump you up a grade, as well as giving the examiner the impression of careful, ordered thinking.

This mark includes credit for good English, but in particular you should aim for:

- Correct, well-organised presentation and layouts
- Logical workings
- Clear explanations and arguments (start with the relevant definitions and facts, and develop them)
- Appropriate names, terms and vocabulary

You may want to jot down an answer like it's on the back of an envelope, but don't forget that this is accounting. Clarity is an essential, not just in the exam but in accounting in general. Examiners will give credit for good presentation, and taking the time to keep your words clear and your columns straight is all it takes.

It may sound like boot camp, but a tidy exam paper is usually a good exam paper.

Note: For the AQA A/S level, you need Unit 1 or Unit 2, plus Units 3 and 4. If you might go on to complete A2, it's recommended you do Unit 1. Please check that you're studying the correct programme of units.

Unit 1

FINANCIAL ACCOUNTING: the accounting information system

The Hall of Mirrors: reflections in accounting 1.1

Financial accounting is all about measuring the money that moves in and out of a business. In Unit 1 we look at the ways we write down the movement of money, and add it all up at the end. At the heart of the way we write down the movement of money is what accountants call the dual aspect concept – or what we can call the Hall of Mirrors.

POINTS TO CONSIDER:

- What are assets and liabilities, and what is capital?
- What is 'double entry'?
- If a debit entry increases an asset, how do we decrease one?
- If a credit entry increases a liability, how do we decrease one?
- If a building is good and a bill is bad, why are they both debit entries?
- If sales are good and creditors are bad, why are they both credit entries?
- Why isn't there a single account for stock? What do we use instead?
- What is a Trial Balance?
- What financial statements can be made from it?

Welcome to the Hall of Mirrors. It's unfortunate that we have to play 'Alice Through the Looking Glass' as soon as we start accounting, but get the hang of it and it makes everything else easier.

Accounting is about listing the money moving into and out of a business. Think of accounts appearing in big books called ledgers, with a page for everything a business buys or sells. Each page is an account. An account will have a left-hand side called debit or 'Dr' and a right hand side called credit or 'Cr'.

Every time you list some money on the debit side of one account, you must also list it on the credit side of another account, and vice versa (this is called 'double entry').

Bank

Dr			*Cr*		
1 Mar	Capital	50,000			

Capital

Dr			*Cr*		
			1 Mar	Bank	50,000

Figuring out which side to put the money is something you will have to learn. It's like a Hall of Mirrors – reflections everywhere.

Now, it's natural to want to think 'left side good, right side bad' or something similarly simple. You will certainly find short cuts to help you. However, when you are tested you will come unstuck if you rely on them. Double entry is a principle that will really help you sort out any problem you face in your exam. Get familiar with it.

1.1.1 ASSETS, LIABILITIES AND CAPITAL

You can navigate the Hall of Mirrors if you remember that accounts measure:

- What a business owns, and
- What a business owes; both to
  1. Other businesses, and
  2. The owners of the business.

- What a business buys, or owns, is called **assets**. Assets can include buildings and machines, money in the bank, and services like electricity.
- What it owes to other businesses is called **liabilities**.
- What it owes to the owners is called **capital**, which is the money originally put in by the **proprietor** or **shareholders**, plus the profit made.

> **proprietor**
> Owner of a business
> **shareholder**
> Owner of a share of a company

This brings us to the accounting equation:

assets = liabilities + capital

You must get your approach to accounting right. Don't think like the owner, who wants to see how much capital he has. For the everyday mechanics of accounting you must put this out of your mind. Accounts measure the money from the point of view of the business. For a business, it's about 'assets' and 'not-assets'. That's it.

Study these lists of assets, liabilities and capital items. If you can't distinguish an asset from a liability you'll be lost.

asset
Property that has value, for example in meeting debts. Something bought and owned by a business.

liability
A debt that a business is required to pay.

capital
The owners' money, for example when used to start a business. Note: this is an especially tricky term to understand. It can mean money loaned to help a business, or even, in economics, assets bought for a business. For now, it means money belonging to the owner or owners.

Examples of asset accounts

Assets, remember, are things the business buys or owns. There are 'current assets'; think of them as part of the money flowing through the business.

- (Money in the) bank
- (Money owed by) **debtors**
- Stock (goods to be sold on, e.g. purchases and returned goods)
- Prepayments – things you've paid for but haven't used yet, e.g. next month's rent

debtors
People or firms who owe you money. If you sell to someone on credit, the money due is yours, even if it's still in their bank account. You are their creditor.

And there are 'fixed assets'. These are bought to be kept and used.

- Buildings
- Vehicles
- Computers
- Fixtures and furniture

Then there are '**expenses**'. These are treated as assets.

- Fuel and power
- Wages
- Interest
- Discounts Allowed
- Depreciation (we'll learn about this in Unit 3)

expense
Money paid. Think of it as the cost of something that has now gone, rather than what you buy, like a shiny new delivery van.

Although an account for an expense seems like money going out of the business, it actually represents something bought by the business. 'Electricity', for example, is the account for the electricity you've bought, not for the money you've paid for it or what you owe the electricity company. Your payments and debts, as we shall see, are the reflections on the credit sides of other accounts.

However, as you'll see, we use the account for 'electricity' to count the money paid for this expense.

Examples of liability accounts

Liabilities, remember, represent outside debts.

There are 'current liabilities' – again, think of money flowing through the business:

- (Money owed to) **creditors** who want paying soon
- Suppliers who sold us stock on credit (buy-now-pay-later)
- Bank overdraft – our bank account is negative and we owe the bank money

creditor
A person or a firm who wants money from you. If you buy from someone on credit, the money due is theirs, even if it's still in your bank. You are their debtor.

And there are long-term liabilities:

- Long-term loans
- Mortgage – a loan to buy a building
- Debenture (another loan – we'll learn about this later)

Note that the 'loan' itself is a liability; the money you've borrowed is in the bank and is an asset. Think also of VAT as a liability account, since a VAT-registered business owes VAT to the government.

Examples of capital accounts

Capital is what the owner can claim.

- Capital/ordinary capital/preference capital (money invested by the owner/proprietor/shareholders)
- Share premium account (extra money raised when shares are sold)
- General reserve
- Drawings is money taken out by the owner/proprietor, but is treated as a Capital account
- Profit kept in the company is capital

This last one is important: remember that profit is added to capital. It's the reason you're in business.

Which side is which?

Here's how to deal with each type of account, and find your way through the Hall of Mirrors. This information is vital.

If an account is an asset, add by putting a number on the debit side (left), take away by putting a number on the credit side (right).

An Asset account

Dr							Cr
			Add money here				Subtract money here

If the account is a liability or capital, do it in reverse: subtract by putting a number on the debit side (left), and add by putting a number on the credit side (right).

A Liability or Capital account

Dr							Cr
			Subtract money here				Add money here

The easiest way to understand double entry is to think like this:

Debit side entries for more assets, less liabilities and less capital

Credit side entries for less assets, more liabilities and more capital

For each entry, consider what you're actually recording. And remember, we always put an amount in the left column of one account *and* in the right column of another. Label each entry with a date, and a reference to the other half of the double entry.

Here are some examples.

Example 1

We buy a van from Joe's Garage for £10,000 on credit.

The van is an asset, so we increase the debit/left side of the Vehicles account. But the money we still owe for the van is a liability, so we increase the credit/right side of the 'Joe's Garage' account.

General Ledger Page 4

Vehicles

Dr							*Cr*
16 Feb 09	Joe's Garage	PL7	10,000				

Purchases Ledger Page 7

Joe's Garage

Dr							*Cr*
				16 Feb 09	Vehicles	GL4	10,000

Dates and folios

See how we also have a column with the date, and a column (called a folio column) with some strange code in it. Although we have the name of the other account, we don't know where it is. The folio column tells us: PL7 means that the account for Joe's Garage is in the Purchases Ledger, page 7. GL4 means that we keep the Vehicles account on page 4 of the General Ledger (we'll learn more about ledgers in section 1.2.1). Folio columns direct you to more information in the accounts.

Example 2

We pay £1,000 towards the van by standing order from the bank.

This is the opposite. By paying for the van we are reducing our liability to Joe's, so we put £1,000 in the debit (left) column.

The money comes from the bank account. Money in the bank is an asset so we reduce the asset by putting £1,000 in the credit (right) column.

Purchases Ledger Page 7

Joe's Garage

Dr							*Cr*
27 Feb 09	Bank	CB14	1,000	16 Feb 09	Vehicles	GL4	10,000

Cash Book Page 14

Bank

Dr							*Cr*
				27 Feb 09	Joe's Garage	PL7	1,000

See how the accounting equation, A = L + C, is always maintained. Typically, when you do business you

- Trade off an asset against a liability (e.g. buying stock on credit, or sending a cheque to pay a bill), or
- Trade one asset for another, like paying cash for stock

1.1.2 STOCK

Now, we really need to understand how **stock** is treated in accounting. Because we buy stock at one price and sell it at another, we don't have a regular account called 'stock'. We have four or five accounts instead, and all of them are asset accounts, since stock is an asset.

stock
Things you buy with the main intention of selling them again. For a CD shop, stock means CDs. For a fashion boutique it means shirts, jeans and earrings. For a used car lot it means used cars. Certainly you may sell the old company computer when you upgrade it, but it doesn't count as stock because you bought it with the main intention of using it, not reselling it.

Purchases means buying stock. We increase the asset of stock by making entries on the debit (left) side. Purchases entries are always in the debit column, and 'purchases' always means stock – that is 'goods for resale'. If you bought a photocopier or a new sign, it would go in an account called 'Office equipment' or 'Fixtures'.

Sales means selling stock. We reduce the asset of stock with an entry in the credit (right) column of the Sales account. The figure for 'Sales' means stock going out.

The figure for 'Sales', however, is used to represent your **revenue**, since the value of the stock going out equals the money coming in for it. As the money comes in, it's entered on the debit side of the cash account.

revenue
Money coming in.

Selling a used vehicle or computer, meanwhile, would also go in the credit column – but of the vehicles account or equipment account, not the Sales account.

Returns can catch you out, but they shouldn't. Returns In, or Sales Returns, is when someone has bought something and then brought it back (because it didn't fit, or didn't work, or whatever). There are two ways to get this right.

1. Returns In is the opposite of Sales, so it goes in the opposite column to Sales, i.e. the debit side.
2. You're adding to the asset of stock, so it still goes in the debit side.

Use whichever gets you through. Returns Out, or Purchase Returns, works in a similar way, of course. These go in the credit side for the same reason that Returns In goes in the debit side.

Now is a good time to mention **discounts**. 'Discounts Allowed' is money off what we sell. It works as the opposite of Sales, so put Discounts Allowed on the debit (left) side. Discounts Received are the opposite of Purchases, so put them on the right.

Example 3

We buy stock worth £100 from Army Surplus Specials.

Buying stock is adding to the asset of stock, so we debit the Purchases account. This is just like buying the vehicle in example 1, except there we debited the Vehicles account (a vehicle isn't stock). The credit entry is increasing the liability to Army Surplus Specials.

General Ledger Page 6

Purchases

Dr							*Cr*
3 June 09	Army Surplus	PL84	100				

Purchases Ledger Page 84

Army Surplus Specials

Dr							*Cr*
				3 June 09	Purchases	GL6	100

In point of fact, we'd probably collect a list of purchases in a day book and move the total to the Purchases account at the end of a suitable period, e.g. every day or every month. However, this is a good illustration of how the balance works.

Example 4

We return stock worth £10 to Army Surplus Specials.

Returning stock is reducing our business's asset of stock, so we credit the Returns Out account. The debit entry is in Army Surplus Specials.

General Ledger Page 19

Returns Outwards

Dr							Cr
				13 June 09	Army Surplus	PL84	10

Purchases Ledger Page 84

Army Surplus Specials

Dr							Cr
13 June 09	Returns Out	GL19	10	3 June 09	Purchases	GL6	100

We'll see later how £10 in the debit side and £100 in the credit side implies a 'credit balance' for Army Surplus of £90. This idea should make sense, even now.

Have a look at the Trial Balance in section 1.5. Most of the debit side entries are assets. Most of the credit side entries are liabilities or capital. The exceptions are the accounts where reductions are recorded, e.g. drawings from capital, or the sale of stock in the Sales account.

Exercises

Now do some exercises. Watching 'Raging Bull' is no substitute for pulling on the gloves and getting in the ring. Exercise is essential for understanding accounting.

1 Make both the debit and credit entries for the following information. A date and folio reference are not required.

- We buy a vehicle by cheque for £18,500.

Bank

Dr							Cr

Vehicles

Dr							Cr

- We buy a computer on credit from Oranges Ltd for £1,140.

Equipment

Dr							*Cr*

Oranges Ltd

Dr							*Cr*

- We sell stock on credit to A. E. Poe Ltd for £350.

Sales

Dr							*Cr*

A. E. Poe

Dr							*Cr*

- We have stock worth £150 returned by A. E. Poe Ltd.

Returns Inwards

Dr							*Cr*

A. E. Poe

Dr							*Cr*

- We pay a creditor, Moon and Sons Ltd, by standing order.

Moon and Sons

Dr							*Cr*

Bank

Dr							*Cr*

- We return the stock from Poe to our supplier, Pitt and Pendulum PLC. It is valued at £95.

Returns Outwards

Dr							*Cr*

Pitt and Pendulum PLC

Dr							*Cr*

- We send a cheque to HM Customs and Excise for £450 in respect of VAT on sales.

VAT

Dr							*Cr*

Bank

Dr							*Cr*

- The proprietor (owner) of the business withdraws £1,000 by cheque to pay off his personal overdraft.

Bank

Dr							*Cr*

Drawings

Dr							Cr

- We find a bank transfer has been made to us from a debtor, J. Wells and S. Kimpton.

Bank

Dr							Cr

Wells Kimpton

Dr							Cr

- We take out £200 cash from the bank account.

Bank

Dr							Cr

Cash

Dr							Cr

- We take out a secured loan from ADBC Bank.

Bank

Dr							Cr

ADBC

Dr							Cr

2 Now do it again – but this time you're not given the names of the accounts to use.
   - We buy a vehicle by cheque for £18,500.
   - We buy a computer on credit from Oranges Ltd for £1,140.
   - We sell stock on credit to A. E. Poe Ltd for £350.
   - We have stock worth £150 returned by A. E. Poe Ltd.
   - We pay a creditor, Moon and Sons Ltd, by standing order.
   - We return the stock from Poe to our supplier, Pitt and Pendulum PLC. It is valued at £95.
   - We send a cheque to HM Customs and Excise for £450 in respect of VAT on sales.
   - The proprietor (owner) of the business withdraws £1,000 by cheque to pay off his personal overdraft.
   - We find a bank transfer has been made to us from a debtor, J. Wells and S. Kimpton.
   - We take out £200 cash from the bank account.
   - We take out a secured loan from ADBC Bank.

1.1.3 ACCOUNTS IN OUTLINE

The AQA exam tests you on many different aspects of accounting for a business. You'd probably like to get on and learn exactly the material you need. However, accounting can be a large, complex, confusing system, with different things going on that don't seem to belong together.

Without going into too much explanation, and before we even learn how to make an invoice, let's take a very simple look at a business running for a month. It may not make complete sense yet, but it will give you an outline of what you need to understand and why.

Example

Harmony Rainbow supplies paint to independent decorating retailers.

1 Rosie Jay, the proprietor, forms the company on 1 March 2010, and puts £50,000 of her own money into it. The money goes in the new Bank account.
2 She buys a new £1,899 computer system on 2 March from Core Solutions on credit.
3 She also buys 2,500 litres of various colours on credit from Carmichael's Chemicals for £1,500.
4 On 3 March she sells 240 litres of Bullfrog and Desert Mist on credit to Local Colour for £240, and 680 litres of various shades of beige to Superior

Interiors for £660.

5 10 litres of Bullfrog was found to be Grasshopper when it was opened. Local Colour sent it back on 10 March.

6 So, Harmony Rainbow sent it back to Carmichael's at the purchase price of 60p per litre on 19 March.

7 On 23 March, Harmony Rainbow pays by cheque wages of £110 and rent of £210.

8 Harmony Rainbow also makes monthly payments to Core Solutions (£300 on 29 March) and Carmichaels (£700 on 30 March), and receives part payment from Local Colour (£120 on the 30 March) and Superior Interiors (£460 on 30 March).

The accounts look like this. See if you can follow them.

General Ledger Page 1

Capital

Dr							*Cr*
				1 Mar '10	Bank	CB1	50,000

Cash Book Page 1

Bank

Dr							*Cr*
1 Mar '10	Capital	GL1	50,000	23 Mar '10	Wages	GL7	110
30 Mar '10	Local Colour	SL1	120	23 Mar '10	Rent	GL8	210
30 Mar '10	Superior Int.	SL2	460	29 Mar '10	Core Sol's	PL1	300
				30 Mar '10	Carmichael's	PL2	700
1 Apr '10	Balance		49,260				

Purchases Ledger Page 1

Core Solutions

Dr							*Cr*
29 Mar '10	Bank	CB1	300	2 Mar '10	Office Equip't	GL2	1,899
				1 Apr '10	Balance		1,599

General Ledger Page 2

Office Equipment

Dr							*Cr*
2 Mar '10	Core Solutions	PL1	1,899				

Purchases Ledger Page 2

Carmichael's

Dr							*Cr*
19 Mar '10	Returns out		6	2 Mar '10	Purchases		1,500
30 Mar '10	Bank	CB1	700				
				1 Apr '10	Balance		794

General Ledger Page 3

Purchases

Dr							*Cr*
2 Mar '10	Carmichael's		1,500				

Sales Ledger Page 1

Local Colour

Dr							*Cr*
3 Mar '10	Sales		240	10 Mar '10	Returns In		10
				30 Mar '10	Bank	CB1	120
1 Apr '10	Balance		110				

Sales Ledger Page 2

Superior Interiors

Dr							*Cr*
3 Mar '10	Sales		<u>660</u>	30 Mar '10	Bank	CB1	460
1 Apr '10	Balance		200				

General Ledger Page 4

Sales

Dr							*Cr*
				3 Mar '10	Local Colour		240
				3 Mar '10	Superior Int.		660
				1 Apr '10	Balance		900

General Ledger Page 5

Returns In

Dr							*Cr*
10 Mar '10	Local Colour		10				

General Ledger Page 6

Returns Out

Dr							*Cr*
				19 Mar '10	Carmichael's		6

General Ledger Page 7

Wages

Dr							*Cr*
23 Mar '10	Bank	CB1	110				

General Ledger Page 8

Rent

Dr							*Cr*
23 Mar '10	Bank	CB1	210				

Note: Sales, Purchases and Returns of stock have no folio reference in this example. For stock accounts, the folio reference is to day books, which are used to record detail.

At the end of this slightly odd month, Rosie decides to see how her business is doing, so she makes up her Financial Statements. There are some accounts with a lot of activity, so first she 'balances' them – she totals both sides and uses the difference. Note that the full procedure for balancing at the end of the month hasn't been shown here (see section 1.3.1), but the result should make sense.

Then Rosie collects all the balances together in one list, called a Trial Balance.

Harmony Rainbow Trial Balance – 31 March 2010

	Dr £	Cr £
Capital		50,000
Bank	49,260	
Debtors and Creditors	310	2,393
Office equipment	1,899	
Purchases	1,500	
Sales		900
Returns in	10	
Returns out		6
Wages	110	
Rent	210	
	53,299	53,299

Rosie still has paint worth £948 in the store.

Now she calculates her Gross **Profit** – profit before expenses, and her Net Profit, which includes expenses.

Her calculation looks like this:

> **profit**
> The difference between the money that's come in and the money that's gone out. For a proper definition of profit, look at section 4.3.2.

Harmony Rainbow Trading and Profit and Loss Account – 31 March 2010

	£	£
Sales		900
Less returns inwards		(10)
		890
Less cost of sales		
Purchases	1,500	
Less returns outwards	(6)	
	1,494	
Less closing stock	(948)	(546)
Gross Profit		344
Less expenses		
Wages	110	
Rent	210	(320)
Net Profit		24

See how £890 is the value of the paint she sold, and £546 is what she paid for it. Out of the Gross Profit of £344 she had to pay £320 expenses, and kept £24 Net Profit to add to her capital.

Then she looks at her assets, liabilities and capital. We've made the accounts based on assets and not-assets, but since, as the owner or proprietor, Rosie's interested in the capital (her money), she rearranges the accounting equation

assets = liabilities + capital

to read:

assets – liabilities = capital

If you have any head for maths you can see that this works. It also makes sense: if she sold all of the assets and paid off her liabilities, the money left over would be her capital.

She arranges these items like this.

Harmony Rainbow Balance Sheet – 31 March 2010

	£	£
Fixed assets		
Equipment		1,899
Current assets		
Stock	948	
Debtors	310	
Bank	49,260	
	50,518	
Less current liabilities		
Creditors	(2,393)	
		48,125
		50,024
Financed by:		
Capital		50,000
Add Net Profit		24
		50,024

As if by magic, the net assets are equal to the capital. As we look properly at Unit 1 now, we'll see this explained in much more detail.

Keep practising this. Getting yourself used to the Hall of Mirrors really is the key to doing well in your AQA A/S accounting exam.

FURTHER READING

Frank Wood and Alan Sangster, *Business Accounting 1*, Chapters 1–4

David Cox and Michael Fardon, *A/S Accounting for AQA*, Chapters 1–3

Ian Harrison *Introducing Accounting for A/S*, Chapters 1 and 6

USEFUL WEB SITES

www.aqa.org.uk/qual/gceasa/acc_assess.html
The most useful web site in the world. Download as many exam papers as your printer will allow – you should expect to complete at least five for each unit. Keep working back through them until they become easy.

If you can't remember the whole web address, go to **www.aqa.org.uk**, and follow Qualifications > GCE AS/A > Accounting, and click on the Assessment Material link at the top of the page.

www.allbusiness.com This site for real businesses has lots of information. In the 'Advice Centres' section, click on 'Finance and Accounting', and have a look round.

www.bized.ac.uk biz/ed has lots of useful resources. The BAIT section in particular has some useful interactive exercises.

www.nrbarton.co.uk This group of accountants has prepared a bookkeeping tutorial section.

www.unisys.com/common/investors/glossary/ You can use this to check many words you might find unfamiliar in business.

www.businesstown.com/accounting/basic-terms.asp Or, to put it another way…

www.google.co.uk When in doubt, put a term you don't know into Google.

Documents, day books and ledgers

1.2

There is usually a simple question in Unit 1 on documents and day books. It tests you on day-to-day bookkeeping. Learn this and you should get a few per cent quickly.

POINTS TO CONSIDER

- What is an invoice?
- What's the difference between a trade discount and a cash discount?
- In which day book would you record the sale of stock?
- What might the Journal be used for?
- In which ledger is the account for Sales?
- What columns might you find in the Cash Book?

A business will buy things and sell things. Unlike a visit to the shops with cash in your pocket, it's normal to buy and sell on credit – 'buy now, pay later'.

Every time you buy, sell, take goods back, put money in the bank etc., it's called a **transaction**. For each transaction a **document** will be issued. Your domestic electricity bill is an example of a document called an **invoice**.

> **document**
> Any official piece of paper.
> **invoice**
> A document requesting payment.

The accountant will take the documents and put the information in a day book. This is where the details of each transaction can be collected in one place.

It's important to note that the information from the day books is 'posted' to a ledger. Not by mail; that's just the action of moving the important information. The ledger is where those T-accounts are, and the information can be used to make the Financial Statements at the end of the year. Here's the flow of information in full:

transaction > document > day book > ledger T-account > Financial Statement

While a document will hold full information on a transaction, each stage in the process loses detail and focuses more on totals. The Financial Statements have very general totals. Folio references are used to direct you from one collection of information to the next, or back to the last. There are examples in sections 1.2.1 and 1.2.2.

1.2.1 PREPARING DOCUMENTS

You may be asked to prepare a document, like an invoice or a credit note. You'll be given a price, how many were bought or returned, whether or not they get a discount, and asked to calculate a total. Whether they ask for the document to be laid out or just calculated, you can't go wrong if you arrange it properly.

Can you see how this invoice works?

Example & Co. Ltd

25th Sept 2009

Sales Invoice – 41178

10 dresses, size 14, at £12.00	120.00
6 pairs of jeans, size 32R, at £30.00	180.00
	300.00
Less trade discount 20%	(60.00)
	240.00
Plus VAT at 17.5%	39.90
Total due	**279.90**

Cash discount of 5% available for payment within 5 working days

See how we've

- Added the cost prices to make a subtotal.
- Put the trade discount in brackets to show that it's subtracted.

Discounts

There's an important point about discounts. There are two kinds: trade discount and cash discount, and the two are treated differently.

Trade discount is where you reduce the price of an item, because, for example, somebody in the trade buys from you regularly. The price is actually reduced. It's a new lower price, it's given on the spot and doesn't change if the goods are returned.

Cash discount is a little trickier. When a customer buys on credit, then for the 30 or so days you're waiting for payment you're missing out on interest. This is just one reason why a cash discount may be offered for payment made within a few days. It's only applied if the payment is made within the time stated. Otherwise it's lost. If it is applied, however, then it is treated as a separate expense, not a reduction of the selling price.

Here's one really fiddly bit that will get you the extra marks you need if you want a good grade. VAT (a tax, usually 17.5%) is calculated on the cash discounted total, whether the discount is taken up or not. Always remember this.

Try an example of a typical question.

The Wright Part sells washing machine supplies. T. Henry & Co. have bought 25 30mm widgets at 84p each, and 10 40mm widgets at £1.12 each. They qualify for a 20% trade discount and a 5% cash discount (7 days). They pay VAT at 17.5%. Prepare a sales invoice.

Your answer should look something like this:

The Wright Part

Sales Invoice – to T Henry

30mm widgets × 25 @ £0.84	21.00
40mm widgets × 10 @ £1.12	11.20
	32.20
Less trade discount 20%	(6.44)
	25.76
VAT at 17.5%	4.28
Total	30.04

5% cash discount available for payment within 7 days

Go through this example with a calculator and it should make sense. Note, especially, that the VAT was charged on the cash discounted price, i.e. £25.76 × 95% × 17.5%. Note also that the bottom line has a double underline, and how the **subtotals** sit below a single line. This line tells you

subtotal
Not the grand total but a total half way through a calculation. A subtotal can show the value of a group within a group, or how much you've added up so far before you add more.

not to add the figures above it again because they're all included in the figure below it.

If you have to prepare a credit or debit note for a return, it will follow a similar format. Keep your wits about you in the exam, try to use what you've learned, and do the exercises. You'll only learn it by practising it. Most importantly, try as many real exam questions as you can – at least four. You can download past papers at www.aqa.org.uk.

How to calculate a percentage on a calculator

Let's say you want to find 20% of £32.20. The routine way is to enter

32.20 × 20 ÷ 100 =

But there's a nice shortcut.

Your calculator should have a % option, often as a 2nd function of the = button. You use this by pressing the 'inv' or 'shift' button to change the function of the = button. Try it.

32.20 × 20 [inv/shift] %

The VAT on this question, meanwhile, would be

25.76 × 95 [inv/shift] % × 17.5 [inv/shift] %

1.2.2 DAY BOOKS AND LEDGERS

You're also likely to be tested on which transaction goes with which document and with which day book (also called 'subsidiary book', or 'book of original entry'). You may even be asked which T-accounts will be affected.

Here's a list. Commit it to memory and you should be OK – try also to understand how it works to be sure in the exam.

1.2 Table 1

Transaction	*Document*	*Day book*	*To debit*	*To credit*
Credit sale	Sales invoice	Sales day book	Debtor/ customer	Sales
Charging VAT	Sales invoice	Sales day book	Debtor/ customer	VAT
Changing the price/ trade discount	Sales invoice			
Giving cash discount	Sales invoice	Cash Book	Discounts allowed	Debtor/ customer
Credit purchase (stock)	Purchase invoice	Purchases day book	Purchases	Creditor/ supplier

1.2 Table 1 (continued)

Transaction	*Document*	*Day book*	*To debit*	*To credit*
Receiving cash discount	Purchase invoice	Cash Book	Creditor/ supplier	Discounts received
Purchase of asset (e.g. vehicle)	Purchase invoice	Journal	Asset (e.g. 'vehicles')	Creditor/ supplier
Expense (e.g. petrol)	Petty cash voucher	Petty Cash book	e.g. 'motor expenses'	Petty Cash
Paying a supplier by cheque	Cheque counterfoil	Cash Book	Creditor/ supplier	Bank
Paying money into a bank	Pay in slip	Cash Book	Bank	Debtor/ customer
Paying money into a bank (not your own)	Bank giro credit	Cash Book	Bank	Debtor/ customer
Returning goods to supplier	Debit note	Returns Out day book	creditor/ supplier	Returns Out Purchase Returns
Goods returned from customer	Credit note	Returns In day book/Sales Returns day book	Returns In/ Sales Returns	debtor/ customer

Every business is different, but this arrangement of books is a good standard.

Day books

- **Sales day book.** This is where you record each sale of stock, using your carbon copies of the sales invoices. The totals are moved to the Sales account and VAT account in the General Ledger (credit side), and the individual debtors' accounts in the Sales Ledger (debit side).

A page might look like this:

Sales Day Book Page 7

Date	*Details*	*Invoice no.*	*Folio*	*Net £*	*VAT £*	*Gross £*
1/11	A. Debtor	98765	SL9	85.11	14.89	100.00
3/11	B. Callum	98766	SL123	340.00	59.50	399.50
4/11	C. Luke	98767	SL14	40.00	7.00	47.00
				[1]465.11	[2]81.39	546.50

[1] This total goes to Sales (credit side).
[2] This total goes to VAT (credit side).

You may not be asked about document numbers and folio references in your exam.

- **Purchases day book**. This is where you record each purchase of stock. You can figure how it works by thinking of the Sales day book in reverse. The date, details, net VAT and gross will be the same, but the folio will direct you towards the Purchases Ledger (PL), and the invoice numbers will take all forms, as they're sent by different suppliers.
- **Returns In day book**. This is where you record the return of an item of stock that you've sold. The value of the returned goods is credited to the debtor's account in the Sales Ledger, and debited in the Returns In and VAT accounts in the General Ledger.

  A page might look like this:

Returns In Day Book Page 12

Date	*Details*	*Credit note*	*Folio*	*Net £*	*VAT £*	*Gross £*
7/11	L. R. O'Kane	4113	SL68	12.00	2.10	14.10
9/11	A. Debtor	4114	SL9	8.51	1.49	10.00
				[1]32.00	[2]5.60	37.60

[1] This total goes to Sales Returns / Returns In (debit side).
[2] This total goes to VAT (debit side).

- **Returns Out day book**. This is where you record the return of an item of stock that you previously purchased. How do you think you move the information to the ledgers?
- **Cash Book**. (see 1.4.1) This is both a day book and a ledger.

1.2 Table 2

Dr											*Cr*
Date	*Details*	*Folio*	*Discount* £	*Cash* £	*Bank* £	*Date*	*Details*	*Folio*	*Discount* £	*Cash* £	*Bank* £
3/11	A. Debtor	SL9	4		96	1/11	A. Creditor		6		194

  As you can see, the T-accounts for Bank and Cash overlap each other on the same page (there's another example of this in the section on balancing off accounts). All movements of money (payments, receipts, putting money in the bank etc.) are recorded here. Small amounts are kept in a separate Petty Cash Book – there are examples in section 1.4.2.

- **The Journal**. This records any other entry, like buying a computer system, and is also used when setting up a business and correcting errors. We'll look at it in more detail in section 1.7.3 on correcting errors. It has its own layout which applies to any entry.

  Note that day books are sometimes called Journals (e.g. Sales Journal) from the French word for day, 'jour'. In this case, the Journal would be called the General Journal.

Ledgers

- **Sales Ledger for debtor/customer accounts**. This ledger just contains the accounts of everyone who buys stock from you on credit. Every sale will be entered on the debit (left) side of the customer's account, and every payment, discount or return will be recorded on the credit side. Think of it as a debtors' ledger. The Sales Ledger does not contain the account for Sales.

Sales Ledger Page 9

Mrs A. Debtor

Dr							*Cr*
Date		*Folio*	*£*	*Date*		*Folio*	*£*
1.1.11	Sales	SB7	100	3.1.11	Bank		96
				3.1.11	Discounts		4
				9.1.11	Returns In	RI12	10

See how the folio columns direct you to the Sales Day Book (Page 7) and the Returns Inwards Day Book (Page 12) where the entry came from, and where more information can be found.

- **Purchases Ledger for creditor/supplier accounts**. This ledger just contains the accounts of everyone who sells stock to you on credit. Every purchase will be entered on the credit side of the supplier's account, and every payment, discount or return will be recorded on the debit side. Think of it as a creditors' ledger. The Purchases Ledger does not contain the account for Purchases.

A. Creditor Ltd

Dr							*Cr*
Date		*Folio*	*£*	*Date*		*Folio*	*£*
5.1.11	Bank		194	1.1.11	Purchases	PB31	200
5.1.11	Discounts		6				
8.1.11	Returns Out	RO29	19				

See how the folio column directs you to the Purchases Day Book (Page 31) and the Returns Out day book (page 19), where the entry came from, and where more information can be found.

- **Cash Book for Bank and Cash**. As we've seen, this is also a day book.
- **General Ledger for all other accounts**. This contains all other accounts, i.e. capital, expenses, assets like delivery vans, and stock accounts like Sales or Purchases. It will also contain the accounts for Discounts Allowed, Discounts Received and VAT.

FURTHER READING

Frank Wood and Alan Sangster, *Business Accounting 1*, Chapters 11, 13–17
David Cox and Michael Fardon, *A/S Accounting for AQA*, Chapters 1, 4 and 6
Ian Harrison, *Introducing Accounting for A/S*, Chapters 7 and 10

USEFUL WEB SITES

www.aqa.org.uk/qual/gceasa/acc_assess.html This is always your most useful web site. Download as many exam papers as your printer will allow.

www.ir35calc.co.uk/how_to_prepare_an_invoice.aspx
This is great – it has some example templates to look at.

www.nrbarton.co.uk This group of accountants has prepared a bookkeeping tutorial section.

www.unisys.com/common/investors/glossary/

www.google.co.uk

SAMPLE QUESTIONS

1.2.1

The table below shows transactions for Ian Heritage Ltd, pottery wholesaler.

Required
Complete the table to show which subsidiary book is used for each transaction, which account will be debited and which credited. The first item has been completed for you.

Transaction	Subsidiary Book	Account to be debited	Account to be credited
Credit sale to H. Potts	*Sales day book*	*H. Potts*	*Sales*
Cheque sent to settle account with World Cups Ltd			
Cash discount given to Ainsley Ltd			
Goods returned to World Cups Ltd			

(9 marks)

1.2.2
Boris's Balalaikas is offering trade and cash discounts.

Required

(a) Explain the reasons for offering each type of discount, and where they are recorded in the day books.

(i) Trade Discounts

(3 marks)

(ii) Cash Discounts

(3 marks)

(b) Boris supplies 4 balalaikas to No Strings Attached for £55 each plus VAT at 17.5%, with a 15% trade discount and a 10% cash discount. Calculate the total of the invoice sent by Boris.

(5 marks)

1.2.3
Required

Use the table below to identify three different subsidiary books. For each, give an example of a document that might be used to make an entry into it. One example has been shown and may not be used.

Subsidiary Book	Source document
Returns Inwards day book	*Credit note*

(6 marks)

1.2.4
Required

In the table below is a list of documents. For each, identify the subsidiary book used to record the information, and the debit and credit accounts which should or could be used for the double entry. The first one has been completed for you.

Document	Subsidiary Book	Account to receive debit entry	Account to receive credit entry
Cheque counterfoil for payment to Fred's Curries	*Cash book*	*Fred's Curries*	*Bank*
Invoice sent with goods to Zitaz Ltd			
Invoice for new computer system received from Bishop's Ltd			
Paying in slip			

(9 marks)

1.2.5
You are preparing invoices on behalf of Gracetune Ltd. They have sold 4 flutes at £170 each and 2 tubas at £190 each to Chotnut. Gracetune charges VAT on all of their instruments, and allows a 5% discount for quick payment. Chotnut are regular customers and are given a 20% reduction.

Required
Prepare an invoice for the above transaction. Show clearly each stage of the calculation and the total, labelling each figure and any discounts that apply,

(7 marks)

1.2.6
Required

For each of the transactions in the table below, identify the document and the Book of Prime Entry used.

Transaction	Document	Book of Prime Entry
Giving a cash discount		
Paying a small expense		
Returning goods to a supplier		
Getting a cash discount		

(8 marks)

1.2.7 (E)
B. E. Jones (Wholesale) has partially prepared the following invoice from the delivery note.

Required

(a) Complete the total amount column of the invoice.

INVOICE

B. E. Jones (Wholesale), 6 Church Road, Middleton, MT4 6AQ

Telephone: 01687 132579
Fax: 01676 123457

VAT Reg. No. 1103987654
Date: 2 January 2002

J. C. Smith
Shopping Centre
Downtown, DT6 9BJ

Account number S26

Your Order No: 123		Delivery Note No: 0678		Invoice No: 12576
Quantity	Details	Price	VAT rate	**Total Amount**
96	Dresses	£8.50 each	17.5%	
20	Coats	£15 each	17.5%	
			Trade discount 20%	
			Subtotal	
			VAT	
			Total	
Terms of trade: cash discount of 5% for payment within 7 days				

(8 marks)

(b) This invoice will be used as a source document by both J. C. Smith and B. E. Jones (Wholesale). Which subsidiary book will be used for the entry:

(i) in the books of J. C. Smith:

(1 mark)

(ii) in the books of B. E. Jones (Wholesale)?

(1 mark)

(c) Explain the terms:

(i) trade discount

(2 marks)

(ii) cash discount

(2 marks)

Total 14%

Source: Assessment and Qualifications Alliance, January 2002

1.2.8 (E)

In the catalogue of Wholesale Car Spares is part number 1063 which has a list price of £45.00 less a trade discount of 25%. VAT is charged at 17.5%.

J. C. Cross Garages, a customer, who is allowed trade discount and a cash discount of 5% for payment in 7 days, returned 23 units of part 1063 which were faulty.

Required

(a) What document will Wholesale Car Spares prepare and send to J. C. Cross Garages?

(1 mark)

(b) Calculate the amount to be recorded on the document clearly showing all the stages in the calculation.

(7 marks)

(c) Name the subsidiary book used by J. C. Cross Garages or the returned parts and show the amounts to be entered.

(4 marks)

Total 12%

Source: Assessment and Qualification Alliance, January 2001

1.3 Balancing accounts and VAT

In the exam you will normally be given at least one T-account to balance. The main idea is simple, but there is also a curious procedure which you have to get used to. We'll be using the VAT account as a working example.

POINTS TO CONSIDER

- What is a balance?
- What do 'balance c/d' and 'balance b/d' mean?
- What do you notice about the dates of these balances?
- On which side will you probably find the balance of a VAT account?
- How can you find the VAT included in a total price?
- What does the balance on a VAT account mean?

1.3.1 BALANCING OFF

You may be given some figures and asked to put them in a T-account – this is where your work in the Hall of Mirrors will help you. First decide whether the account is an asset account or a liability/capital account. Now decide whether each figure is adding to the account or reducing it. Most marks can be had just for putting each figure on the correct + or – side of the T. The trick is to remember what's an asset, what's a liability, and which way round they go (see section 1.1.1).

Don't forget to put in the date and details of the other T-account in the double entry. If in doubt about a date, use the end-of-period date at the start of the question. Finally, find the **balance**.

balance
You will see the term 'balance' a lot in accounting. The easy definition is that it's the difference between the totals on each side. To be more accurate, it's a 'balancing figure' added to one side of an account to make the debit and credit totals the same. At the same time, it's the net figure on the other side, which is still there if you continue the account.

Let's look at a simple question.

Using these figures complete the account for Ludwig's Vans, a supplier, for the month ended 31 July 2011. Balance off the account.

7 July Buy a vehicle: £9,000

26 July Make a payment: £1,200

Ludwig's Vans

Dr					*Cr*
26 Jul '11	Bank	1,200	7 Jul '11	Vehicles	9,000
31 Jul '11	Balance c/d	[2]7,800			
		[1]9,000			[1]9,000
			1 Aug '11	Balance b/d	[3]7,800

So how did we get this finished account?

First, of course, we make a credit entry for the money owed on the van, and a debit entry for the payment against it. Now we still owe £7,800. We need to calculate this figure to 'balance off the account'.

How we write this down is the curious bit.

1 First, add up the debit and credit sides. See which total is bigger (it will normally be the debit side on an asset account, or the credit side on a liability or capital account). Leaving a gap under the last entries, put the bigger total under both columns.

Ludwig's Vans

Dr					*Cr*
26 Jul '11	Bank	1,200	7 Jul '11	Vehicles	9,000
		[1]9,000			[1]9,000

2 But one total is incorrect, so add in the difference (£7,800) on the smaller side for the totals to make sense. This is the balance at the end of the month (or year, or whatever), and it needs to be 'carried forward' or 'carried down' to the next period. Call it 'Balance c/d'.

Ludwig's Vans

Dr					*Cr*
26 Jul '11		1,200	7 Jul '11	Vehicles	9,000
31 Jul '11	**Balance c/d**	[2]**7,800**			
		9,000			9,000

3 But, the balance should be 'brought down' or 'brought forward' on the bigger side, so under the total on the bigger side start the new period with the same 'Balance b/d'.

Ludwig's Vans

Dr					*Cr*
26 Jul '11	Bank	1,200	7 Jul '11	Vehicles	9,000
31 Jul '11	Balance c/d	7,800			
		9,000			9,000
			1 Aug '11	**Balance b/d**	[3]**7,800**

This is not too difficult if you practise the procedure, but you do have to recognise the difference between assets and liabilities or capital, and add and subtract by inserting the figures on the correct side.

This was a liability account. Balancing an asset account will normally work like a mirror image of this one with the balance on the left. Remember Local Colour, debtors from Harmony Rainbow in 1.1.3? We saw their balance like this:

Sales Ledger Page 1

Local Colour

Dr						*Cr*
3 Mar '10	Sales	240	10 Mar '10	Returns In		10
			30 Mar '10	Bank	CB1	120
1 Apr '10	Balance	110				

Now we know how to balance an asset account off properly:

Sales Ledger Page 1

Local Colour

Dr						Cr
3 Mar '10	Sales	240	10 Mar '10	Returns In		10
			30 Mar '10	Bank	CB1	120
			31 Mar '10	**Balance c/d**		**110**
		240				**240**
1 Apr '10	Balance	110				

As always, pay attention to clear, detailed presentation.

1.3.2 VAT

You could be asked to balance almost any kind of account, but it's typical to tackle the **VAT** account. In any case it makes a good example.

Small companies won't be registered for VAT, but there's likely to be a VAT registered company in your exam that needs it sorting out somehow.

Here's the trick. VAT behaves like a liability account.

When you sell your stock and charge VAT you are collecting money for the government (HM Customs and Excise). You owe them the money, and so you put VAT-on-sales on the credit side (the right side, the same as your Sales balance). However, when you bought the stock, you paid VAT to the manufacturer or wholesaler. This part of the VAT has already been paid, and is taken away by putting VAT-on-purchases on the debit side (the left – the same side as purchases). Payments to Customs and Excise also go on the debit side, as they reduce your liability to them.

VAT

Value added tax has to be paid on almost everything. Food and children's clothes are rare examples of VAT-exempt goods. Ultimately the end user pays all of the VAT. However, right along the supply chain, each business has to pay the VAT-inclusive price (usually cost plus 17.5%), and then claim the VAT back.

For example, if a factory sells you an item for £100 + VAT, you'll have to pay them £117.50, and the factory will send the £17.50 to the government. Now say you sell the item on for £1,000 + VAT = £1,175. That's £175 VAT you've charged, but since you've already paid £17.50 to the supplier, you only have to pay up the remaining £157.50 (= £175–£17.50).

VAT is normally 17.5% in the UK, but there are lower rates, like 8% or 5%, payable on products and services the government doesn't want to penalise too much.

Cash sales

This is fairly straightforward if you can handle liability accounts, but there's one tricky one they might put in.

What happens if you have a cash sales total, and you need to find how much of it is VAT? Adding VAT of 17.5% is easy, but extracting it from a total? You can't just find 17.5%! The calculation is not rocket science if you have a head for maths and logic, but if you don't, just use 14.89361702% or 0.1489361702. It looks long and horrible, but it's just like a magic phone number: 01489 361 702. For smaller figures, 0.148936 is sufficient. Use it like this:

0.148936 × Total = VAT

Understanding the VAT in a sales total

We want to find the fraction of the total that's made up by VAT.

If the total = the net price plus VAT (100% + 17.5% = 117.5%), then the fraction of the total made by VAT is 17.5% / (117.5%).

To find the VAT use this formula:

VAT = 17.5 / 117.5 × Total

This gives us 0.148936 × the total. It can of course be adapted to calculate VAT at any rate. Try it.

Here's how a question might appear.

> **Using these figures complete the VAT account for the month ended 31 January 2008. Balance the account.**
>
> **VAT on sales: £87,654**
>
> **VAT on purchases: £43,210**
>
> **VAT on petty cash expenses: £4,321**
>
> **Total cash sales are £54,321 including VAT.**

So how do we answer this? On which side does VAT on sales go? VAT on purchases? Petty cash expenses is a form of purchase, so you can figure which side that goes. Finally, extract the VAT on cash sales using your magic phone number, and put it on the same side as your other VAT on sales. Now you can balance it.

Answer:

Cash sales working out: 54,321 × 0.1489361702 = 8,090.36

Or: 54,321 × 17.5 ÷ 117.5 = 8,090.36

VAT

Dr					Cr
31 Jan '08	Purchases	43,210.00	31 Jan '08	Credit sales	87,654.00
"	Petty Cash	4,321.00	"	Cash sales	8,090.36
"	Balance c/d	48,213.36			
		95,744.36			95,744.36
			1 Feb '09	Balance b/d	48,213.36

One thing to remember – the balance on the VAT account represents money owing to HM Customs and Excise.

VAT and T-accounts

There's one more thing to be aware of. You should understand how the whole of a transaction is dealt with in the accounts. Look at this example.

You have a purchase invoice in your exam from Roobarb and C'stard Ltd for £100 + VAT. What would you enter into the accounts? Well, we have to pay Roobarb and C'stard £117.50, so naturally that's entered into the credit side of their account. But we make two debit entries: £100 in Purchases and £17.50 in VAT.

Roobarb and C'stard Ltd

Dr					Cr
			9 Apr '12	Purchases	117.50

Purchases

Dr					Cr
9 Apr '12	Roobarb & C'stard	100.00			

VAT

Dr					Cr
9 Apr '12	Roobarb & C'stard	17.50			

In point of fact, we'd actually collect the information in the purchases day book, and enter the purchase and VAT totals in the accounts, but this single transaction gives a simple illustration of the principle.

FURTHER READING

Frank Wood and Alan Sangster, *Business Accounting 1*, Chapters 5 and 19
David Cox and Michael Fardon, *A/S Accounting for AQA*, Chapters 5 and 7
Ian Harrison, *Introducing Accounting for A/S*, Chapter 8

USEFUL WEB SITES

www.aqa.org.uk/qual/gceasa/acc_assess.html This is always your most useful web site. Download as many exam papers as your printer will allow.

www.bized.ac.uk biz/ed has lots of useful resources. BAIT 4 gives you some interactive balancing off exercises.

www.workbox.demon.co.uk/C5.htm This page has a lot of extra information on VAT

www.unisys.com/common/investors/glossary/

www.google.co.uk

SAMPLE QUESTIONS

1.3.1

The books of the Iccing Bike Co. show that the following figures were collected during the month of May 2009. VAT is calculated at 17.5%.

Credit sales	£2,300
VAT on credit sales	£402.50
Credit purchases	£1,800
VAT on Credit purchases	£315
Cash sales inc VAT	£822.50
New racks purchased, including VAT	£423

Required

(a) Calculate the balance of VAT due to HM Customs and Excise from the month of May 2009. There are marks available for clearly presented calculations.

(9 marks)

(b) On which side of the VAT account will this balance appear?

(1 mark)

1.3.2

Lynne's Cane Furniture has an account with Ig Glue Ltd. The following transactions took place with Ig Glue up to 31 January 2010:

Credit sales	1,720
Cash sales	190
Returns Inwards	220
Regular monthly credit	
Payment received	950

Required

Enter the relevant information into Ig Glue's account for Lynne's Cane Furniture, and bring down the balance for the start of February.

Lynne's Cane Furniture

Dr *Cr*

Date		£	Date	£
01.01.10	Balance b/d	1,100		

(8 marks)

1.3.3

Hayley's Comics have extracted the following information from their books for the month ended October 2012:

	Goods (£)	VAT (£)	Total (£)
Purchases day book	4,320	756	5,076
Returns out day book	320	56	376
Sales day book	7,180	1,256.50	8,436.50
Returns in day book	130	22.75	152.75

VAT inclusive cash sales totalled £2,373.50, and VAT inclusive expenses amounted to £1,104.50. All VAT is charged at 17.5%.

Required

(a) Complete the VAT account for October 2012, and show the balance clearly.

VAT Account

Dr *Cr*

		£		£

(8 marks)

(b) How much should Hayley's Comics pay HM Customs and Excise to settle their account?

(1 mark)

1.3.4 (E)

Required

(a) Using the figures below, complete the VAT account for the three months ended 31 March 2002 for R Masters. Bring down the balance on the account.

	£
VAT on credit sales	3216.58
VAT on credit purchases	2198.45
VAT on the petty cash expenses	39.27
Payments made to HM Customs and Excise by cheque	846.39

You are also informed that the cash sales for the three months are £8671.96 and that this figure **includes** VAT at 17.5%.

(7 marks)

VAT Account

Dr *Cr*

Date 2002	**Details**	**£**	**p**	**Date 2002**	**Details**	**£**	**p**
				1 Jan	Balance b/d	456	87

(b) What does the balance on the VAT account represent and in which section of the balance sheet at 31 March 2002 will the balance be shown?

(3 marks)

Total 10%

Source: Assessment and Qualifications Alliance, May 2002

The Cash Book and Petty Cash Book 1.4

The Cash Book has the T-accounts for Bank and for Cash. Just remember that Bank and Cash are asset accounts, and that you add by debiting and subtract by crediting, and you'll have little trouble if you're a thoughtful student. The Cash Book is both day book and ledger. The Petty Cash Book takes care of small amounts and relieves the Cash Book from too much detail.

POINTS TO CONSIDER

- Why might a prompt payment or receipt be split across two columns in the Cash Book?
- What is the Imprest system?
- What are the debit and credit columns of the Petty Cash Book called?
- What can the totals of the petty cash analysis columns be used for?
- Identify two methods commonly used to check the accuracy of the Petty Cash account.

1.4.1 CASH BOOK

One curiosity of the Cash Book is that is that the accounts for Bank and Cash regularly appear on the same page. There's a debit side with Cash and Bank columns, and a credit side with the same.

There are a couple of points which may baffle you. You should be able to see the Cash and Bank columns on each side. But what's the Discount column? And the Folio?

Cash Discounts are given for fast payment, as we saw in section 1.2.1 on invoices. Say Standard Hunter Ltd is expecting £100, but allowing a 5% cash discount. The credit entry when we made the credit purchase would have been £100. Their debit entry, then, as we send them our cheque, has to match the credit entry for the account to be balanced.

1.4 Table 1

Cash Book

Dr											Cr
Date	*Details*	*Folio*	*Discount* £	*Cash* £	*Bank* £	*Date*	*Details*	*Folio*	*Discount* £	*Cash* £	*Bank* £
1/12	Cash	C			50.00	1/12	Standard Hunter	PL159	5.00		95.00
						1/12	Bank	C		50.00	

Standard Hunter Ltd

Dr					*Cr*
1 Dec	Bank	95	28 Nov	Purchases	100
"	Discount	5			

But the cheque was only for £95, which we enter on the credit side for Bank. We put the other £5 in the credit Discounts column – which represents Discounts Received. In this way the cash book is acting as a day book. At the end of the accounting period (e.g. the end of the month) we move the Discounts column total to the credit side of Discounts Received. The same happens in mirror image for prompt Sales receipts and Discounts Allowed.

The Folio column is not common in exams, but is useful to understand. It tells you where to find the other half of the double entry; not just the name of the account but the ledger and page number too. See how personal accounts can be found in, for example, PL172, which is Purchases Ledger page 172, and how Rent is found GL05, or General Ledger page 5. C stands for 'contra', meaning 'against' or 'opposite', and is used for transfers between Bank and Cash on the page.

the Petty Cash Book and the Imprest system

This is used to record minor expenses, like petrol claims, paying the window cleaner, milk and sugar, etc. The French word 'petit' means 'small'. Someone other than the cashier or accountant can handle this, and it keeps fiddly details out of the Cash book and other accounts.

Petty Cash uses the Imprest system. Here's how it works. The Petty Cashier is given a cash 'float' from the main Cash Book to use for minor payments. You may have worked in an office with a little grey cash tin. When the float is running low, it's topped back up again, and the Cash book only has to record the top-up total.

1.4.2 PETTY CASH BOOK

Petty Cash Book questions are about as big and bad as a T-account gets. For one thing, Petty Cash is not a standard T-account.
Let's take a look at one of these nasty questions.

1. **Enter the following information into the Petty Cash Book shown below.**
2. **Complete and total the analysis columns, and make the necessary entries to restore the Imprest.**

10 May	Milk & coffee	£3.16 inc. VAT
13 May	Cleaner	£55 inc. VAT
16 May	Postage	£4.19 excl. VAT
17 May	Travel and hospitality	£74.19 plus VAT

Answer:

Received[1]	Date	Details	Total[2]	VAT[3]	Office[3]	Other[3]
£ p	2013		£ p	£ p	£ p	£ p
200 00	1 May	Balance b/d				
	2 May	Petrol	37 78	5 63		32 15
	9 May	Postage 8	15		8 15	
	10 May	**Milk & coffee**[4]	**3 16**	**0 47**	**2 69**	
	13 May	**Cleaner55**	**00 8**	**19 46**	**81**	
	16 May	**Postage 4**	**19**	**4**	**19**	
	17 May	**Travel etc.**	**87 17**	**12 98**		**74 19**
			[5]**195 45**	**27 27**	**61 84**	**106 34**
		Balance c/d	[6]**4 55**			
200 00			200 00			
[7]**4 55**	**17 May**	**Balance b/d**				
[8]**195 45**	**17 May**	**Cash**				

Well, what's all this? First, see how the work in **bold** type is what you'll have to write. The rest is a head start.

1 Treat the 'Received' column as a debit column. See how we start with a balance on this side (petty cash is an asset). This balance represents the float in a cash tin.
2 Treat the 'Total' column as a credit column – petty cash going out decreases the asset of cash. As you can see, both sides share the date and details columns.
3 The group of subtotal columns on the right are new. These are analysis columns. They run parallel to the main account and provide the breakdowns for accounts like VAT, motor expenses or **miscellaneous** expenses.
4 See how each expense from the question is listed in the Total column, and then categorised in one or more analysis columns: e.g. milk and coffee has the VAT extracted (see VAT), and the price without VAT is an Office Expense. Watch out for the last expense – it needed VAT adding to it.
5 Find the total for each column, including the analysis columns.
6 Balance off the Petty Cash account.
7 Bring the balance down.
8 Finally the float needs more cash. The Petty Cashier is given the total money

miscellaneous and sundry
Miscellaneous expenses, sundries, other expenses and general expenses are all the same thing with different names.

that's been paid out, and this is entered in the Received column. We're back to £200 in the little grey tin and ready to go again.

The replacement cash comes from the Cash account. See how the double entry for the debit entry in Received would be a credit entry in Cash. The analysis column totals can be entered in the various expense accounts.

You can check if the Petty Cash account is right in a couple of ways.

1 Count the money to see if it matches the balance
2 Add the analysis column totals – these can be 'cross cast' and shown to match the total of the Total column. Casting is just adding.

FURTHER READING

Frank Wood and Alan Sangster, *Business Accounting 1*, Chapters 13 and 18
David Cox and Michael Fardon, *A/S Accounting for AQA*, Chapters 8 and 9
Ian Harrison, *Introducing Accounting for A/S*, Chapters 11–13

USEFUL WEB SITES

www.aqa.org.uk/qual/gceasa/acc_assess.html This is always your most useful web site. Download as many exam papers as your printer will allow.

www.unisys.com/common/investors/glossary/

www.google.co.uk

SAMPLE QUESTIONS

1.4.1 (E)

The following items have yet to be recorded in the Cash Book of J A Summerfield for the first week in January 2002:

January		**£**	
1	Balance in cash account	50.00	
1	Overdrawn bank balance	263.67	
Cheque counterfoils show:			
3	J B Smith Ltd (cash discount taken – £4.00)	120.00	Cheque amount
4	A E Evans Ltd	146.59	Cheque amount
5	K L M Spares (cash discount taken – £3.96)	127.45	Cheque amount
6	Restoring the petty cash imprest	45.67	Cheque amount
Paying in counterfoils show:			
3	M S Supplies	136.98	Amount banked
4	J O Jones (cash discount taken – £4.67)	246.89	Amount banked

The following additional items should also be recorded in the Cash Book:

The bank statement shows:	£
Direct debit payment Shop Insurances plc	100.00
Credit transfer received ABC Traders	120.56
Bank charges	23.98
Bank interest paid	46.97

The week's till rolls show cash receipt totals of	467.23
There were cash payments of:	
Part time wages	40.00
Postage stamps	27.00

It is the business's policy to retain a cash float of £50 at the end of each week and pay the rest of the cash into the bank. This was done on 7 January 2002.

Required

(a) Record this information in the cash book below and balance the cash book at 7 January 2002.

Cash Book of J A Summerfield

Date 2002	Details	Discount Allowed £	Cash £	Bank £	Date 2002	Details	Discount Received £	Cash £	Bank £
Jan					Jan				

(21 marks)

(b) What method or technique can be used to verify:
   (i) the cash balance; (1 mark)
   (ii) the bank balance? (1 mark)

(c) Explain the term 'petty cash imprest' (2 marks)

Total 25%

Source: Assessment and Qualifications Alliance, January 2002

1.4.2 (E)

The petty Cash Book for the Taj Mahal Restaurant has been only partly completed for the week ended 12 January 2003.

Required

(a) Complete their petty Cash Book (below) for the week from the following details:

Jan 9	Petrol	£12.50	(including VAT)
Jan 10	Postage on parcels	£8.50	(no VAT)
Jan 11	Saturday help	£20.00	(no VAT)

(5 marks)

(b) Balance their petty Cash Book and total the analysis columns. Make the necessary entries to restore the imprest to £120.00

(5 marks)

(c) Explain how the balance shown in the petty Cash Book can be checked for accuracy.

(2 marks)

Petty Cash Book

Received	Date	Details	Voucher number	Total	VAT	Motor expenses	Stationery	Postage	Sundries
£ p	2003			£ p	£ p	£ p	£ p	£ p	£ p
120.00	Jan 6	Balance b/d							
	Jan 7	Petrol	27	23.00	3.43	19.57			
	Jan 8	Postage	28	15.00				15.00	
	Jan 8	Envelopes	29	10.00	1.49		8.51		
	Jan 8	Cleaner	30	15.00					15.00

(d) Give two benefits of using a petty cash book.

Benefit 1..

Benefit 2..

(4 marks)

Total 16%

Source: Assessment and Qualifications Alliance, January 2003

1.4.3(E)

Country Fair Stalls has partly completed its petty Cash Book, as shown below, for the week ended 8 May 2004.

Required

(a) Complete the entries for the week by recording the following items.

May 4	Voucher number 003	Petrol £16.49 including VAT at 17.5%
May 6	Voucher number 004	Window cleaning £15.00 no VAT
May 7	Voucher number 005	Envelopes £16.00, VAT at 17.5% to be added
May 7	Voucher number 006	Parcel post £10.00 no VAT

(10 marks)

(b) Total the petty Cash Book, carry down the balance and restore the imprest.

(3 marks)

(c) In which section (subheading) of the balance sheet would the closing balance of petty cash appear?

(1 mark)

Country Fair Stalls' Petty Cash Book

Dr **Cr**

Received		Date	Details	Total	VAT	Stationery	Postage	Motor expenses	Cleaning
£	**p**	**2004**		**£ p**	**£ p**	**£ p**	**£ p**	**£ p**	**£ p**
100	00	May 1	Cash float (balance down)						
		May 2	Petrol 001	20 43	3 04			17 39	
		May 3	Postage 002	5 45			5 45		

(d) How could the closing balance of petty cash be checked? (3 marks)

Total 17%

Source: Assessment and Qualifications Alliance, June 2004

The Trial Balance 1.5

This bit's easy – if you know your assets from your liabilities and capital. Make sure you are happy with the Hall of Mirrors in general, and the lists in section 1.1.1 in particular.

You've seen how to balance off an account and carry the balance forward to the next period. Well, at the end of an accounting period (at least every year) you collect the balances from all of the accounts and put them in a list called a Trial Balance. We did this for Harmony Rainbow in section 1.1.3.

POINTS TO CONSIDER

- Why do we make a Trial Balance?
- Which item is always found as a note outside the Trial Balance?
- If a building is good and bill is bad, why are they both debit entries?
- If Sales is good and Creditors is bad, why are they both credit entries?
- Can you explain why Carriage In and Carriage Out are both debit entries?
- Can you explain why Returns In is a debit entry and Returns Out is a credit entry?
- Capital balances are on the credit side – so why is Drawings (a capital account) on the debit side?
- Which errors won't be shown by the Trial Balance?

There are two good reasons to make a trial balance.

1. If the sides don't match then there may be a mistake in your books (see section 1.5.1 on errors).
2. It makes it easier to use the balances to calculate your profit and publish your Financial Statements (see section 1.6).

Here's a Trial Balance for Jonama Trading, who buy and sell fashion items wholesale. They've drawn up a Trial Balance for the year ended 31 July 2007, which we'll use in the next section.

Jonama Trading – Trial Balance – 31 July 2007

	Dr £	*Cr* £
Sales		845,000
Purchases	781,000	
Returns In	4,000	
Returns Out		3,300
Capital		125,000
Drawings	19,000	
Mortgage		210,000
Stock (01.08.06)	26,000	
Bank	21,000	
Cash	1,500	
Building	220,000	
Vehicles	56,000	
Equipment etc.	14,500	
Electricity etc.	1,500	
Bank charges	1,000	
Discounts Allowed	2,500	
Discounts Received		2,000
Carriage Inwards	1,800	
Carriage Outwards	500	
Debtors and Creditors	117,000	82,000
	1,267,300	1,267,300

Note: Closing stock was valued at £24,000

Do you understand every entry (they're all explained in the Hall of Mirrors)? Is it on the side you would expect? What does each entry represent? Remember the rules and it'll make sense:

- The debit side (left) is where you add to assets and expenses, or reduce liabilities and capital.
- The credit side (right) meanwhile, is where you reduce assets, and increase liabilities and capital.

In most accounts you're putting the balances on the + side. That's why electricity and vehicles have a balance on the left (increasing an asset) while capital and creditors are on the right.

Go back the Hall of Mirrors if you're unsure – you don't want to be found out in the exam.

Accidents waiting to happen

- Look at the entries for debtors and creditors. Which is which? Debtors represents money owed to you – your money – an asset.
- It's easy to get discounts and returns mixed up, so be careful. Discounts Allowed are an expense, Discounts Received count as extra income. Returns In and Returns Out are the opposites of Sales and Purchases.
- Carriage In and Carriage Out are both expenses on the debit side.
- When you add to Drawings, you decrease the Capital in the business.
- What would it mean if the entry for Bank was on the credit side?

1.5.1 ERRORS

Now, because every debit entry (left side) has a corresponding credit entry (right side), the totals of the debit and credit sides should be the same. If they're not, you know there's an error in your bookkeeping. Perhaps there's a single entry. Maybe an account has been added up incorrectly (**overcast** or **undercast**). If you absolutely can't find the error when your debit and credit sides don't match, put the difference in a suspense account until the error is found (see section 1.7.2).

overcast
Added up wrongly to give too big a figure, e.g. 2+3=7.

undercast
Added up wrongly to give too small a figure, e.g. 2+5=6.

But there are some errors that won't show up, because both sides still balance. This is often examined, so learn these names and be able to explain them. You should also be able to record the errors in the Journal (see section 1.7.3).

Errors not shown by a trial balance

- Errors of omission: both entries of a transaction have been left out completely.
- Errors of original entry: similar to omission, the wrong figure is used for both entries, because of an incorrect invoice for example.
- Errors of commission: a sale has been made to P. Kay Ltd, but entered into the account of K. Pea Ltd. The figure is on the correct side of the wrong account.
- Compensating errors: you make the same adding mistake on both the debit and credit sides.
- Errors of principle: similar to errors of commission. This is where the new van was

▶

put in Purchases instead of Vehicles, or a return out is entered as a discount received. The figure is on the correct side of the wrong type of account.

- Complete reversal of entries: somebody has used the correct accounts, but put the debit entry on the credit side and the credit entry on the debit side: e.g. we send off a cheque and put it on the debit side of Bank and the credit side of the creditor.
- Transposition errors: £201 is entered as £210 in each account, or similarly £577 is entered as £557 both times.

You could try to memorise the list like this:

Om Or   Com Comp   Prince Rev Trans

How might a question look?

Explain one benefit of drawing up a trial balance. Outline two limitations of this procedure.

You can see if there are errors in the accounts if they don't balance. However, some errors won't show up, like:

- Errors of omission, where both entries of a transaction have been left out completely, and
- Errors of commission, where stock has been bought by J. Smith Ltd, but entered into the account of K. Smith Ltd.

Another benefit, as we've seen, is that you it's easier to draw up your financial statements like the Trading and Profit & Loss Account. Let's look at them next.

FURTHER READING

Frank Wood and Alan Sangster, *Business Accounting 1*, Chapters 6 and 32
David Cox and Michael Fardon, *A/S Accounting for AQA*, Chapter 5
Ian Harrison, *Introducing Accounting for A/S* Chapter 9

USEFUL WEB SITES

www.aqa.org.uk/qual/gceasa/acc_assess.html This is always your most useful web site. Download as many exam papers as your printer will allow.

www.bized.ac.uk This has a good section on Trial Balances. Choose 'accounting' as your subject and look at the Pizza Package.

www.unisys.com/common/investors/glossary/

www.google.co.uk

SAMPLE QUESTIONS

1.5.1
In the table below is a list of items which might be found in a Trial Balance.

Required

(a) Complete the table by showing for each item whether you would expect to see a debit or a credit balance. The first one is done for you.

	Dr	Cr
General expenses	✓	
Sales		
Returns outwards		
Carriage inwards		
Discounts received		
Interest paid		
Carriage outwards		
Drawings		
Creditors		
Capital		
Last year's closing stock		

(10 marks)

1.5.2
A Trial Balance is often used to make the final accounts easier to prepare.

Required

(a) Name one other benefit of making a Trial Balance

(1 mark)

(b) Identify the main limitation of this benefit, explaining three examples:

Limitation:

Example 1:

Example 2:

Example 3:

(10 marks)

1.5.3

The following trial balance extract has been prepared for Chris 'n' Jack Muzic. Some of the balances have been brought down on the wrong side of the account.

Required

(a) Identify in the grid below which items have been entered incorrectly. The first two have been completed for you.

Chris 'n' Jack Trial Balance – 31 March 2009

	Dr £	Cr £	
Sales		512,000	✔
Returns inwards		2,800	✘
Purchases	242,000		
Debtors	93,000		
Creditors		49,000	
Discounts allowed	1,700		
Discounts received	1,100		
Bank overdraft		23,000	
Cash		1,700	
Premises	120,000		
Electricity etc	800		
Carriage inwards		700	
Carriage outwards	600		
Returns outwards	2,100		
Stock (01.04.08)	17,000		
Capital	180,000		
Drawings	22,000		

(15 marks)

1.5.4

(a) What is a trial balance, when defined in terms of the source of the figures?

(2 marks)

(b) Identify one kind of error this allows an accountant to verify?

(2 marks)

(c) Identify and describe any kinds of error this does not allow an accountant to verify?

(14 marks)

1.5.5 (E)

The trial balance of H G Patel, as at 30 April 2003, has been partially completed. The following balances have now to be included:

	£
Purchases	38 900
Sales	98 000
Returns outwards	3 698
Carriage inwards	367
Carriage outwards	450
Discount received	2 135
Drawings	6 900

Required

(a) Complete the trial balance.

(7 marks)

(b) Total the trial balance and enter any difference in the suspense account.

(1 mark)

H G Patel: Trial Balance as at 30 April 2003

Account	**Debit £**	**Credit £**
Wages	23 890	
Administration costs	6 000	
Capital		60 000
Premises	65 000	
Motor vehicles	5 000	
Motor expenses	1 650	
Purchases		
Sales		
Returns Outwards		
Carriage Inwards		
Carriage outwards		
Discount received		
Drawings		
Suspense		
TOTAL		

(c) There are many reasons for the error(s) giving rise to the suspense account.

From the following list of bookkeeping errors, tick the Yes or No box to indicate whether or not the error could be responsible for the difference in the trial balance.

An example has been given.

Error	Yes	No
A balance has been entered in the wrong column of the trial balance.	✓	
An error of principle has occurred.		
The sales account has been totalled incorrectly.		
An invoice has been omitted from the books.		
A cheque has been debited in the Cash Book as £150 but credited in the customer's account as £105.		

(4 marks)

Total 12%

Source: Assessment and Qualifications Alliance, June 2003

Financial Statements 1.6

You will definitely get examined on this, and there should be a lot of marks available. Furthermore, the skills will carry forward to Unit 3. Most students find that there's a 'right answer' to aim for and that they can learn enough to get a good mark.

POINTS TO CONSIDE

- What do we calculate in a Trading Account?
- Which kind of accounts are almost exclusively found in the Trading Account?
- What do we calculate in a Profit and Loss Account?
- Which kind of accounts are almost exclusively found in the Profit and Loss Account?
- How do we rearrange the accounting equation to make the Balance Sheet?
- What is liquidity?
- How do you treat a Bank balance on the credit side?

finance

Noun: money, especially for business activity (rather than personal activity).

Verb: to provide finance.

There isn't an account for profit. Cash in the bank, for example, is not a meaningful indicator of how well your business is doing. At the end of the year, you have to compile your end-of-year Financial Statements:

- Trading Account to find your **Gross Profit**
- Profit and Loss Account to find your **Net Profit**
- Balance Sheet to take a freeze-frame look at your assets, liabilities and capital.

The Trading Account and Profit and Loss Account may be examined separately, although in a business they always go together, one straight after the other. Always start a Balance Sheet on a new sheet.

In Unit 3 we'll also look at
- Manufacturing Accounts, and
- Appropriation Accounts

for limited liability companies.

gross profit

The money you keep if you sell something for more than you paid for it, although you still have to pay expenses from this. In an exam you can call it 'the difference between revenue and trading costs, before you take away general expenses'.

net profit

'Net' anything means what's left at the end after you've paid everything. Net profit is revenues less all expenses.

Financial statements are made from your Trial Balance. Remember, this is a list of the balances on the accounts, and all of these balances are asset, liability or capital accounts. As well as knowing which is which, you need to know your Fixed Assets from your Current Assets and your Expenses, and you'll need to be able to separate your Current Liabilities from your Long-term Liabilities.

We saw briefly in section 1.1.3 how Harmony Rainbow made their financial statements. Let's look more carefully now at how to do it from the Trial Balance in the last section. We'll add some twists in Unit 3.

Jonama Trading – Trial Balance – 31 July 2007

	Dr £	*Cr* £
Sales		845,000
Purchases	781,000	
Returns In	4,000	
Returns Out		3,300
Capital		125,000
Drawings	19,000	
Mortgage		210,000
Stock (01.08.06)	26,000	
Bank	21,000	
Cash	1,500	
Building	220,000	
Vehicles	56,000	
Equipment etc.	14,500	
Electricity etc.	1,500	
Bank charges	1,000	
Discounts Allowed	2,500	
Discounts Received		2,000
Carriage Inwards	1,800	
Carriage Outwards	500	
Debtors and Creditors	117,000	82,000
	1,267,300	1,267,300

Note: Closing stock was valued at £24,000

How do we show this in the Financial Statements?

1.6.1 TRADING ACCOUNT

First, we make the Trading Account to find Gross Profit. This is all about your stock accounts. If you're asked for one of these in the exam, make sure it looks like this:

Trading Account – Jonama Trading – 31 July 2007

	£	£
Sales		845,000
Less Returns Inwards		(4,000)
		841,000
Less Cost of Sales		
Opening Stock	26,000	
Purchases	781,000	
Carriage Inwards	1,800	
Less Returns Outwards	(3,300)	
	805,500	
Less Closing Stock	(24,000)	(781,500)
Gross Profit		59,500

Study this example carefully.

- Learn the layout of the Trading Account. You will need to reproduce it from memory. Two columns are used, but they are NOT debit and credit columns. The outer column is for important figures, the inner column for less important detail. Labels for the inner column e.g. Closing Stock should be indented. Let the names of the outer-column figures stand out. You may choose to use a 3-column format to make subtotals clearer.
- Remember the title, and the £ at the head of each column.
- Understand that the figure in the Trial Balance for stock is opening stock (note the date). Since there is no 'stock account' as such, you can only find closing stock by stock taking, i.e. counting up what you haven't sold. The figure for closing stock will always be in an additional note.
- See how figures to be subtracted are in brackets.
- See also how subtotals often appear below underlines, and must be labelled when a name exists. You'll drop marks if you forget to put in Gross Profit, for example. Use a double underline for the Gross Profit (bottom line) figure.
- Note that not all items in the Trial Balance are used in the Trading account. We'll come back to them later. Also, if there are any items you expect to see that are not in the Trial Balance, just leave then out of the Trading account.

Understanding the Trading Account

We've put the stock items in the Trading Account to calculate the Gross Profit, which is profit before expenses are taken out (we'll look at expenses in the Profit and Loss Account). Your business buys stock for one price and sells it for a higher price. In a very simple model, you start with Sales, take away the Purchases, and you have your Gross Profit.

In real life, however, it's a bit more complex than that.

- If you already had some stock at the start of the year, you've sold it by now. Add the value of **Opening Stock** to your figure for Purchases.
- If you have unsold stock left over at the end of this year, meanwhile, you have to subtract the value of **Closing Stock** from your figure for Purchases, since you can't count it against sales. Note that this figure is always in a separate note from the Trial Balance.
- If you sell something and it's brought back, you haven't sold it any more. Subtract the value of **Returns In** or **Sales Returns** from your figure for Sales.
- If you buy something and it's later sent back, you haven't really bought it. Subtract the value of ***Returns Out*** *or* ***Purchase Returns*** from your figure for Purchases.
- A supplier can include delivery in the purchase price, or can leave you to pay for it. To account for these deliveries in the same way, expenses for delivery to your business are included as a trading expense. Add the value of **Carriage Inwards** to your figure for Purchases.

Be careful with this last item. All stock items go in the Trading Account, and all Trading Account items are stock, except Carriage Inwards. It's the only expense included in the Trading Account. Carriage Out, meanwhile, never goes in the Trading Account.

1.6.2 PROFIT AND LOSS ACCOUNT

So you have your Gross Profit. But your business activity isn't just stock. **Expenses** go in the Profit and Loss account, where you calculate Net Profit, which is the money the owner can keep. Net Profit adds to Capital.

expense
Money you have to pay to help your business run.

If you're asked to prepare a Profit and Loss account, just add the expenses like this:

Profit and Loss Account – Jonama Trading – 31 July 2007

	£	£
Gross Profit		59,500
Discounts received		2,000
		61,500
Less Expenses		
Electricity etc.	1,500	
Bank charges	1,000	
Discounts allowed	2,500	
Carriage outwards	500	(5,500)
Net Profit		56,000

- First thing in your Profit and Loss Account, add any money coming in that wasn't part of your trading. This will include discounts received, interest received and any other income. Add each item to the Gross Profit and make a new subtotal.
- Now take care of any expenses, as shown in the example. It's not too important what order they go in. Add the expenses in the inner column and put the total in the outer column, with brackets to indicate that it has to be subtracted. Take the total for expenses away and you have your Net Profit.

Remember:

- The figures you use here are the here-and-gone figures mostly expenses (a type of asset).
- The Profit and Loss Account normally goes directly under the Trading Account, with no need for a new title. Exam questions, however, can just test you on the Profit and Loss Account on its own.
- Net Profit adds to the capital of the owner or owners of the company.

You've probably noticed that the Trading Account and Profit and Loss Account don't look much like the T-accounts we've been studying. That's because they're in the recommended vertical form of presenting your figures. Have a look at section 3.3 in Unit 3 if you'd like to understand better how we make them work.

1.6.3 BALANCE SHEET

Take another look at the Trial Balance in the question. The stock figures have been used, and the expenses. All that's left are the other assets, the liabilities and the capital. They go in the Balance Sheet – a freeze-frame look at the state of the business. If you're asked for one of these, its general form should be like the 2-column example for Harmony Rainbow in section 1.1.3, or like this 3-column example:

Balance Sheet – Jonama Trading – 31 July 2007

	£	£	£
Fixed Assets[1]			
Building	220,000	0	220,000
Vehicles	56,000	0	56,000
Equipment etc.	14,500	0	14,500
			290,500
Current Assets[2]			
Stock	24,000		
Debtors	117,000		
Bank	21,000		
Cash	1,500	163,500	
Less Current Liabilities[3]			
Creditors	82,000	(82,000)	
Working Capital			[4]81,500
Less Mortgage			[5](210,000)
			[6]162,000
Financed by:			
Capital	125,000		
Add Net Profit	56,000		
	181,000		
Less Drawings	(19,000)		
	162,000		

So, what are we doing?

Remember the accounting equation, **assets = liabilities + capital**? Since the owner wants to see how much money he has, we rearrange this to read **assets – liabilities = capital**. This is the same equation.

So, we're going to add the assets, subtract the liabilities, and this should match the capital.

1 First we list the Fixed Assets, that we buy to use and don't change from year to year. Note how three £ signs are used. We'll need them for calculating depreciation in Unit 3, so learn to use them now. Put the cost price under the first £ and the current value under the third one. In Unit 1 these will both be the same – you could just use the third column. You may encounter a two £-sign form of Balance Sheet in the exam (see 1.1.3). Just combine the first two columns into one.

2 Now we list the current assets, whose value changes from year to year. We list these in order of increasing liquidity, which means how easy it is to spend. Stock is hard to spend, cash is easy, so memorise the mantra 'stock, debtors, bank, cash'. Put each amount in the first column and the subtotal in the second column.

3 Now list the current liabilities. This is money that should be paid within the next year, so don't include long-term loans like mortgages. In Unit 1 current liabilities should just be creditors and possibly a bank overdraft. Again, put the subtotal in the second column, remembering to put brackets around it to indicate it needs to be subtracted.
4 Take the liabilities subtotal from the current assets subtotal and put that total in the important third column. Give it a label. This amount is called **Working Capital**, or Net Current Assets, and it's the amount of money moving around the business, i.e. working for the company and not tied up in buildings and so on.
5 Any long-term liabilities are entered next in the third column, with brackets to indicate that they're subtracted. We have now added all of our assets and subtracted our liabilities.
6 Now the total is calculated. This important figure can be called **Capital Employed**, as it is equal to the capital being used in the business, although it's often left unlabelled. Don't forget to double underline the figure to show it's a grand total.
7 Finally we enter the figures for Capital, Drawings (in brackets) and Net Profit (which adds to capital). Some accountants use the first column to make the bottom lines clearer (as shown here), although most text books will show these figures in the third column. Choose the way you like and stick to it. The total should be the same as the Capital Employed, since **assets – liabilities = capital**. If it is, there's a fair chance you've just picked up most or all of the marks for the question; and there are usually quite a few on offer. To get these marks, you'll probably have to practise making five or ten balance sheets. Learn by doing – these financial statements are central to accounting.

Overdrawn bank balances

To see how the Current Liabilities subtotal works properly, assume that you're told you have a bank overdraft. As a student, you're probably familiar with the term 'overdrawn' – it means you owe money to the bank. Alternatively, you might see that the Trial Balance figure for Bank is on the credit side. Watch out for this one – it's easy to miss – a credit balance means you've taken more out of the account than you've put in. Both of these pieces of information mean the same thing.

Look what happens to the Balance Sheet when the figure for Bank is an overdraft. This is quite likely to be what your answer is aiming at.

	£	£	£
Current Assets			
Stock	24,000		
Debtors	117,000		
Cash	1,500	142,500	
Less Current Liabilities			
Creditors	82,000		
Bank	21,000	(103,000)	
Working Capital			39,500

FURTHER READING

Frank Wood and Alan Sangster, *Business Accounting 1*, Chapters 7–9
David Cox and Michael Fardon, *A/S Accounting for AQA*, Chapter 12

USEFUL WEB SITES

www.aqa.org.uk/qual/gceasa/acc_assess.html This is always your most useful web site. Download as many exam papers as your printer will allow.

www.bized.ac.uk Choose 'accounting' as your subject and look at the Pizza Package.

www.allbusiness.com This site has some other financial statements. In the 'Advice Centres' section, click on 'Finance and Accounting', and look at 'common financial reports'.

www.unisys.com/common/investors/glossary/

www.google.co.uk

SAMPLE QUESTIONS

1.6.1

Prepare a Trading Account for Francine and Debbie for the year ended 31.12.11 using the following information. Label each stage of your calculation where appropriate.

	£	£
Sales		48,000
Returns inwards	3,000	
Stock (31.12.11)	9,000	
Purchases	22,000	
Carriage inwards	600	
Returns outwards		2,000

Closing Stock was £5,000

(6 marks)

1.6.2

Prepare a Profit and Loss Account for Francine and Debbie for the year ended 31.12.11 using the Gross Profit figure from Question 1.6.1 and the following information. Label each stage of your calculation where appropriate.

	Dr £	Cr £
Discounts received		1,000
Discounts allowed	1,500	
Power	900	
Bank charges	800	
General expenses	1,600	
Carriage outwards	500	
Motor expenses	1,100	

(8 marks)

1.6.3

Prepare a Balance Sheet for Francine and Debbie at 31.12.11, using the Net Profit figure from Question 1.6.2 and the following information. Label each section and subsection where appropriate.

	Dr £	Cr £
Building	140,000	
Vehicles	19,000	
Equipment	11,000	
Bank	2,000	
Cash	1,000	
Debtors	8,000	
Creditors		7,000
Capital		70,000
Drawings	16,000	
Mortgage		110,000

Closing Stock was £5,000

(15 marks)

1.6.4

Prepare a Trading and Profit and Loss Account and Balance Sheet for Hurle and Pennington at 31.08.08, using the Trial Balance below. Label each section and subsection where appropriate.

Hurle and Pennington – Trial Balance – 31.08.08

	Dr £	Cr £
Capital		600,000
Mortgage		800,000
Premises	1,250,000	
Vehicles	89,000	
Equipment	224,000	
Bank	14,000	
Cash	2,000	
Sales		390,000
Purchases	140,000	
Carriage inwards	1,000	
Carriage outwards	6,000	
Returns outwards		11,000
Returns inwards	12,000	
Stock (31.12.11)	28,000	
Discounts received		6,000
Discounts allowed	5,000	
Electricity	4,000	
Gas	3,000	
General expenses	5,000	
Drawings	38,000	
Motor expenses	7,000	
Debtors	61,000	
Creditors		82,000
	1,889,000	1,889,000

Closing Stock £21,000

(30 marks)

1.6.5

Sandra Warden has extracted the balances from her books for 30.04.10. including the following:

	£
Sales	692,000
Purchases	354,000
Carriage inwards	900
Carriage outwards	1,200
Stock (01.05.09)	48,000
Stock (30.04.10)	51,000
Returns inwards	3,000
Returns outwards	2,000
Discounts allowed	1,000
Discounts received	4,000

Required

Using the relevant information, prepare the Trading Account for Sandra Warden, showing clearly the cost of sales and gross profit.

(12 marks)

1.6.6

DWR Productions trade in art equipment. They have produced the following figures at 30.11.07.:

	£
Carriage inwards	800
Purchases	23,000
Stock (01.12.06)	1,300
Discounts received	90
Electricity	640
Sales	61,000
Carriage outwards	1,900
General expenses	2,200
Returns inwards	1,000
Returns outwards	1,100
Motor expenses	850
Discounts allowed	140
Stock (30.11.07)	1,260

Required

(a) Prepare a Trading and Profit and Loss Account for DWR Productions.

(14 marks)

(b) State in which section of the Balance Sheet the following would be found:
(i) Drawings
(ii) Cash

(iii) Premises
(iv) Bank overdraft

(4 marks)

1.6.7

Required
Explain the following Balance Sheet sections, providing one example for each:

(i) Fixed assets:
Example:

(ii) Current assets:
Example:

(iii) Current Liabilities:
Example:

(iv) Long Term Liabilities:
Example:

(v) Capital/financed by:
Example:

(15 marks)

1.6.8 (E)

On 30 April 2004 the following figures were extracted from the ledgers of Country Crafts.

	£
Bank loan (repayable 2010)	20 000
Bank overdraft	3 900
Buildings	85 000
Capital at 1 May 2003	113 160
Creditors	4 700
Debtors	6 900
Drawings	16 250
Net profit for the year	6 940
Plant and machinery	22 500
Stock at 30 April 2004	7 850
Vehicles	10 200

Required
Prepare a balance sheet as at 30 April 2004.

(12 marks)

Total 12%

Source:Assessment and Qualifications Alliance, June 2004

1.6.9 (E)

Required
From the following figures complete the balance sheet for A to Z Engineering Supplies as at 31 March 2003. Clearly show the fixed and current assets and long-term and current liabilities. To complete the balance sheet calculate the proprietor's capital.

	£
Net profit for the year	23 460
Stocks at 31 March 2003	14 905
Debtors	6 500
Creditors	4 590
Premises	50 000
Motor vehicles	14 560
Bank overdraft	3 400
Petty cash	56
Drawings	13 000
Mortgage on premises	25 000

(12 marks)

Total 12%

Source: Assessment and Qualifications Alliance, June 2003

1.6.10 (E)

The following balances are taken from the books of James Cadwallader showing totals for the year ended 31 December 2002.

	£
Sales	67 945
Purchases	34 981
Returns inwards	2 945
Returns outwards	1 367
Carriage inwards	679
Carriage outwards	386
Stock at 1 January 2002	5 780
Stock at 31 December 2002	6 590
Wages	12 056
Other expenses	4 650

Required
Prepare the trading and profit and loss account for the year ended 31 December 2002.

James Cadwallader

Trading and Profit and Loss Account for the year ended 31 December 2002

(15 marks)

Total 15%

Source: Assessment and Qualifications Alliance, January 2003

1.6.11 (E)

Mary Arbuthnot runs Mary's Doll Shop and is preparing her balance sheet but has problems with allocating **four** items.

Required

Using the memorandum below, advise her as to which section/sub-heading of the balance sheet the items should appear under. Give detailed reasons for your choice.

MEMORANDUM

Date...

To ....

From...

Subject ....

(Headings: 1 mark)

1 Cost of new delivery van

Section: ....

(1 mark)

Reasons:...

(5 marks)

2 Stock of dolls for resale

Section: ....

(1 mark)

Reasons:...

(2 marks)

3 Telephone bill due to be paid in one month's time

Section: ....

(1 mark)

Reasons:...

(3 marks)

4 Drawings for the year

Section: ....

(1 mark)

Reasons:...

(4 marks)

Total 19%

Source: Assessment and Qualifications Alliance, January 2003

1.6.12 (E)

R Masters has completed his trading account for the year ended 31 March 2002.

Required

From the following information:

(a) (i) prepare the profit and loss account for the year ended 31 March 2002.

	£
Gross profit	56 231
Wages	23 980
Discount received	350
Carriage outwards	3 600
Motor expenses	4 500
Bank charges	450
Drawings	12 500
Capital	36 790

R Masters

Profit and Loss Account for the year ended 31 March 2002

(7 marks)

(ii) prepare the capital account as at 31 March 2002.

Dr **Capital Account** **Cr**

Date 2002	Details	£	Date 2002	Details	£

(4 marks)

(b) Explain two possible causes of a change in the balance of the capital account over the course of a year's trading.

(4 marks)

Total 15%

Source: Assessment and Qualifications Alliance, May 2002

1.6.13 (E)

The subsidiary books of Amaryllis Trading show the following totals for the month of December 2001.

Totals for the month	Goods	VAT	Total
	£	£	£
Sales day book	4560.30	798.05	5358.35
Returns inwards day book	236.91	41.46	278.37
Purchase day book	2769.56	484.67	3254.23
Returns outwards day book	127.50	22.31	149.81

The balances in the general ledger, made up of the totals for October and November 2001, are:

	£
Sales account	16 493.27
Returns inwards account	1 269.43
Purchases account	10 276.41
Returns outwards account	1 039.41

Required

(a) From the information given above enter the necessary data into the following accounts. The accounts need not be balanced.

Dr **Sales Account** **Cr**

Date 2001	Details	£	p	Date 2001	Details	£	p

Dr **Returns Inwards Account** **Cr**

Date 2001	Details	£	p	Date 2001	Details	£	p

Dr **Purchases Account** **Cr**

Date 2001	Details	£	p	Date 2001	Details	£	p

Dr **Returns Outwards Account** **Cr**

Date 2001	Details	£	p	Date 2001	Details	£	p

(8 marks)

The following information is also given:

	£
Stocks on 1 October 2001	2560.87
Stocks on 31 December 2001	2640.96
Carriage inwards for the 3 months	871.26

Required

(b) Prepare the trading account for the three months ended 31 December 2001.

Amaryllis Trading

Trading Account for the three months ended 31 December 2001

(8 marks)

(c) Using the figures from the trading account, state the totals of the following items:

	£
(i) Cost of goods sold	
(ii) Goods available for sale	
(iii) Turnover	

(3 marks)

Total 19%

Source: Assessment and Qualifications Alliance, January 2002

1.6.14 (E)

Joe Kinsworth, owner of Joe's Supplies, made profits of £24 000 and took drawings of £12 000 during the year ended 28 February 2001.

Required

(a) (i) Complete the trial balance with the details given.
(ii) Calculate the opening capital for Joe's Supplies.

Trial Balance as at 28 February 2001

	DR £	CR £
Vehicles	14 600	
Buildings	120 000	
Office Furniture	13 000	
Bank Loan		46 000
Bank		4 600
Debtors and creditors	27 500	34 000
Stock at 28 February	15 873	

(4 marks)

(b) Draw up the balance sheet from the trial balance to show clearly fixed assets, current assets, current liabilities, long term liabilities and capital.

(15 marks)

Total 19%

Source: Assessment and Qualifications Alliance, June 2001

1.6.15 (E)

Required

(a) In the following trial balance for the month ended 30 September 2000 enter, where necessary, the remaining balances given and calculate the capital account balance.

	£
Returns inwards	4 783
Returns outwards	3 791
Carriage outwards	4 796
Carriage inwards	396
Salaries	16 894
Stock at 1 September 2000	4 792
Stock at 30 September 2000	2 289
Petty cash	94
Bank overdraft	3 671

Wholesale Car Spares
Trial Balance as at 30 September 2000

	£	£
Sales		102 578
Purchases Trade creditors	56 453	 5 239
Trade debtors Discount allowed	7 824 452	
Discount received Rent and rates	 12 689	896
Fixtures and fittings	20 000	
Motor vehicles	13 000	
Buildings	80 000	
Drawings	3 568	
Returns inwards		
Returns outwards		
Carriage outwards		
Carriage inwards		
Salaries		
Stock		
Petty cash		
Bank overdraft		
Capital		

(9 marks)

(b) Prepare the trading account for the month ended 30 September 2000.

(9 marks)

Total 18%

Scurce: Assessment and Qualifications Alliance, January 2001

Detecting and correcting errors[A]

1.7

We've seen already that a Trial Balance can be used to spot certain types of error in the accounts (have a look at section 1.5.1). You will get a question on errors, and if it's not on the trial balance it should be about one of the techniques we're about to look at.

Whichever one it is, it'll probably be less straightforward than the material we've covered so far, so make sure you get that nailed down before you worry about this new section. These marks are often harder to get, especially if you don't know how to get the marks we've already studied for. This is why I've put the [A] on the title. It means 'Don't go for an A grade yet if you're not sure you've got a Pass or a B nailed right down'.

POINTS TO CONSIDER

- What's the difference between the Bank account and your account at the bank?
- Why do we have to make a bank reconciliation statement if our Bank account and the bank's account are measuring the same thing?
- Why might you make a Suspense account?
- Why is a Suspense account entry a single entry?
- What is the double entry required to cancel a suspense item?
- What do 'overcast' and 'undercast' mean?
- How do the entries in a Journal appear differently from those in most other day books?
- What do the Sales and Purchases Control Accounts check?
- On which side would you find an entry for 'Returns Out' and why?
- How would you record a contra entry?
- Why make control accounts?

1.7.1 BANK RECONCILIATION STATEMENTS

Whenever money is moved into and out of your firm's bank account, you record each transaction in the account for Bank in the Cash Book. Since money in the bank is an asset, you collect it on the debit (left) side, and pay it out on the credit side.

But your bank also has an account for you (i.e. your bank account), and they'll be recording the same transactions.

Banking through the looking glass

You are a customer of the bank, and the bank has an account for you, as they would for any supplier or customer. Your bank will record money going in and out on the opposite sides of the account to you; i.e. money goes out of the company account on the debit side.

Think of it from the point of view of the bank as a business. Money you put in the bank is money they'll have to pay back. To them you're a creditor and a liability. Or, if you're paying off an overdraft, they'll reduce the asset of debt on the credit side. Meanwhile, any money you borrow makes you a debtor: it's an asset to be reclaimed.

Look at your own bank statement and you'll see it working as a mirror to the way it should look for a firm's asset.

A bank statement is the bank's record for your account. When you get your bank statement you should check it against your own records. So what happens if their record doesn't match yours? Any differences need to be tackled by the accountant. Perhaps we put a cheque in but the money hasn't arrived. Maybe an automatic payment's been made that we didn't know about.

Terms in banking

There is some terminology used in banking which you may not know. You need to understand how to deal with each item:

Drawer: Someone who writes a cheque – they are drawing their funds

Payee: Someone who receives a cheque (has it written to them) – the opposite of a payer

Lodgement: Money put into your bank account

Clearing: The process of moving money from the drawer's account to the payee's account

Bank charges: What you pay the bank for running your account

Unpresented (cheque): A cheque you've written to someone that hasn't been claimed yet

Dishonoured (cheque): Someone's cheque to you doesn't have the funds to back it up

Standing order: An automatic instruction from you to pay a regular fixed amount. This will mean money coming out from your account.

Direct debit: An automatic instruction to allow a variable amount to be taken from your account.

Credit transfer: Money paid automatically into an account. In your exam you'll often find this is receiving money not paying it.

To 'reconcile' is to get two things to agree, so a bank reconciliation statement is where you use new information to make your account for Bank match the bank statement, possibly updating your Bank account in the process.

The exam paper will probably tell you the balance in your Cash Book and/or the balance on your bank statement, and give you some items that are not included in one or other. You have to build a bridge between the two. Normally you will start with your own figure and adapt it to match that of the bank statement, although you can work back from the bank's figure to your own if that's the way it's presented in the question.

Now, assuming we start with the balance in the Cash Book, we can either add or subtract a figure in response to four situations:

Our books say:	The bank statement says:	**Action:**
We recorded a payment	The payment didn't go out, e.g. unpresented cheque	**Add the payment back on (temporarily)**
We didn't record a payment	A payment was made e.g. bank charges	**Take the payment away**
We recorded a receipt	The receipt didn't happen e.g. dishonoured cheque	**Take the receipt away (temporarily)**
We didn't record a receipt	A receipt happened e.g. credit transfer	**Add the receipt on**

To go from the bank statement to the Cash Book, add instead of subtract and vice versa.

Here's a question. First we'll tackle each item one at a time in a simple one-column format:

> **Autumn Chill kilt manufacturers have a debit balance of £4,397 in their Cash Book for the month ended March 2006. A statement from Gordon's Bank records the balance as being £5,019. An inspection reveals the following information:**

Automatic bank charges not yet entered	**£35**
Unpresented cheque to Black Sheep Barbers	**£545**
Dishonoured cheque from The Little Sock Shop	**£357**
Standing order to Never Say Dye	**£146**
Credit transfer from IBC Costumes	**£615**

Prepare a bank reconciliation statement.

Answer:

Bank reconciliation statement for Autumn Chill – 31 March 2006

Balance in cash book	4,397
Bank charges	(35)
	4,362
Unpresented cheque	545
	4,907
Dishonoured cheque	(357)
	4,550
Standing order	(146)
	4,404
Credit transfer	615
Balance on bank statement	5,019

Commentary:

We start with £4,397 in our books. How would we change our books if we knew what we know now?

- The bank charge is easy. We didn't know it had gone out so we just subtract it now.
- The unpresented cheque is *to* Black Sheep. The money is still in the bank. This doesn't mean more money for us, it just means we recorded money going out, and have to add it again temporarily to make it look like the bank statement.
- The dishonoured cheque would have been recorded in the cash book when the cheque was paid in. But if the money's not there we have to subtract it again, and probably phone the debtor.
- The standing order. We should have known this one was coming. Never mind, we'll record the money going out now. Note how 'standing order' is a detail we'd expect to have for movement from our account. A standing order into our account would probably appear as a credit transfer.
- And here is a credit transfer, and it says 'from' just to make it easier. Just add the money on.

If you're feeling bold you can adopt the 2-column approach:

Bank reconciliation statement for Autumn Chill – 31 March 2006

Balance in cash book		4,397
Add		
Unpresented cheque	545	
Credit transfer	615	1,160
		5,557
Less		
Bank charges	35	
Dishonoured cheque	357	
Standing order	146	(538)
Balance on bank statement		5,019

One sneaky thing you should look out for. If your Bank account has a credit balance (i.e. you're overdrawn) you'll be starting with a negative figure. Apart from this the actions remain the same. Remember – a credit balance on the bank statement means you have money. A debit balance is an overdraft. This is the opposite way round to the appearance in your account for Bank.

Dress to Kill make safety clothing for paintballing centres. Their Cash Book says their Bank account has a credit balance of £12,000, but the bank statement lists a debit balance of £13,854.

Use the following information to make a bank reconciliation statement.

Automatic bank charges not yet entered	**£86**
Unpresented cheque to Pull the Wool	**£920**
Dishonoured cheque from Bigg Events	**£2415**
Standing order to Electric Blue	**£493**
Credit transfer from Bang Bang Pop Pop	**£220**

Answer:

Bank reconciliation statement for Dress to Kill

Balance in Cash Book		(12,000)
Add		
Unpresented cheque	920	
Credit transfer	220	1,140
		(10,860)
Less		
Bank charges	86	
Dishonoured cheque	2415	
Standing order	493	(2,994)
Balance on bank statement		(13,854)

1.7.2 SUSPENSE ACCOUNTS

You're not likely to get a question just on suspense accounts, but you should know how they work as they may be included in another question.

What happens if you finish a Trial Balance, and the debit and credit sides don't match? Well, first you add them again. Still don't match? Well, there's obviously been an error. So you try to find the error. Maybe there's a single entry somewhere. Maybe one account has been added up incorrectly (undercast or overcast). If you really can't find the mistake, you put an entry in the Suspense account, just to make the trial balance totals balance. It's that rarest of things: a single entry. The theory is that the other half already exists, lurking somewhere as a mistake in the books.

When you find the mistake, you can

- record the correction in the Journal, and
- make the correction in the books:
  - with an entry to correct the mistake, and
  - an entry to neutralise the entry in the Suspense account.

Any exam question is likely to test this skill, and depends on your ability with double entry. However, don't forget you're in the Hall of Mirrors.

See in this example how we deal with two errors.

The Trial Balance (extract) reads:

	Dr	*Cr*
Total Credit balances		792,300
Suspense		7,700
	800,000	800,000

The Suspense account reads:

Suspense

Dr			*Cr*
		Balance	7,700

We can now make our Financial Statements, although when we get to the Balance Sheet we record the Suspense account figure as a current liability (or a current asset for a debit figure).

We later find that there has been an undercast (added up too small) of £1,300 in the Sales Returns account (debit side), and an interest payment of £9,000 left off the Cash Book (credit side). This accounts for the original excess on the credit side of £7,700. We're going to have to make these entries into the accounts where they belong as described above, so that they're now correct, and we have to make the corresponding double entries to balance off the Suspense account.

The Suspense account now reads:

Suspense

Dr			*Cr*
Bank	9,000	Balance	7,700
		Sales Returns	1,300
		9,000	9,000

Note how the corrections appear to be on the 'wrong' side – because of course they're the other half of the belated double entry:

Bank

Dr			*Cr*
		Suspense	9,000

Sales Returns

Dr			*Cr*
Suspense	1,300		

If you're given a Suspense Account to complete, it'll probably be this last stage. You should understand that a Suspense account has

- a balancing figure, and
- the other halves of the belated corrections.

1.7.3 THE JOURNAL

The Journal is a day book used to record irregular events, like buying fixed assets, adding capital, **writing off** debts and so on.

> **to write off**
> To let go of something because its value can't be reclaimed.

It's also used to record the correction of errors – especially the errors not shown up by the Trial Balance. If you find you've added up the Purchases account incorrectly, you'll make a note of the problem in the Journal. But you must follow this format:

		Dr	Cr
		£	£
Date	Account to be debited	x.xx	
	Account to be credited		x.xx
	Narrative (description)		

This isn't a double entry account, just a list of double entries. The Journal is a day book, remember, and the information is then moved to other accounts.

Let's see some questions in action:

C. Higson bought some oversized purple trousers (item no. 4321) for £50, but the purchase was debited to C. Hignett. The mistake has been noticed. Show the Journal entry required.

	Dr	Cr
	£	£
C. Higson	50	
C. Hignett		50
Sale of oversized purple trousers no. 4321		
Correction of entry in wrong personal account		

Oops – an error of commission. Note how the debit entry that Higson should have had has now been entered, and how the credit entry for Hignett cancels out the debit entry that was made by mistake.

The Purchases day book has been overcast by £90. The discrepancy was recorded in the Suspense account but has now been noticed. Show the Journal entry required.

	Dr	Cr
	£	£
Suspense	90	
Purchases		90
Correction of overcast recorded in suspense account		

Overcasting means over-adding up (undercasting means under-adding up). If we over added by £90 there would have been £90 too much in Purchases on the debit side of the Trial Balance. We'd have needed a credit entry in Suspense to level things up. Now we can undo it – a debit entry in Suspense to cancel it, and a credit entry in purchases to eliminate the overcast.

A cash payment of £25 was received from F. Giles, but was recorded as £35 in both Cash and Giles's accounts. Show the journal entry required to correct this.

	Dr	Cr
	£	£
F. Giles	10	
Cash		10
Reduction of figure entered for cash payment		

Nasty! Now we're undoing things. F. Giles had paid us £25 to reduce his debt (a credit entry in his account). We gained £25 cash (debit entry in the Bank account). The £35 we entered both times were too high. Now we have to put £10 into the opposite side to counter the error. Put £10 back onto the debit side of Giles' account, and £10 off cash with a credit entry.

Discounts Received has been debited with a sum of £80, when the Cash Book shows there should have been an entry for £8. A suspense entry was made pending the discovery of the mistake. Make the Journal entries now required to record the corrections.

	Dr	Cr
	£	£
Suspense	88	
Discounts Received		88
Correction of Suspense entry		

Who was working with figures of £72? They've bowled you a real late spinner this time! This question takes the Hall of Mirrors into another dimension.

Discounts Received should be a credit entry. It's described as a debit entry. It was the wrong amount and it was on the wrong side. How sneaky is that? The Trial Balance had a mistaken £80 entered on the debit side, and was missing £8 on the credit side. This would have required an £88 credit entry in Suspense. Now that we've fixed it, we debit Suspense to balance it off, and credit Discounts Received with the original £8, plus £80 to eliminate the error. You can make two journal entries of £80 and £8 if you prefer.

This is about as hard as it gets in Unit 1. Get something like this right in your exam and you're on course for an excellent score.

1.7.4 CONTROL ACCOUNTS

If it comes up in your exam, do this question last. The principle is straightforward, but executing it can be as confusing as hell. In fact, you'll struggle with this if you can't do double entry really well; although if you can do this on top of the other stuff you're on course for a very good grade.

A Control Account is a kind of Trial Balance for one ledger, and runs in parallel to the regular accounts. It's based on the fact that all entries are double entries – each transaction gets put in the books twice. This means we can use the totals from one half of the double entry to check the totals of the other half.

In an exam you could be offered a Sales Ledger Control Account, or a Purchases Ledger Control Account.

Remember that:

- The Sales Ledger is a ledger for Debtors (NOT Sales).
  - The Sales Ledger Control Account is a Total Debtors Account.
- The Purchases Ledger is a ledger for Creditors (NOT Purchases).
  - The Purchases Ledger Control Account is a Total Creditors Account.

A question might look like this:

Use the following list of balances to complete the Sales Ledger Control Account for 29 February 2012.

Credit Sales	**£94,200**
Cash Sales	**£10,100**
Credit Sales Returns	**£ 2,300**
Cash Sales Returns	**£400**
Payments Received	**£89,020**
Contra set-off from Purchases Ledger	**£280**
Bad debts written off	**£40**
Discounts allowed	**£30**
Refunds for overpayment	**£20**
Closing Debit Balance	**£17,090**
Closing Credit Balance	**£50**

(Total Debtors Account)

Sales Ledger Control Account

Dr					*Cr*
1.2.12	Balance b/d	14,650	1.2.12	Balance b/d	60
29.2.12	Credit Sales	94,200	29.2.12	Credit Sales Returns	2,300
"	Refunds	20	"	Receipts	89,020
"	Credit Balance c/d	50	"	Contra set-off	280
			"	Bad debts	40
			"	Discounts allowed	30
			"	Debit Balance c/d	17,190
		108,920	"		108,920
1.3.12	Debit Balance b/d	17,190	1.3.12	Credit Balance b/d	50

See how it might be confusing?

An easy trick is to enter the information on the 'wrong' side: For example, we expect to see a Sales balance on the credit side, so we put 'Sales' on the debit side. But why?

We're checking the balances in the accounts of our debtors. Every time a debtor increases the money they owe us by buying something (debit entry), we put a Hall of Mirrors credit entry in Sales as well. So, to check our total for the amount of debt incurred in the Sales Ledger, we can go and add up all of the totals in the Sales Day Book for Sales. This is why a figure called Sales appears on the debit side – it represents 'debts incurred'.

Similarly, if a debtor has decreased their debt (a credit entry) by making a return we use the day book figures for Returns In – normally seen on the debit side.

When you look at each figure, just think how it would be reflected in the account for Debtors or for Creditors and it'll keep you on track. In fact, before you answer the question, change the heading to 'Total Debtors Account' or 'Total Creditors Account'.

Note that the opening balance is on the side you'd expect for Debtors or Creditors. Any additions to sales and purchases should go on the same side as the opening balance, while reductions (e.g. returns, payments, discounts and debts written off) should go on the other side.

Exceptions to the opening balance rule can happen. If you sell 100 handkerchiefs at £1 each to Thar She Blows, what happens if they pay you the full £100 and later return £20 worth of stock? Well, for one thing you hope it's unused. But also, you will find a balance of £20 on the credit side, as well as the larger balance for all other debtors on the debit side.

Cash, contra and errors of commission

One item to be wary of is cash sales or purchases. The Sales and Purchases ledgers are for debtors and creditors. Ignore cash transactions.

Contra items may be new to you. Say you supply lunches to the local radio station, and they supply advertising for you. You'll have them down as a debtor for the lunches (say, £45) and as a creditor for the advertising (say, £250). It's normal at the end of the month to set off one account against the other. Start by balancing off the smaller account as if full payment had been made (e.g. credit entry of £45 to bring the debtor's account to zero). Now make the corresponding entry in the larger account (debit entry also of £45). This reduces it by the amount of the offset and leaves a balance still owing (in this case a credit balance of £205). We're interested in the amount you've set off (£45). This shows up in both the Sales and Purchases Control Accounts. It behaves like a payment in both, and goes on the same side as a payment.

Also, if you're presented with any errors, take care with errors of commission, for example, or other errors not affecting the balance. If you're told that the cheque from Tom Jones was entered into the account for John Thomas, then you'll wonder all day how it makes the control account wrong. It doesn't – the overall balance stays the same. Nor does it affect the Suspense Account, although you may record the correction in the Journal.

Why control accounts?

If each of the ledgers, Sales, Purchases and General, is being looked after by a team of accountants, then the head of the team will use each ledger's totals to:

- Double check accuracy except errors not affecting a Trial Balance
- Localise a mistake, thus saving time crawling through all of the books
- Reduce the risk of fraud

FURTHER READING

Frank Wood and Alan Sangster, *Business Accounting 1*, Chapters 17, 30, 31, 33
David Cox and Michael Fardon, *A/S Accounting for AQA*, Chapters 10, 13 and 14
Ian Harrison, *Introducing Accounting for A/S* Chapters 9, 14, 15

USEFUL WEB SITES

www.aqa.org.uk/qual/gceasa/acc_assess.html This is always your most useful web site. Download as many exam papers as your printer will allow.

www.bized.ac.uk Choose 'accounting' as your subject. There are BAIT interactive tests on Control Accounts and Suspense Accounts.

www.allbusiness.com In the 'Advice Centres' section, click on 'Finance and Accounting', and choose the Bank Reconciliation worksheet. Note that the Americans write cheque as 'check'.

www.turbocashuk.com Turbocash offer some theory to back up their products. The last entry on the menu bar is Help Topics. From here the sections on Control Accounts and Bank Reconciliation are quite helpful.

www.unisys.com/common/investors/glossary/

www.google.co.uk

SAMPLE QUESTIONS

1.7.1

Accountants acting on behalf of Tony and Lucy have prepared a bank reconciliation statement and control accounts in order to check their books. They have also used the journal to record errors kept in a suspense account.

Required

(a) What is a bank reconciliation statement used for?

(b) Which ledgers might be verified by a Control Account?

(c) Why might a Suspense account be used?

(6 marks)

1.7.2

The Little Octopus Café chain has drawn up a Trial Balance, whose debit side total was greater than its credit side total by £890. They opened a Suspense account. The following errors have since been discovered:

- The Sales account was undercast by £620.
- A cheque for £52 received from Joe Davis was entered into the account for Davy Jones.
- The Returns Outwards balance should have been £420, but had been brought down as £240.
- The Discounts Received balance of £80 had been left out entirely.
- A £40 invoice for Carriage Inwards had been entered into Carriage Outwards.

Required

(a) Make the necessary entries into the Suspense account, and identify any balance remaining.

Suspense

Dr	£		Cr £
		Balance	890

(6 marks)

(b) Identify three types of error which would not affect the Trial Balance, with examples.

(6 marks)

(c) Why would these errors not need to be recorded in a Suspense account?

(2 marks)

1.7.3

Required

(a) Use the following list of balances to complete the Purchase Ledger Control Account for 31 July 2007.

	£
Credit Purchases	72,900
Cash Purchases	850
Credit Purchase Returns	1,800
Cash Purchase Returns	110
Discounts received	60
Refunds for overpayment	30
Credit Payments Made	69,150
Contra set-off from Sales Ledger	70
Debit Balance	30
Credit Balance	?

Purchase Ledger Control Account

Dr					Cr
2007		£	2007		£
1/7/07	Balance b/d	20	1/7/07	Balance b/d	12,390

(6 marks)

(b) What does the closing credit balance represent?

(2 marks)

1.7.4 (E)

James Baker has received a bank statement for his business and is preparing a bank reconciliation statement.

Required

(a) Why are bank reconciliation statements prepared?

....

(3 marks)

(b) The bank statement includes he following entries. Explain the meaning of each of them. Identify the ledger entries James Baker will have to make.

Standing order paid to Perfect Insurance Co. £200

Explanation:..

(3 marks)

Debit:...

(1 mark)

Credit: ....

(1 mark)

Credit transfer from The Magnificent Garden Centre £700.47

Explanation:..

(3 marks)

Debit:...

(1 mark)

Credit: ....

(1 mark)

Bank charges £43.27

Explanation:..

(3 marks)

Debit:...

(1 mark)

Credit: ....

(1 mark)

Total 18%

Source: Assessment and Qualifications Alliance, June 2004

1.7.5 (E)

Here is a bank statement for the month of November 2003 which has been received by James Jolly and Co. A junior clerk has checked the Cash Book against the bank statement, and has ticked (✓) the items that appear in both.

WESTBANK LTD 27–43–56

WESTOWN BRANCH

Account 4569823

James Jolly and Co.

STATEMENT OF ACCOUNT

Date 2003	Details £	Payments £	Receipts £	Balance
Nov. 1	Balance b/f			2659.35
2	Cheque 345	200.00 ✓		2459.35
3	Counter credit		234.00 ✓	2693.35
4	Cheque346	134.37 ✓		2558.98
4	Cheque 347	276.89 ✓		2282.09
5	Counter credit		4361.00 ✓	6643.09
9	Cr.tfr. J. Black Ltd		246.98	6890.07
12	S/o Business rates	547.90		6342.17
15	Cheque 349	3781.95 ✓		2560.22
18	S/o Proper Ins. Co.	145.65		2414.57
23	Counter credit		560.00 ✓	2974.57
23	Bank charges	45.89		2928.68
27	Cheque 350	139.43 ✓		2789.25
27	Cheque 348	92.50 ✓		2696.75

Note
Cr.tfr. – credit transfer
S/o – standing order

Required

(a) Update the following Cash Book on 30 November with any necessary entries and calculate the new bank balance.

Cash Book extract

Date 2003	Details	Bank £	p	Date 2003	Details	Cheque number	Bank £	p
Nov 1	Balance b/d	2459	35	Nov 1	Banks Ltd	11346	134	37 ✓
Nov 3	Toys for You	234	00 ✓	Nov 1	Books & Paints	11347	276	89 ✓
Nov 5	B. J. Patel	3219	00 ✓	Nov 10	Wages	11348	92	50 ✓
Nov 5	Dolls and things	1142	00 ✓	Nov 12	Jones and Son	11349	3781	95 ✓
Nov 23	J. A. Smith Ltd	560	00 ✓	Nov 23	Smith and Son	11350	139	43 ✓
Nov 26	Cash banked	340	00	Nov 25	HGF Finance	11351	256	00
				Nov 25	Toy Designs	11352	1245	98
				Nov 30	Balance c/d		2027	23
		7945	35				7945	35
Nov 30	Balance b/d	2027	23					

(5 marks)

(b) Prepare a bank reconciliation statement as at 30 November 2003.

(8 marks)

Total 13%

Source: Assessment and Qualifications Alliance, January 2004

1.7.6 (E)
James White uses several methods to verify his records.

Required
Write a report to Bill Bennett explaining one benefit of each of the following methods. Give an example of one error which will be revealed in each case.

REPORT

To:..

From:...

Date: ....

Subject: ....

(Report headings: 1 mark)

(a) Bank reconciliation statement

Benefit: ....

(3 marks)

Example: ....

(1 mark)

(b) Sales ledger control account

Benefit: ....

(3 marks)

Example: ....

(1 mark)

(c) Trial balance

Benefit: ....

(3 marks)

Example: ....

(1 mark)

Total 13%

Source: Assessment and Qualifications Alliance, June 2003

1.7.7 (E)

When reconciling bank statements the adjustments will include entries in the cash book for standing orders, direct debits and credit transfers.

Required

(a) Explain what each of these terms means and whether they will be **debited** or **credited** to the bank account in the business's books.

(i) Standing orders.

....

(3 marks)

(ii) Direct debits.

....

(3 marks)

(iii) Credit transfers.

....

(3 marks)

The bank statement received by A Smith and Co shows a debit balance of £600 at 31 March 2001. The accountant checks it against the cash book and makes the following discoveries:

(1) The bank statement shows the following items not shown in the cash book:
- a standing order for £230 in favour of Planet Insurance:
- a direct debit payable to Electric Supplies £420;
- a credit transfer has been received from The Best Co for £540;
- a cheque for £265 is debited on the bank statement, which A Smith and Co are querying;
- bank charges of £46 have been levied.

(2) The cash book has an overdrawn balance of £378 and shows the following items not shown on the bank statement:
- unpresented cheques amounting to £469;
- uncleared bankings of £270.

Required

(b) Make any necessary entries in the cash book.

Dr **Cash Book – Bank Account** **Cr**

	£		£

(7 marks)

(c) Prepare a bank reconciliation as at 31 March 2001.

Bank Reconciliation Statement as at 31 March 2001

(7 marks)

Total 23%

Source: Assessment and Qualifications Alliance, June 2001

1.7.8 (E)

R Masters has drawn up a suspense account at 31 March 2002 following the discovery of errors.

Required

(a) Name **two** accounting techniques which may have been used to detect the presence of errors in the books

....

(2 marks)

(b) Make the necessary entries in the journal below to correct the following errors. Narratives are **not** required.

(1) The sales day book has been overcast by £270.

(2) The returns inwards has been entered as a credit of £500. In fact it only totalled £300.

(3) A discount received of £400 was entered in the cash book but omitted from the general ledger.

(4) A cheque paid to J Jones of £350 was entered in the account of A Jones in error.

JOURNAL

Account	**Debit** £	**Credit** £

(10 marks)

Total 12%

Source: Assessment and Qualifications Alliance, May 2002

1.7.9 (E)

Required

(a) From the following list of balances extracted from the books of BJ Patel on 30 November 2003 complete the sales and purchases ledger control accounts. Bring down the balance on each account.

	£
Sales on credit	26 500
Purchases on credit	19 600
Returns inwards	590
Returns outwards	450
Amounts received from customers	18 900
Amounts paid to suppliers	16 300
A debit balance set off from the sales ledger to the purchase ledger (contra)	400

Debit — Sales Ledger Control Account — Credit

Date 2003	Details	£	Date 2003	Details	£
Nov 1	Balance b/d	5476			

Debit — Purchases Ledger Control Account — Credit

Date 2003	Details	£	Date 2003	Details	£
			Nov 1	Balance b/d	2960

(10 marks)

(b) Explain how control accounts are used to verify the balances in the sales ledger and purchase ledger accounts.

....

(4 marks)

(c) What is the main limitation of using a control account to verify these ledger accounts?

....

(3 marks)

Total 17%

Source: Assessment and Qualifications Alliance, January 2004

1.7.10 (E)

Required

(a) Advise Wholesale Car Spares of two benefits they would gain from keeping control accounts.

BENEFIT 1: ....

BENEFIT 2: ....

(3 marks)

The sales ledger control account for the month ended 31 October 2000 did not agree with the sales ledger balances list total.

The following errors have been discovered.

1. The sales day book was undercast by £540.
2. The return inwards day book includes £100 which is actually for returns outwards
3. A discount allowed of £37 has been omitted from the books completely.
4. A cheque received from J C Cross Garages for £1479 was entered in the account of A B Cross Ltd in error.
5. The opening balances brought down should have been £25 080.

Required

(b) Enter the necessary corrections in the control account. Balance the account.

Dr SALES LEDGER CONTROL ACCOUNT Cr

2000			£		2000		£
Oct	31	Balance b/d	25 800				

(7 marks)

(c) Explain the main limitation of control accounts using two examples to illustrate your answer.

(5 marks)

Total 16%

Source: Assessment and Qualifications Alliance, January 2001

Computers in accounting 1.8

We've been looking at how accounts might be presented on paper, although most businesses will do a lot of the work we've seen on computers. Day books, ledgers and so on are all stored on a computer. This doesn't affect the principles of accounting. You'll probably be asked about computers in accounting in your exam, and typically you'll be asked to discuss a situation where a new computerised system is being considered.

POINTS TO CONSIDER

- What can computers be used for in a business?
- What decisions face a manager buying a new system?
- What do computers do better than entries by hand?
- What problems might you face with a new system?
- How can computers help managers make decisions?
- How does a new system affect staff?

There is plenty you could learn about computers, but at this stage it's probably sufficient to learn the key points shown here. As with any essay-style question, start with the key facts, and show how they apply to the situation in the question. The information is shown here in bullet point form to make it easy to learn. You'll get marks for showing you know the bullet points, but write an answer properly if you can.

Different computer packages and systems you could use

- Spreadsheets (e.g. Excel)
  - Display plans and results in table form

  - Calculate tax / interest and statistics easily
  - Can convert currency
- Sage Instant Accounting
  - A widely used package specifically for accounting
- AIS (accounting information systems)
  - Can be linked to EPOS (electronic point of sale) and stock control
- Workstations / LANs (local area networks) / WANs (wider area networks) / intranet

Software: what should you choose?

- 'Off-the-shelf' package – a general system that fits most businesses
  - Less expensive
  - But is it exactly what you want?
- Bespoke/customised package
  - Can be designed to work exactly for the way your business wants
  - Could be expensive

Benefits / advantages of using computers

- Does the same job, but better
  - Input is only necessary once
    - Can be done via EPOS/laser scanning or document scanning
  - Calculations are made automatically
  - Passwords can improve security
  - Skilled staff are more productive
- Increases
  - Speed (saves time)
  - Accuracy (more automation reduces the opportunity for error)
  - Efficiency
  - Consistency
- Produces reports automatically; quicker; more reliable; more professional appearance
  - Customer statements
  - Financial statements
  - Cash flow analysis
  - Pay rolls
  - Stock reports
- Error detection / Exception reporting (automatically flags problems)
  - Credit limits – are your customers buying more than they can pay for?
  - Budget control – are limits being broken?

  - Low levels of stock – is it time to re-order?
  - Delivery times – are we meeting all of our performance targets?
- Management Information System (MIS) helps decision-making
  - More job satisfaction
  - Information can be
    - Stored in a smaller space
    - Accessed and cross referenced easily
    - Copied/backed up easily in case of accident

Problems / disadvantages

- Any change brings stress and needs management
- Expense
- Staff will need new training, although accounting skills are still more important than computing skills.
- Must comply with Data Protection Act 1998
- Care must still be taken when inputting data/GIGO (garbage in garbage out)
- Increased reporting efficiency can bring information overload
- Will better efficiency mean that redundancies are necessary?

Other issues

- Should the new computer system replicate the old paper system, or be redesigned?
- Can you adapt an off-the-shelf package?
  - May need to adapt existing terminology / functions to fit an off-the-shelf package
- Who's in charge of the new system?
- Time scales
  - Development
  - Testing
  - Introduction
    - Swap over date or
    - Run in parallel for an overlap period?
- Costs and benefits

Here's how you might use these ideas for an exam question. This answer is as full as you'd normally be able to write in the time and space available. Try to include at least one valid point for each mark available, and remember that if you're asked a question in two parts you need to answer both. Note that some information hasn't been used here: we're not asked about software, for example, so there are no marks available for talking about it.

The managers of Ben Downe Fruit Picking are considering a comprehensive new computer system to replace their existing one which just holds payroll records.

Write a report to the management:

1. **Advising them on two new uses for a new computerised system**
2. **Assessing the advantages and disadvantages to both the business and its staff**

To: Management of Ben Downe Fruit Picking
Date: (The date of your exam will do here)
From: (Your name here)
Subject: New computer system

- The new system can be used to automate the accounting of the company; the day books and ledgers could be held on a computer with many advantages.

  The new system can also be used as a Management Information System (MIS) to help with decision making.

- This plan has many advantages, as a computerised system increases speed, accuracy, efficiency and consistency. Calculations are automatic and staff are more productive. The new system can be linked to an EPOS (electronic point of sale) system to manage stock, and input information with a scanner gun.

  It produces reports automatically, e.g. customer statements, financial statements and cash flow analysis. These will look more professional as well as being more reliable.

  A Management Information System (MIS) saves routine work and offers more job satisfaction. Information can be backed up easily in case of an accident, and passwords can improve security. It can be used for error detection and exception reporting, e.g. credit limits, budget control, low levels of stock and delivery times. This will reduce risk and improve service.

  However, there may be problems and disadvantages. For one thing it will be expensive and there will need to be change management. You must comply with the Data Protection Act 1998, and care must still be taken when inputting data, as garbage in means garbage out. Also, for an MIS, increased reporting efficiency can bring information overload.

  There will need to be training for staff, although accounting skills are still more important than computing skills. Staff may also worry about redundancies if the new system does their job more cheaply.

You'll need to be able to reproduce this information; as always, practice applying it to the exam questions.

FURTHER READING

Frank Wood and Alan Sangster, *Business Accounting 1*, Chapters 22–23
David Cox and Michael Fardon, *A/S Accounting for AQA*, Chapter 11

USEFUL WEB SITES

www.aqa.org.uk/qual/gceasa/acc_assess.html This is always your most useful web site. Download as many exam papers as your printer will allow.

www.workbox.demon.co.uk/C12.htm This firm of chartered accountants has produced a practical summary of using computers.

www.turbocashuk.com This company has lots of images of what a computerised package might look like, and how it works. Please note that this book does not endorse any one computerised system over any other. This site was selected for the pictures in the online help.

www.google.co.uk

SAMPLE QUESTIONS

1.8.1

Quiller's Racy Magazine Co. currently uses a computer for word processing and for publishing motor magazines.

Required
Advise Quiller's on how they might expand their system to include accounting functions. You should consider issues such as what software would or would not be relevant to a publishing company, and how it might help them to deal with suppliers and retailers.

(10 marks)

1.8.2

Mayglyn Motorbikes is considering upgrading the computer system used for their store.

Required
Write a report to Mayglyn, outlining the uses they could make of such a system, the issues they need to consider, and the advantages that can be gained.

To: ....

From: ....

Date: ....

Subject: ....

(Headings 1 mark, total 11 marks)

1.8.3
Rhys's Teapot Shop currently uses a simple spreadsheet package to manage accounts. Rhys is considering the best way to handle stock, payroll and financial reporting.

Required
Write a report advising Rhys about the options available, the advantages of expanding his computer system, and the problems he should be prepared for.

(10 marks)

1.8.4
Wrod's Quads are concerned about the time taken and mistakes made by their staff at various stages of their accounting process, including purchasing, sales and the preparation of final accounts.

Required
Advise Wrod's Quads on how they can use computerisation to improve staff efficiency.

(10 marks)

1.8.5
Legs By Liz is a rapidly expanding wholesale clothes business. Liz Simmonsen has always prepared her accounts by hand because she doesn't understand computers.

Required
Describe the different options available to Liz, including the types of hardware and software she can choose, possible applications such as stock control, and issues such as cost.

(12 marks)

Unit 2

FINANCIAL ACCOUNTING:
published accounts of limited companies

Foundation for Unit 2

2.0

Are you sure you're doing the right Unit?

For the AQA AS level, you need Unit 1 or Unit 2, plus Units 3 and 4. If you might go on and complete A2, it's recommended you do Unit 1 instead of Unit 2. If you've done Unit 1 already, you need to flick forward to Unit 3 and leave this part alone.

Much of the work you'll do in Unit 2 is actually covered elsewhere in Units 1 and 3, and you'll find yourself directed to those relevant sections for most of this unit. You might find it effective to download as many exam papers as possible first, to focus your attention on exactly what's required.

To start, you should study section 1.1 The Hall of Mirrors. If you want a crash course, '1.1.3 Accounts in outline' may be sufficient. You won't be tested on this material directly, but you will find it easier to understand the material that you are tested on.

Section 1.1 shows that everything we buy or sell is listed in 'accounts'. When we have collected the money in these lists, we can calculate how much money we have, how much we owe, and many other things we might want to know abut the business.

You can look at the web sites for more information.

When you have a grasp of section 1.1, come back and look at section 2.1, The Trial Balance.

FURTHER READING

David Cox and Michael Fardon, *A/S Accounting for AQA*, Chapter 15

SAMPLE QUESTION

2.0.1 (E)

Required
The table below lists some items which can be found in a Trial Balance.

(a) State from which ledger each account is taken and whether it will be a debit or credit entry in the Trial Balance.

An example has been given.

	Account	**Ledger**	**Debit/credit**
e.g.	*Business rates*	*General*	*Debit*
1	Trade debtor		
2	Sales		
3	Cash		

(6 marks)

Source: Assessment and Qualifications Alliance, January 2003

You should also attempt the questions at the end of section 1.1.

2.1 The Trial Balance

You're going to go back to Unit 1 to learn about this, but not without some guidance.

Learn section 1.5 The Trial Balance, and then come back for some exam questions. As you go through it consider:

- Where did these numbers come from? Look again at section 1.1.3 if you're unsure.
- What are the two main reasons for making a Trial Balance?
- What does a Trial Balance look like?
- Does it matter in what order we put things? (No)
- Does it matter which side we put things? (Very much so!)
- If there are mistakes, what types will and will not be shown in a Trial Balance?

After you've studied the next section on Financial Statements you'll also be able to consider these points:

- If there are mistakes in the Trial Balance, how do they affect the profit calculations we make from it? For example, if the figure for an expense is too big, does that make our profit higher or lower?
- How will these mistakes affect the Balance Sheet?

Learn also section 1.7.2 Suspense accounts. We make one of these if the Trial Balance totals don't agree, and you may be asked to sort out some mistakes that have been found.

You can look at the web sites in both sections for more information, and then come back and try these exam questions.

FURTHER READING

David Cox and Michael Fardon, *A/S Accounting for AQA*, Chapter 16

SAMPLE QUESTION

2.1.1 (E)

On 30 April 2004 China Products plc prepared a trial balance. The trial balance totals did not agree. A suspense account was opened.

The following errors have been discovered:

(1) The sales account had been overcast by £200.

(2) A purchases invoice for £500 had been entered in both the supplier's account and the purchases account as £50.

(3) Rent paid of £650 had been correctly entered in the Cash Book, but had been entered in the rent account as £400.

Required

(a) Make appropriate entries in the suspense account. Show the opening balance.

Suspense Account

Dr **Cr**

Date 2004	Details	£	Date 2004	Details	£

(3 marks)

(b) Give an example of an error of commission. Explain why it will not be revealed by a trial balance.

Example:..

(2 marks)

Explanation: ....

(3 marks)

(c) Identify **two** reasons for preparing a trial balance

Reason 1:...

(2 marks)

Reason 2: ....

(2 marks)

Total 12%

Source: Assessment and Qualifications Alliance, June 2004

You should also attempt the questions at the end of section 1.5.

2.2 Financial Statements

By choosing Unit 2 you've opted to learn about accounts for larger firms, and you'll see that there is a lot of detail in Unit 1 you won't study: sections 1.2 to 1.4 for instance. We'll make up for that by learning some extra stuff about Limited Liability Companies in section 2.3.

In this section, however, we'll start by learning the simpler layouts for the Financial Statements of one-owner businesses (sole traders). Now study section 1.6 Financial Statements. Bear in mind that some comments about study in Unit 3 will actually apply to you in this unit.

Although it's not in your exam, you might want to try some of the Unit 1 exam questions before you tackle the next section, and familiarise yourself with the layouts you need to know. Whether or not you do this, get ready for plenty of practise at the end of Section 2.3.

When you're sure about Trading and Profit and Loss Accounts and Balance Sheets for sole traders, and you've practised the material there, move on.

FURTHER READING

David Cox and Michael Fardon, *A/S Accounting for AQA*, Chapter 18

SAMPLE QUESTION

2.2.1 (E)

The following balances are taken from the books of James Cadwallader Ltd showing totals for the year ended 31 December 2002.

	£
Sales	67 945
Purchases	34 981
Returns inwards	2 945
Returns outwards	1 367
Carriage inwards	679
Carriage outwards	386
Stock at 1 January 2002	5 780
Stock at 31 December 2002	6 590
Wages	12 056
Other expenses	4 650

Required
Prepare the trading and profit and loss account for the year ended 31 December 2002

James Cadwallader Ltd
Trading and Profit and Loss Account for the year ended 31 December 2002

(15 marks)

Total 15%

Source: Assessment and Qualifications Alliance, January 2003

You should also attempt the questions at the end of section 1.6.

Limited Liability Companies 2.3

Before you can attempt most Unit 2 exam questions, you'll need to learn some extra material for Limited Liability Companies. Look at Chapter 3.6 Limited Liability Companies. Whilst most of it is examined again in Unit 3, nearly all of it is useful for Unit 2 – especially sections 3.6.1 to 3.6.5 on types of capital.

When you've got that, you're ready for some questions.

FURTHER READING

David Cox and Michael Fardon, *A/S Accounting for AQA*, Chapters 19 and 21

SAMPLE QUESTION

2.3.1

The directors of Sheng Motors want to revalue their premises, which were bought for £130,000 several years ago, but are now valued at £180,000.

(a) In which section of the Balance Sheet is the asset of premises found?

(1 mark)

(b) How would the subtotal of this section change after the revaluation?

(1 mark)

(c) What other change will need to be made to the Balance Sheet?

(2 marks)

2.3.2

The draft Net Profit for Isabel & Owen Ltd at 30 June 2010 was £107,000. The following errors have since been discovered:

- Discounts Received of £1,000 were deducted from Gross Profit as expenses.
- A Motor Expense balance of £2,500 was omitted from the accounts.

- A new £21,000 computer system was recorded in the Purchases account.
- Business Rates were entered into the Profit and Loss Account as £12,000. The balance was in fact £21,000.
- The figures for Returns In (£3,000) and Returns Out (£4,500) have been used in each other's place.

(a) Calculate the correct figure for Net Profit for Isabel & Owen Ltd at 30 June 2010.

(6 marks)

(b) Identify any changes that need to be made to the Balance Sheet.

(4 marks)

2.3.3 (E)

Country Fair plc is financed by the following:

1 500 000 issued ordinary shares of £1 each fully paid;
£400 000 7% debentures repayable in 2010.

For the year ended 31 March 2004:

The debenture interest has been paid;
The directors have proposed a dividend of 13p per share.

Required

(a) Calculate the debenture interest paid (show workings).

Interest paid: £ ....

(2 marks)

Workings: ....

(b) Calculate the proposed dividend (show workings).

Proposed dividend: £..

(2 marks)

Workings: ....

(c) Identify in which section (subheading) of the balance sheet each of the following would appear.

Issued shares: ....

(1 mark)

Debentures: ....

(1 mark)

Proposed dividend:..

(1 mark)

(d) Explain **two** benefits of owning debentures rather than ordinary shares.

Benefit 1:..

(2 marks)

Benefit 2:..

(2 marks)

(e) Explain **two** benefits the company gains from issuing ordinary shares rather than debentures.

Benefit 1:..

(2 marks)

Benefit 2:..

(2 marks)

Total 15%

Source: Assessment and Qualifications Alliance, June 2004

2.3.4 (E)

The following balances have been extracted from the books of Positive Advertising plc at 31 December 2003:

Issued share capital:	
Ordinary shares of £1 each fully paid	2000
6% Preference shares of £1 each fully paid	500
Profit and loss account balance as at 1 January 2003	65
Revaluation reserve	70
Trade creditors and accrued expenses	35
Profit before tax for the year ended 31 December 2003	694
Taxation for the year ended 31 December 2003	208

The directors propose the following:

A full year's dividend on the preference shares;

An ordinary share dividend of 4 pence per share.

Required

(a) Prepare the profit and loss appropriation account for the year ended 31 December 2003.

(8 marks)

(b) Prepare the capital and reserves section of the balance sheet.

Positive Advertising plc balance sheet extract as at 31 December 2003

(5 marks)

(c) Prepare the current liabilities section of the balance sheet.

Positive Advertising plc balance sheet extract as at 31 December 2003

(4 marks)

When preparing a balance sheet it is important to distinguish between long-term and current liabilities.

(d) Give **one** example of a long-term liability.

(1 mark)

(e) Explain why it is important to distinguish between long-term and current liabilities.

(4 marks)

Total 22%

Source: Assessment and Qualifications Alliance, January 2004

2.3.5 (E)

Required
From the following figures complete the balance sheet for A to Z Engineering Supplies Ltd as at 31 March 2003. Clearly show the fixed and current assets and long-term and current liabilities. To complete the balance sheet calculate the issued share capital.

	£
Profit and loss account at 31 March 2003	19 031
Stocks at 31 March 2003	14 905
Debtors	6 500
Creditors	4 590
Premises	50 000
Motor vehicles	14 560
Bank overdraft	3 400
Petty cash	56
Dividends proposed	13 000
10% debentures	25 000

(12 marks)

Total 12%

Source: Assessment and Qualifications Alliance, June 2003

2.3.6 (E)
The balance sheet of Highfield Products Ltd shows capital reserves and revenue reserves.

Required
Explain the nature of these reserves, giving **one** example of each.

(a) Capital reserves

Explanation...

(3 marks)

Example...

(1 mark)

(b) Revenue reserves

Explanation..

(3 marks)

Example...

(1 mark)

(c) Will reserves be shown on the debit or credit side of the general ledger accounts?

(1 mark)

Total 9%

Source: Assessment and Qualifications Alliance, June 2003

You should also attempt the questions at the end of section 3.6.

Matters not covered in Units 1 and 3 2.4

Very little material in Unit 2 is exclusive. There are, however, some items not covered elsewhere that you ought to know.

2.4.1 INTANGIBLE FIXED ASSETS

You'll have seen already that a building, a vehicle or a machine is a fixed asset. It's owned by the company, and next year it's likely still to be there. They're called Tangible Assets – tangible meaning you can touch them.

Say, however, that you're buying the entire business of McDonald's restaurants. You buy the buildings, the kitchen fittings and the delivery vans, but you're not allowed to use the big yellow 'M'. The distinctive 'M' design isn't tangible – except when it's stuck on a sign – but it's plainly of great value to the company. A trade mark is an example of an Intangible Asset. A patent is also an example, or a licence to broadcast on a radio frequency.

'Goodwill' is another example. This is the fact that people know about your company and are willing to trade with it. Maybe you've invested in a skilled workforce, or the improvement of local communications has improved its prospects. Normally goodwill only appears on the Balance Sheet if a company has actually been bought for a price greater than that of its recognised assets.

Be careful, however. Some American assessments will describe intangibles as 'an ability to work efficiently with a regulatory body' or similar; since you can sell a patent they'd say it wasn't intangible!

You might care to examine FRS 10, a rule covering intangible assets. Just put 'FRS 10' into a search engine.

Investments also count as fixed assets. Just as a mortgage or a debenture are counted as long-term liabilities, lending money to get a return in the future counts as a long-term asset.

2.4.2 DIRECTORS' REPORTS

In many companies, especially large ones, shareholders may not be involved with the operation of the business. Companies are obliged to tell shareholders what's happening with the company they're investing in, and for many shareholders this happens when the Directors' Report lands on their doormat. Many reports are published on the web, and a search for Directors' Report will bring up many examples for you to compare.

You'll see that they include:

- Financial performance for the last year, for example:
  - Revenue
  - Profit
  - Debt
  - Share prices
  - Dividends
- Transfers to reserves
- Assets that have been acquired or disposed of
- The names and shareholdings of directors active in the last year
- Business activities
- Policies on
  - Employment
  - Training
  - Welfare
  - Creditor payment
  - Corporate responsibility
- Donations to charity
- Any other significant activity
- Announcements for the AGM (annual general meeting)
- Prospects for the coming year

Auditors' report

The Directors' Report may refer to the Auditors' Report. The auditors for the company are a kind of referee. Their report should:

- Describe their responsibilities, and those of the directors
- Describe the basis of their assessment of the financial statements
- Confirm that the financial statements:
  - Have been prepared in accordance with the Companies Act 1985
  - Give a true and fair picture of the company's affairs

2.4.3 CASH FLOW STATEMENTS[A]

You've seen that a Trading and Profit and Loss account shows you how much profit you've made. But what about cash? Cash and profit are not the same thing. A company will publish a Cash Flow Statement with its Trading and Profit and Loss Account and Balance Sheet to show movements of cash that can't be seen in these other statements.

There are lots of reasons why profit and cash might be different. You can buy a vehicle for £20,000 cash in one year, for example, but spread the expense (depreciate it) against profit over a number of years. This is just one case:

- You can increase cash without changing profit by selling shares, for example, or by selling off an asset.
- You can decrease cash without changing profit by paying dividends, for example, or paying back a loan.
- You can increase profit without changing cash by reducing provision for doubtful debt, for example, or selling an asset for more than you thought it was worth.
- You can decrease profit without changing cash by allowing for more depreciation, for example, or selling an asset for less than you thought it was worth.

Some of these terms may be unfamiliar to you. You'll learn about them in Unit 3, but they may be worth memorising for now.

These items are dealt with in two stages; the Cash Flow Statement is the second.

Reconciliation statement

Before you make a cash flow statement, you have to make a reconciliation statement. This starts with your Net Profit (i.e. net cash generated through regular business activity), and adds and takes away items other than trading that affect it, for example, depreciation, cash used or claimed in increasing or decreasing stock levels, cash used or claimed in increasing or decreasing debtors and creditors, profits or losses on the disposal of fixed assets.

You'll see in Unit 3 that provisions for depreciation and debt are included in the Profit and Loss Account, and so they affect Net Profit. For now, you just need to know that you should allow for them to find the Net Cash Flow From Operating Activities.

Contents of Cash Flow Statements

Now you can continue with the Cash Flow Statement proper. Start with

- Net Cash Flow From Operating Activities as found in your reconciliation statement.

For A/S level you should then allow for:

- Returns on investments and servicing of finance (receiving and paying interest)
- Tax (this happens after profit, but still requires cash movement)
- Capital expenditure and financial investment (buying and selling fixed assets, making and reclaiming long term loans)
- Equity dividends (these are just ordinary dividends)
- Management of liquid resources (making investments that can be reclaimed quickly – or reclaiming them)
- Financing (issuing shares, or issuing and redeeming debentures)

By allowing for these figures against the Net Cash Flow From Operating Activities, you'll find the final Net Cash Flow for the period.

Reasons and uses for Cash Flow Statements

There are several reasons to examine cash flow. For one, there is a rule called FRS 1, which makes it compulsory for all but the smallest businesses to make a statement. For another, it helps everyone interested in the company to make sure it remains 'liquid' – able to pay its bills. Poor cash flow is a major cause of businesses closing.

It also gives a fuller view of the position of the company than the Trading and Profit and Loss Account can on their own, it shows up the differences between profit and cash, and it shows where the money is actually coming from and going to. Also, by keeping to the recognised format, businesses can be compared in different years and against other businesses.

2.4.4 STAKEHOLDERS

A stakeholder is anyone with an interest in the business: owners, employees, customers, suppliers, investors, the tax man. All of these groups use accounting information, since all of them have a stake in the performance of the company. This is one key reason why the concepts of accounting have been established – it means that information from different businesses from different years can be compared, and that anyone investing time, money or effort in the business has some idea of how things are going.

For example:

- Investors want to see how safe their money is and how much extra money it's making for them (return)
- The Inland Revenue wants to see how much tax is due
- New suppliers want to see if existing creditors are getting paid
- Banks need to be sure their loans can be repaid
- Even competitors would want an idea of how they could be improving their business.

All of these stakeholders have an interest in the company, so make sure you present your information in a clear and meaningful way, according to the rules and conventions of accounting, both in your exam and in real life.

FURTHER READING

David Cox and Michael Fardon, *A/S Accounting for AQA*, Chapter 21 and 22

USEFUL WEB SITES

www.aqa.org.uk/qual/gceasa/acc_assess.html This is always your most useful web site. Download as many exam papers as your printer will allow.

www.accaglobal.com/publications/studentaccountant/30993 This is an extensive article on goodwill and intangible assets.

www.google.co.uk Any web search for 'directors' report', 'auditors' report' or 'cash flow statement' will bring up genuine examples for you to study.

www.tutor2u.net has lots of useful advice if you click on Accounting and Finance Revision Notes in the menu bar. This includes notes on stakeholders and users of accounting information.

www.unisys.com/common/investors/glossary/ You can use this to check many words you might find unfamiliar in business.

SAMPLE QUESTION

2.4.1

Required
Explain the importance of publishing an annual cash flow statement, including the difference between cash and profit, the rules governing the procedure and the relevance to stakeholders.

(5 marks)

2.4.2

Required
Discuss the contents of the annual reports produced by the director of a company and the company's auditors.

(6 marks)

2.4.3

Required
In which section of a balance sheet will you find intangible fixed assets?

(1 mark)

Identify **one** intangible fixed asset that might be found on a balance sheet, and explain why it is classed as an asset.

(3 marks)

2.4.4

Required
Identify **two** types of stakeholder who might have conflicting interests in a business, and explain why each might use the published accounts.

(6 marks)

2.4.5 (E)

Required
Explain briefly the value of the published report and accounts to:

(a) Potential shareholders;

(2 marks)

(b) Potential debenture holders.

(2 marks)

Total 4%

Source: Assessment and Qualifications Alliance, June 2003

2.4.6 (E)

Required
The managing director of Supermarket Supreme plc has asked you to prepare a short report explaining to shareholders the purpose of producing a cash flow statement each year.

To ....

From ....

Date...

Subject...

(heading 1 mark)

(report 7 marks)

Total 8%

Source: Assessment and Qualifications Alliance, January 2004

2.4.7 (E)

Required
Both directors and auditors have duties with regard to the accounts of limited companies. Explain what their duties are.

(a) Directors' duties are:

(3 marks)

(b) Auditors' duties are:

(3 marks)

Total 6%

Source: Assessment and Qualifications Alliance, January 2004

Computing in accounting 2.5

This part of Unit 2 is the same as the computing section of Unit 1. Study section 1.8 Computers in accounting in Unit 1 and you should be well covered. You should attempt the questions at the end of section 1.8.

Unit 3

FINANCIAL ACCOUNTING: determination of income

Valuing stock 3.1

First, some good news. Some questions in Unit 3 are similar to Unit 1 (i.e. Trading and Profit and Loss Accounts), but with some new bits. Also, much of your understanding of the Hall of Mirrors will still stand you in good stead. Some of the calculations are trickier, and you will have to understand and learn some more of the rules of accounting. You'll also learn about accounts for larger companies, and you need to figure out how making a change affects your profit, the capital and so on.

Let's learn something straightforward and predictable first.

POINTS TO CONSIDER

- What is closing stock?
- Is it valued using its purchase price or expected sale price?
- If an item of stock is worth less than what you paid for it, how do you value it?

You may be asked some quite sophisticated questions about how 'concepts' relate to valuing stock. We'll deal with that in the next section. First some practicalities.

You remember on the Trading Account, your closing stock was given as a note, not as an entry in the Trial Balance. Where did this figure come from? The simple answer is that someone with a clipboard went and added up the stock, using its purchase value (not selling price). Or they used computerised stock control in a similar way. The less simple answer, for A/S level, is that we're interested in both the cost and what's called the **net realisable value**.

Let's say you paid £10 for something. You intend to sell it but you still have it in the shop, so it'll be deducted as closing stock at £10. However, if for some reason you can only sell it for £8, you have to find a figure called net realisable value. This is how much you can sell it for, less any payments to make it saleable: typically repairs or delivery costs. When we learn about the 'prudence concept' in section 3.5.3, we'll see that we have to choose the lower of cost and net realisable value (be sure to mention concepts if you're asked to explain about this).

Let's look at a question.

> **Gnome-man's-land sells garden gnomes. They have an unsold batch of 10 cement figures: 'gnome fishing out of a leaky bucket'. These were purchased for a total of £55.00, and normally sell for £8.50 each. However, one gnome was splashed with paint. This cost £2.50 to clean up, after which it was priced at £6. How much is the stock worth?**

Ten figures for £55.00 means £5.50 per figure. Nine figures are worth 9 × 5.50 = £49.50. But what about the painty gnome?

The net realisable value is £6 minus £2.50 = £3.50. This is lower than £5.50, so we use this value for the closing stock. Note that the normal selling price of £8.50 doesn't affect our calculation.

Your answer should look something like this:

£55.00 / 10 = £5.50   9 × £5.50 = £49.50

£6.00 – £2.50 = £3.50

£49.50 + £3.50 = <u>£53.00</u>

This may look easy, but practise to be sure you get it right if it comes up.

FURTHER READING

Frank Wood and Alan Sangster, *Business Accounting 1*, Chapter 29
David Cox and Michael Fardon, *A/S Accounting for AQA*, Chapter 26

USEFUL WEB SITES

www.aqa.org.uk/qual/gceasa/acc_assess.html This is always your most useful web site. Download as many exam papers as your printer will allow.

www.thetimes100.co.uk/theory/theory.php?tID=302 Extra information.

www.google.co.uk

SAMPLE QUESTIONS

3.1.1

Instone Music has been stocktaking, and has raised questions about three items which have needed work to make them saleable.

	Purchase cost	Cost to make item saleable	Selling price
Amplifier	£120	£15	£160
Guitar	£80	£25	£99
Snare drum	£49	£8	£75

Required

(a) What name is given to the figure you should calculate using the selling price and the cost to make item saleable?

(1 mark)

(b) Advise Instone Music of the value they should record for each item.

(3 marks)

(c) Which accounting concept governs the valuation of stock?

(1 mark)

3.1.2

Colin Gloss, owner of Majestic, is stocktaking for the year. Colin requires advice on valuing certain items of stock.

Required

Determine the value to be recorded in the books for each of the following:

(a) The Hatichoo ZW-54 was bought for £39 and sells at £59.

(1 mark)

(b) The Smith Q91 was bought for £48.50, and normally sells for £72. However, it was scratched during unpacking, and Colin will sell it for £59.

(1 mark)

(c) Colin bought 6 Rokkarola sound-synchronised gyrating Elvis figurines for £360. He's only sold two in the last year for the RRP of £99, and has now reduced the remaining 4 figurines to £39 to clear.

(2 marks)

(d) A batch of 10 Workytalky AM portable radios were bought for £30 and then left in the rain. It cost £20 to fix them. They will sell for £4.99 each.

(2 marks)

Adjustments and provisions 3.2

In Unit 3 you're likely to be tested on the Trading and Profit and Loss Account and Balance Sheet again. The good news is that the format is essentially the same as you learned for Unit 1. However, there are some trickier items you'll need to include. These items are important, mostly because of the Concepts of Accounting – like rules or guidelines. We'll look at these rules properly in section 3.5, after we've learned some practical applications.

POINTS TO CONSIDER

- Which items in the Profit and Loss Account are not simple expenses?
- How does depreciation affect net profit for the year?
- If the sale of an asset brings in cash greater than the net book value, how does this affect the accounts?
- What's the difference between 'Bad Debt' and 'Provision for Doubtful Debt'?
- How do Accruals and Prepayments affect gross and net profit?

Let's look at a bigger and more difficult example of the Jonama Trading Trial Balance from Unit 1. Some new items have been added in **bold** type. See how much sense you can make of it before you read the explanations.

Jonama Trading – Trial Balance – 31 July 2007

	Dr £	*Cr* £
Sales		845,000
Purchases	781,000	
Returns In	4,000	
Returns Out		3,300
Capital		100,000
Drawings	19,000	
Mortgage		210,000
Stock (01.08.06)	26,000	
Bank	21,000	
Cash	1,500	
Building	220,000	
Vehicles	56,000	
Equipment etc.	14,500	
Provision for depreciation (vehicles) 1.8.06		**16,800**
Provision for depreciation (equipment) 1.8.06		**2,900**
Bad debts	**1,100**	
Bad debts recovered		**1,400**
Provision for doubtful debt 1.8.06		**5,000**
Electricity etc.	1,500	
Bank charges	1,000	
Discounts Allowed	2,500	
Discounts Received		2,000
Carriage Inwards	1,800	
Carriage Outwards	500	
Debtors and Creditors	117,000	82,000
	1,268,400	1,268,400

Notes:

- Closing stock was valued at 24,000
- **Depreciation is to be carried out as:**
  - **15% straight line for Vehicles**
  - **20% reducing balance for Equipment**
- **Provision for doubtful debt is to increase to 5% of closing debtors**
- **Electricity owing amounted to £500, while prepaid Bank charges amount to £200**

None of the new information affects the Trading Account (the only change from Unit 1 is that Capital is reduced by £25,000), so we'll assume that the Trading Account and Gross Profit are the same as in Unit 1.

The new Profit and Loss Account looks like this:

Profit and Loss Account – Jonama Trading – 31 July 2007

	£	£
Gross profit		59,500
Discounts received		2,000
Bad debts recovered		**1,400**
		62,900
Less expenses		
Electricity etc. (1,500 + 500)	**2,000**	
Bank charges (1,000 – 200)	**800**	
Discounts allowed	2,500	
Carriage outwards	500	
Depreciation (vehicles) (56,000 × 15%)	**8,400**	
Depreciation (equipment) ((14,500 – 2,900) × 20%)	**2,320**	
Bad debts	**1,100**	
Provision for doubtful debt (117,000 × 5% – 5,000)	**850**	**(18,470)**
Net profit		44,430

If you're a good accounting student, you'll be able to examine this and the Trial Balance and see how it all works, even if some of the reasons mystify you for now. You should be able to see that the recovered debt is extra revenue, so we add it on. The bad debt, meanwhile, is like us giving stock away for free. Treat it as an expense. From the notes you can see how we got the figures for depreciation, and the £5,000 for doubtful debt comes from last year's provision. See how we've also allowed for accruals and prepayments. All will be explained.

Next, of course, is the Balance Sheet. Can you see how this works?

Balance Sheet – Jonama Trading – 31 July 2007

	£	£	£
Fixed assets			
Building	220,000	**0**	**220,000**
Vehicles	56,000	**25,200**	**30,800**
Equipment etc.	14,500	**5,220**	**9,280**
			260,080
Current assets			
Stock	24,000		
Debtors	117,000		
Less provision for doubtful debt	**(5,850)**		
Prepayments	**200**		
Bank	21,000		
Cash	1,500	157,850	
Less current liabilities			
Creditors	82,000		
Accruals	**500**	(82,500)	
Working capital			75,350
Less mortgage			(210,000)
			125,430
Financed by:			
Capital	100,000		
Add net profit	44,430		
	144,730		
Less drawings	(19,000)		
	125,430		

Note that in the fixed assets section, we've put total depreciation (last year's provision plus this year's) in the second column, to find the value of the asset on the date of the Balance Sheet. Note also that we've added prepayments and subtracted the provision for doubtful debt from the debtors.

Some systems use the middle column to add the current assets (and liabilities). This allows the left column to be used for calculations like 'Debtors less Provision'. It would look like this:

Balance Sheet (extract) – Jonama Trading – 31 July 2007

	£	**£**	**£**
Current assets			
Stock		24,000	
Debtors	**117,000**		
Less provision for doubtful debt	**(5,850)**		
		111,150	
Prepayments		200	
Bank		21,000	
Cash		1,500	
		157,850	

Let's look at how each of these new procedures works.

3.2.1 DEPRECIATION

Let's say you buy a machine, or a delivery van, or a computer. Now let's assume it lasts four years, or six years, or twenty years, and is then worthless. How do we deal with the expense of using this asset? Is it appropriate to include the entire cost of an asset in the first year's expenses and ignore it afterwards? Not at all, which is why we haven't seen it in the Profit and Loss Account. We have to depreciate it, and the **depreciation** is the expense of using an asset. Let's take a computer, bought at the start of a firm's accounting year in January 2011, and costing £1,000. It'll last four years before it becomes bug-ridden and obsolete, and you give it to the secretary's teenager to play Skull Driver 2.

depreciation

The act of reducing the value of an asset in your accounts because it is not new any more.

The value lost by an asset.

£1,000 over four years means that it costs £250 each year to keep it working, if we use 'straight line' depreciation. This is the expense of having an asset, and as such it will appear each year in the Profit and Loss Account.

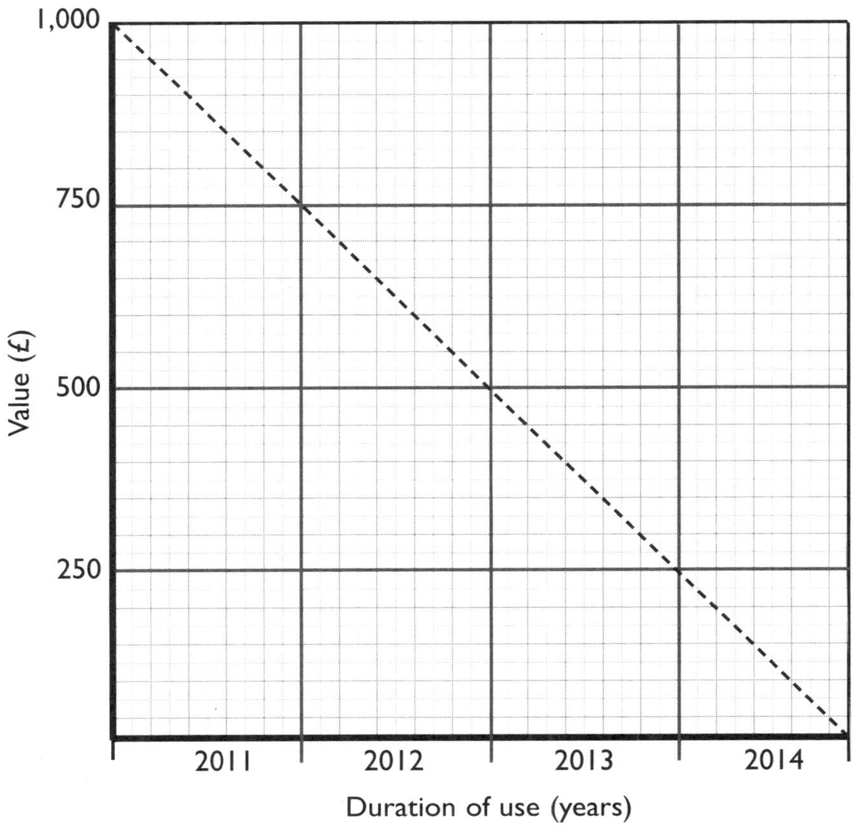

Every year, you put the £250 lost value on the credit side of the Provision for Depreciation account – the debit entry is a reduction of your Net Profit. Depreciation is necessary because things get old, worn out, obsolete, broken, and just plain closer to the end of their life (see section 3.5 on Concepts).

How depreciation affects the accounts

We'll start with the Balance Sheet, where we do something which can be confusing. Study it carefully and practise it. It's tricky but important.

We put the original cost in the first column as before. In the second column, we add together this year's depreciation and the provision for depreciation up to last year, to find total provision.

This seems to baffle some students – for some reason they struggle to understand how this figure works. When you find the total depreciation, subtract it from the original cost and put the result in the third column. It represents the current value.

A note will tell you how to calculate this year's depreciation. It's an expense – the expense of using the asset, i.e. this year's share of the fall in value. It goes in the Profit and Loss Account with the other expenses.

Straight line or reducing balance

If the note tells you that depreciation is 'on cost' or 'straight line' with the yearly depreciation percentage, then this year's expense is simply that percentage of the cost of the item. Beware – don't accidentally calculate a percentage of last year's depreciation. It's 'on cost', so use the original cost figure from the Trial Balance.

If, however, the note says the item is to be calculated using the 'reducing balance' method, it's slightly trickier. You'll need to calculate a percentage of the current value. To do this, just subtract the depreciation so far (last year's provision) from the original cost. Now you can find this year's percentage.

On cost:	original cost	× percentage = expense
Reducing balance:	(original cost – depreciation last year)	× percentage = expense

Residual value: selling an asset after you've used it

You may be able to sell an asset on after its useful life, say by putting it on eBay. An exam question may ask you to calculate the profit or loss on the disposal of the asset.

Start by subtracting all of the depreciation from the original cost of the asset. The result is the **net book value**: what it should be worth, or at least what your books say it's worth. If you sold your old asset for more than this, you've made a profit on the disposal. Often you sell it for less than the net book value, and make a loss. You must state in your calculation if the answer is a profit or a loss.

This loss is an expense in the Profit and Loss Account – or the profit is an addition with the discounts received and other income.

Depreciation is an example of the accruals concept in action. To see why we have to depreciate, look at section 3.5 on Concepts.

3.2.2 BAD DEBTS

Some of your debtors won't pay their bills. That's business. Maybe they're plain dodgy – you should have precautions to protect you against this. Maybe they're refusing to pay a disputed bill, or they just had a bad run and had to fold their business. Whatever the reason, you have to deal with it.

You should have an account for Bad Debts. When you write off a debt, you credit the debtor's account (usually to close it), and debit the Bad Debts account; Bad Debts are an expense. Effectively you're swapping the asset of Debtors for the expense of Bad Debts.

But you'll also have a Provision for Doubtful Debt account. Some of your current debtors will default during the coming year (you can only estimate how many), and you must account for that now. See the notes in the Concepts section (3.5 – especially Prudence) to see why. This account gets credited with a provision, which pretty much sits there as a buffer. The value of the provision is deducted from the Debtors in the Current Assets section of your Balance Sheet. It's important but straightforward.

However, if your estimate is likely to be low, you must increase the provision, and this increase is an expense. Just calculate the increase and put it in the Profit and Loss Account.

Bad Debts Recovered is another account you could be tested on. If somebody sheepishly sends you a cheque that you'd written off last year, then you undo the bad debt by debiting the debtor and crediting Bad Debts Recovered. Now you can credit the debtor and debit Bank as normal.

3.2.3 ACCRUALS AND PREPAYMENTS

We'll see in the section on Concepts (section 3.5.4) that the Accruals concept is one of the most important rules governing the way you make your accounts. For now, we'll concentrate on the practicalities.

Accruals is one of those words that has more than one meaning in similar situations (like 'depreciation', or most terms in cricket). Here, accruals means 'money owing – something that should have been paid for in this period but hasn't'.

We've seen in the new example of Jonama Trading, that: 'Electricity owing amounted to £500…'

Put simply, we used electricity worth £500, but we haven't paid for it yet. Remember, accounts measure transactions, and paying this last bill is one transaction that, for whatever reason, hasn't been concluded yet. However, if we're making up the accounts for the year, we must include all of the expenses for the year. If there is any money owing, add it on. Just add the £500 to the £1,500 we have paid, and use the total of £2,000 as this year's expense.

'…while prepaid Bank charges amount to £200.'

Prepayments works in the same – but opposite – way. Perhaps you pay £1000 a month rent, three months in advance. If you pay on 1 November, then your accounts on 31 December will show a transaction for £3000, when you've only used your premises for two months. £1000 is an expense for next year, not this year. Deduct it.

3.2.4 GOODS TAKEN FOR OWN USE[A]

Ready for some more hard stuff? If the proprietors (owners) of a business take money from the business for private use, they decrease their capital. We have a Drawings account for this. Debit Drawings and credit Bank or Cash.

However, what if the proprietor takes goods for private use? The answer: debit Drawings and credit Purchases. It's a rare thing, a credit entry in Purchases – it's like we didn't make the purchase at all.

If Goods for Own Use is offered in the exam as an adjustment, put it in the Trading Account with Returns Out etc.

3.2.5 THE EFFECT ON PROFIT AND CAPITAL[A]

Your exam question may skip the Financial Statements, and just ask you what effect these adjustments have on your profit, assets, capital etc. You should be able to figure it out. Can you follow this table?

If you can make real sense of it, it'll be of more use in the hot-house of the exam.

3.2 Table 1

	Gross Profit	*Net Profit*	*Capital*	*Fixed Assets*	*Current Assets*	*Current Liabilities*
Depreciation	0	Decreases	Decreases	Decreases	0	0
Bad debt	0	Decreases	Decreases	0	Decreases	0
Increasing provision for doubtful debt	0	Decreases	Decreases	0	Decreases	0
Accruals	0	Decreases	Decreases	0	0	Increases
Prepayments	0	Increases	Increases	0	Increases	0
Selling a fixed asset at net book value	0	0	0	Decreases	Increases	0
Selling a fixed asset above net book value	0	Increases	Increases	Decreases	Increases	0
Selling a fixed asset below net book value	0	Decreases	Decreases	Decreases	Increases	0
Other income	0	Increases	Increases	0	0	0
Goods for private use[1]	Increases	Increases	0	0	0	0

[1] Assuming that closing stock is unaffected.

Let's look at how these work.

- Depreciation is an expense. Expenses reduce Net Profit. Any change to Net Profit will affect capital (note how the Net Profit and Capital columns are almost identical). Depreciation also reduces the value of fixed assets, but has no effect on Gross Profit or liabilities.
- Bad debts are an expense. Therefore they reduce Net Profit, and so reduce capital. Writing off a bad debt also reduces the current asset of debtors. Provision does the same, and will also appear as a reduction in debtors in the Balance Sheet.
- Accruals also add to expenses. Therefore, they also reduce Net Profit and capital. They appear as liabilities in the Balance Sheet.
- Prepayments reduce expenses – for this year at least (they'll be an expense for next year). Less expense means more Net Profit, and so more capital. Prepayments appear as Current Assets in the Balance Sheet.
- Selling a fixed asset just converts bricks or metal into cash – so reduce fixed assets and increase current assets. If you make a profit on the sale (i.e. sell

above net book value), you'll add to your Net Profit and hence your capital. If you make a loss you reduce them both.

- Other income (for example, discounts received) increases Net Profit and capital.
- Goods for private use are taken away from Purchases. We'll assume that the figure for closing stock was found after the goods were taken and doesn't need to be changed. Reduced Purchases means reduced Cost of Sales and increased Gross Profit. This has an exact knock-on effect and increases Net Profit. Normally this would also increase capital – except the goods taken are a drawing, which reduces the capital by the same amount. It's as if the proprietor bypassed the business all along.

You could try to memorise this table – or just try to understand how making changes to one part of the accounting system has a knock-on effect on the bottom line.

FURTHER READING

Frank Wood and Alan Sangster, *Business Accounting 1*, Chapters 25–28
David Cox and Michael Fardon, *AS Accounting for AQA*, Chapters 23–25
Ian Harrison, *Introducing Accounting for A/S*, Chapters 16, 18 and 19

USEFUL WEB SITES

www.aqa.org.uk/qual/gceasa/acc_assess.html This is always your most useful web site. Download as many exam papers as your printer will allow.

www.bized.ac.uk Choose 'accounting' as your subject. There are BAIT interactive tests on Accruals and prepayments.

www.unisys.com/common/investors/glossary/

www.google.co.uk

SAMPLE QUESTIONS

3.2.1

Shaun Wayne sells cricketing memorabilia. He has recently sold his van.

Required

(a) Using the information below, calculate the profit or loss on Shaun's van:

Purchased for:	£27,000
Depreciation:	25% straight line.
Life of van	3 years
Sold for:	£5,999

(4 marks)

(b) How is this profit or loss recorded in the final accounts?

(2 marks)

(c) Calculate the profit or loss if the depreciation had been 40% reducing balance instead of 25% straight line.

(1 mark)

3.2.2

Steve De'ath, producer of gymnasium equipment, is considering how to depreciate his new machinery at the end of his trading year on 31 December 2009. It was purchased at the beginning of 2009 for £14 000, and is expected to last for three years. He is considering using the straight-line method at 30% pa, or the reducing balance method at 50% pa. He wants to know the effect of each method on his reported accounts.

Required

(a) Calculate the depreciation for the first year using each method.

(1 mark each)

(b) How would the choice of method of depreciation affect Steve's cash flow?

(2 marks)

(c) Which method would show the greater net profit for 2009?

(1 mark)

(d) Which method would show the greater value for fixed assets for the end of 2009?

(1 mark)

(e) Which method would show the greater amount of capital for the end of 2009?

(1 mark)

(f) Calculate the final net book value using each method.

(1 mark each)

3.2.3

The following is a summarised trial balance extract for Lee Noogan, after the trading account has been prepared.

Lee Noogan – Trial Balance 31 May 2009

	£	£
Building	230 000	
Machinery at cost	10 000	
Provision for machinery depreciation 1.6.08		2 000
Vehicles at cost	19 000	
Provision for vehicle depreciation 1.6.08		5 700
Bad debts	100	
Provision for doubtful debt 1.6.08		4 000
Recovered debts		300
Discounts	600	1 500
Other expenses	30 200	
Debtors and creditors	60 000	41 000
Bank		1 000
Capital		240 000
Drawings	18 500	
Gross profit		74 700

Additional information:
- Closing stock 31.5.09 was £1 800
- Machinery is depreciated at 20% per year straight line
- Vehicles are depreciated at 30% per year reducing balance
- Provision for doubtful debt is to increase by £500
- There are wages owing of £4 000 and a prepayment of rates of £1 500

Required

(a) Prepare the Profit and Loss Account for the year ended 31 May 2009 to show Lee's Net Profit.

(10 marks)

(b) Prepare the Balance Sheet for the year ended 31 May 2009, clearly indicating the value of Lee's fixed assets, net current assets and capital.

(16 marks)

3.2.4 (E)

The following trial balance has been extracted from the books of account of Siobhan Hugget on 30 April 2004.

	£	£
Vehicles at cost	160 000	
Fixtures and fittings at cost	85 000	
Provisions for depreciation		
Vehicles		80 400
Fixtures and fittings		21 000
Provision for doubtful debts		310
Stock 1 May 2003	7 800	
Debtors and creditors	9 000	7 150
Purchases and sales	149 400	293 100
Wages and general expenses	116 200	
Business rates	13 510	
Bad debts	750	
Bank balance		11 450
Drawings	18 500	
Capital		146 750
	560 160	560 160

Additional information and instructions

(1) At 30 April 2004 stock had been valued at cost, £8700. However, Siobhan believes that it could be sold for £11 500.

(2) No adjustment has been made for goods taken from the business by Siobhan, cost price £3000, for her private use.

(3) On 17 January 2004 Siobhan purchased fixtures for £23 000. This amount is included in the purchases figure on the trial balance.

(4) Wages and general expenses accrued and due at 30 April 2004 amounted to £1600.

(5) Business rates paid in advance on 30 April 2004 amounted to £180.

(6) Depreciation is to be provided on the value of fixed assets held at the financial year end as follows:

Fixtures and fittings 10% straight line;

Vehicles 40% reducing balance.

(7) Provision for doubtful debts is to be maintained at 3% on debtors outstanding at the financial year end.

Required

(a) Prepare a trading and profit and loss account for the year ended 30 April 2004.

(20 marks)

Source: Assessment and Qualifications Alliance, June 2004

Parts (b) and (c) of this question can be found in Section 3.3

3.2.5 (E)

The draft balance sheet for Atul Patel's business as at 31 December 2003 has been prepared. However, adjustments need to be made for the following items.

(a) No entry has been made for rent accrued and unpaid £400.
(b) A bad debt £900 has not yet been written off.
(c) £250 business rates for the period 1 January – 31 March 2004 has been entered in the profit and loss account for the year ended 31 December 2003. No other entries were made in the final accounts.
(d) A vehicle with a net book value of £1500 was sold for £900 cash. No entries have been made in the books of account.
(e) Repairs to a machine £1600 had been included in the machinery account.

Required

Show in the table below how each of the items listed above will affect the balance sheet. An example has been given.

	Fixed assets	Current assets	Current liabilities	Capital
Item 1	No change	No change	Increase by £400	Reduce by £400
Item 2				
Item 3				
Item 4				
Item 5				

(16 marks)

Total 16%

Source: Assessment and Qualifications Alliance, January 2004

3.2.6 (E)

The following is an extract from the business balance sheet of Gorg Hammann as at 31 December 2002.

Fixed assets	**£**	**£**
Machinery at cost	170 000	
Depreciation to date	105 000	65 000

On 31 December 2003 Gorg purchased a new machine.

The cost of the machine was £30 000. To be settled as follows:

	£
Old machine trade-in	8 000
Deposit paid on 31 December 2003	11 000
Instalment to be paid on 31 May 2004	11 000

The old machine cost £24 000 on 1 January 2001 and had been depreciated by £18 000 up to 31 December 2003.

Required

(a) Calculate the profit or loss on disposal of the old machine.

....

(5 marks)

Workings..

(b) Prepare a balance sheet extract as at 31 December 2003 showing **all** items relating to machinery. (No depreciation is to be charged on the new machine.)

Gorg Hammann
Balance sheet extract as at 31 December 2003

(8 marks)

Total 13%

Source: Assessment and Qualifications Alliance, January 2004

3.2.7 (E)[A]

Jock McIntyre has produced a draft profit and loss account for the year ended 31 March 2003. As yet no entries have been made in the profit and loss account for the following information.

	£
Payments to local authority for business rates during the year	1950
Payments to landlord for rent of premises during the year	4200
Receipts from Qualwen plc for commission receivable during the year	600

Additional information

	Year ended 31 March 2002		**Year ended 31 March 2003**	
		£		**£**
Payments to local authority	In advance	70	In arrears	80
Payment to landlord	In arrears	60	In advance	120
Commission received from Qualwen plc	In arrears	50	In arrears	40

Required

Calculate the amounts to be entered in the profit and loss account for the year ended 31 March 2003. Indicate in the table below the amount and whether it should be subtracted from or added to the profit of the business.

	Amount to be *subtracted* from draft net profit £	**Amount to be *added* to draft net profit £**
Business rates		
Rent of premises		
Commission receivable		

Workings ....

(12 marks)

Total 12%

Source: Assessment and Qualifications Alliance, June 2003

3.2.8 (E)

The following is the summarised draft balance sheet of Vlasmin plc as at 31 March 2002.

	Cost	Depreciation	Net
	£000	**£000**	**£000**
Fixed assets	1000	620	380
Current assets		420	
Less current liabilities		360	60
			440
Ordinary share capital			200
Profit and loss account			240
			440

Depreciation has been charged on all fixed assets at 20% per annum using the straight-line method.

After preparing the draft balance sheet the directors of Vlasmin plc have decided to incorporate the following changes in the final accounts.

(a) Wages due but unpaid at the year end amounted to £12 000.
(b) Depreciation on all fixed assets is to be charged at 15% per annum using the straight-line method.
(c) A transfer of £25 000 to a general reserve.
(d) A final dividend on the ordinary share capital of £43 000.

Required

Using the table below show the effect that any amendments resulting from notes (a) to (d) above will have on the balance sheet of Vlasmin plc.

If you believe that there is no amendment necessary write *no change*.

Note (a) has been completed as an example.

Note	Net profit before appropriations	Retained profits	Shareholders' funds	Current assets	Current liabilities
(a)	decrease £12 000	decrease £12 000	decrease £12 000	no change	increase £12 000
(b)					
(c)					
(d)					

(15 marks)

Total 15%

Source: Assessment and Qualifications Alliance, May 2002

3.2.9 (E)

The following trial balance was extracted from the books of Abel Brown as at 31 December 2001.

	Dr £	Cr £
Capital 1 January 2001		78 570
Fixed assets	150 000	
Provision for depreciation of fixed assets 1 January 2001		90 000
Purchases	153 900	
Sales		278 400
Wages	74 750	
Rent	2 500	
Other expenses	25 120	
Debtors	16 100	
Creditors		8 400
Bank balance	1 700	
Drawings	18 600	
Stock 1 January 2001	12 700	
	455 370	455 370

At 31 December 2001 the following additional information was available:

(i) stock in trade was valued at £14 100;
(ii) one week's wages £650 was owed to staff;
(iii) two week's rent amounting to £220 had been paid in advance;
(iv) depreciation is provided on fixed assets at the rate of 10% per annum on cost using the straight line method.

Required

(a) Prepare a trading and profit and loss account for the year ended 31 December 2001 for Abel Brown.

Abel Brown

Trading and Profit and Loss Account for the year ended 31 December 2001

(13 marks)

Abel is considering changing his method of providing depreciation on fixed assets from the straight line method to the reducing (diminishing) balance method.

(b) What would Abel's net profit for the year ended 31 December 2001 have been if he had used the reducing balance method of providing for depreciation on fixed assets at 20% per annum instead of using the straight line method?

The net profit would have been £ ....

Workings ....

(6 marks)

Total 19%

Source: Assessment and Qualifications Alliance, January 2002

3.2.10 (E)

Mary Khan owns and runs a jewellery store. Her financial year end is 30 April. During the week ended 30 April 2001 the following business transactions took place. They have not been included in Mary's final accounts.

(1) Mary purchased stock for resale on credit at a cost of £1000.
(2) At the year end 30 April 2001, buildings insurance paid in advance amounted to £190.
(3) Sale of a diamond ring £2400 on credit. Mary purchased this ring for £1200.

Required

Complete the following grid to show how each of the transactions detailed should be categorised in the final accounts for Mary's business and the financial effect. The first one has been completed for you.
Indicate no entry by inserting N.

	Capital £	**Fixed assets £**	**Current assets £**	**Long term liabilities £**	**Current liabilities £**
(1) Purchase of stock	N	N	+1000	N	+1000
(2) Buildings insurance paid in advance					
(3) Sale of diamond ring					

(11 marks)

Total 11%

Source: Assessment and Qualifications Alliance, June 2001

Additional insight into Financial Statements[A]

3.3

There are some things we've looked at which may baffle you. You're told that we don't have an account for stock, yet there's an account for Opening Stock in the Trial Balance. And what's happening with those Provision accounts – do they have a double entry?

A look at the full process of making the Financial Statements should answer this, and help you get your answers right in the exam.

POINTS TO CONSIDER

- What sorts of accounts are reset to zero at the end of the accounting year?
- How would you separate capital expenditure from revenue expenditure?
- How do the horizontal Trading and Profit and Loss Accounts help you understand the double entry of final accounts?

Personal, Real and Nominal accounts

Some accounts, 'Personal accounts' and 'Real accounts', carry their balances forward to the new accounting year. Personal accounts are for people or businesses: the debtors in the Sales Ledger and the Creditors in the Purchases Ledger. Real accounts measure real things, mainly fixed assets. These are the accounts you find in the Balance Sheet.

Other accounts, like Sales or Utilities, are 'closed off' at the end of the year. This allows us to start the new accounting year from scratch. Harrods, for example, would find no use in their 2009 accounts for 160 years of accumulated sales balances and gas bills! These are examples of 'Nominal Accounts', which include stock accounts like Purchases and Returns, income accounts like Discounts Received, and expense accounts like petrol and wages. All need to be closed off and reset for the new year, and are dealt with in the Trading Account and Profit and Loss Account.

Beware, however, that items like Long-Term Liabilities and Capital are also examples of Nominal accounts, but are not closed off.

Capital and revenue expenditure

In Unit 3 you may encounter the terms 'capital expenditure' and 'revenue expenditure'. Expenditure is just a fussy way of saying 'spending'. Or perhaps you'll be asked about 'capital and revenue receipts' or 'capital and revenue income'.

Revenue expenditure goes on expenses. We can say that revenue expenditure or income applies to the items that get closed off in Nominal accounts: sales, purchases, expenses like motor repairs etc. – all the things that go in the Trading Account or Profit and Loss Account.

Capital expenditure, meanwhile, goes on buying or improving assets to be used in the business. You can think of Capital income and expenditure applying to the things you find in the Balance Sheet, like loans and fixed assets.

You can get grey areas. A new burglar alarm is capital expenditure, because it improves an asset (your building). Paying a security guard to run round with a torch, meanwhile, is revenue expenditure, since staff wages are an expense. Similarly, if your local garage fits a new roof rack to your van and replaces the brake pads, the first is capital expenditure, while the second is revenue expenditure. Selling off old office furniture and old stock, meanwhile, count as capital income and revenue income respectively.

Trading and Profit and Loss T-accounts

Now that we've identified which accounts need to be closed off, we can look again at our Financial Statements. First we make a T-account Trading account. This has the same name as the one we saw in section 1.6 and it contains the same information, but it's a slightly different beast.

Here's how Jonama Trading looks, with one example of a nominal account, and the new Trading T-account:

Returns Inwards

Dr					*Cr*
30.6.07	Balance b/d	3,000	31.7.07	Trading	4,000
12.7.07	Adams	200			
18.7.07	Black	300			
25.7.07	Cuthbertson	500			
		4,000			4,000

Note: we assume that this account has been balanced off each month until June.

Trading

Dr					Cr
31.7.07	Returns Inwards	4,000	31.7.07	Sales	845,000
,,	Stock 01.08.06	26,000	,,	Returns Outwards	3,300
,,	Purchases	781,000	,,	Closing Stock	24,000
,,	Carriage Inwards	1,800			
	Gross Profit c/f to Profit and Loss	59,500			
		872,300			872,300

Here's what we've done.

- Debit the Sales and Returns Outwards accounts to close them off, and put corresponding credit entries in your new Trading T-account.
- Do the same for the closing stock, where we need to make an account for Closing Stock to Debit it.
- Credit the Purchases, Returns Inwards and Opening Stock accounts (the example shows Returns In) to close them off, and put corresponding debit entries in the new Trading T-account.

The balance on the new Trading T-account should be the same as the Gross Profit in the vertical Trading Account we saw in Unit 1.

Now we can do the same with a Profit and Loss T-account. Here's one example of an expense and a provision, with the new Profit and Loss T-account:

Carriage Outwards

Dr					Cr
30.6.07	Balance b/d	460	31.7.07	Profit and Loss	500
14.7.07	Cash	40			
		500			500

Note: We assume that this account has been balanced off each month until June.

Provision for Depreciation (Vehicles)

Dr					Cr
31.7.07	Balance c/d	25,200	01.8.06	Balance b/d	16,800
			31.7.07	Profit and Loss	8,400
		25,200			25,200

Profit and Loss

Dr					Cr
31.7.07	Electricity etc.	2,000	31.7.07	Gross Profit	59,500
,,	Bank charges	800	,,	Discounts received	2,000
,,	Discounts allowed	2,500	,,	Bad debts recovered	1,400
,,	Carriage outwards	500			
,,	Depreciation (vehicles)	8,400			
,,	Depreciation (eq'nt)	2,320			
,,	Bad debts	1,100			
,,	Provision for d'ful debt	850			
,,	Net Profit to Capital	44,430			
		62,900			62,900

Here we:

- credit the various expense accounts (e.g. Carriage Outwards) to close them off, and put the corresponding debit entries in our new Profit and Loss T-account
- credit our various provision accounts (e.g. Depreciation (Vehicles)), and put the corresponding debit entries in our new Profit and Loss T-account.
- debit the various income accounts (e.g. Discounts Received) to close them off, and put the corresponding credit entries in the new Profit and Loss T-account
- make a credit entry for the Trading T-account balance (which is Gross Profit), in effect carrying the balance forward.

The balance is the same as the Net Profit in the vertical Profit and Loss Account.

Capital

Dr					Cr
31.7.07	Drawings	19,000	01.8.06	Balance b/d	100,000
	Balance c/d	125,430	31.7.07	Profit and Loss	44,430
		144,730			144,730

Now we can carry the Net Profit to Capital, and everything's back to zero ready for the new accounting year.

FURTHER READING

Frank Wood and Alan Sangster, *Business Accounting 1*, Chapters 7, 11 and 24
David Cox and Michael Fardon, *AS Accounting for AQA*, Chapters 12 and 24
Ian Harrison, *Introducing Accounting for A/S*, Chapters 3–5

USEFUL WEB SITES

www.unisys.com/common/investors/glossary/

www.google.co.uk

SAMPLE QUESTIONS

3.3.1

Lucia Walters has recently improved the front of her coffee bar. Her expenditure is shown below:

	£
Repainting woodwork	150
Replacing broken glass	80
Installing new sign	210
Extending the patio	950
New tables, chairs and parasols	720
Extra labour	90
Hire of outdoor heaters	55

Required

(a) What is 'capital expenditure'? (2 marks)

(b) What is 'revenue expenditure' (2 marks)

(c) Calculate the capital expenditure by Lucia for this project (3 marks)

(d) Calculate the revenue expenditure by Lucia for this project (4 marks)

3.3.2 (E)

The following trial balance has been extracted from the books of account of Siobhan Hugget on 30 April 2004.

	£	£
Vehicles at cost	160 000	
Fixtures and fittings at cost	85 000	
Provisions for depreciation		
Vehicles		80 400
Fixtures and fittings		21 000
Provision for doubtful debts		310
Stock 1 May 2003	7 800	
Debtors and creditors	9 000	
Purchases and sales	149 400	
Wages and general expenses	116 200	
Business rates	13 510	
Bad debts	750	
Bank balance		11 450
Drawings	18 500	
Capital		146 750
	560 160	560 160

(b) Identify **one** example of capital expenditure and **one** example of revenue expenditure from the final accounts of Siobhan.

An example of capital expenditure is ....

(1 mark)

An example of revenue expenditure is ....

(1 mark)

(c) Explain why it is important to distinguish between capital and revenue expenditure when preparing a set of final accounts.

It is important to distinguish between capital and revenue expenditure because

....

(5 marks)

Source: Assessment and Qualifications Alliance, June 2004

(Part (a) of this question can be found in section 3.2)

3.4 Manufacturing Accounts

In the Trading Account, we calculated the Gross Profit from buying and selling things. But what if you *make* and sell things? What figure do you use for purchases? You have to calculate the cost of making things and use that. For this we need a **Manufacturing Account**.

POINTS TO CONSIDER

- What kinds of stock might you find in a manufacturing business?
- If one electricity supply is used for manufacturing and for administration, where is the expense accounted for?
- How do you define direct and indirect costs?
- What do you do with 'sales expenses' in a Manufacturing Account?
- Why don't we see Purchases in the Trading Account of a Manufacturing Business?

A Manufacturing Account works like a Profit and Loss Account, except it doesn't add general expenses, just factory expenses. It goes right at the start of the Financial Statements, before the Trading Account.

to manufacture
To make something, especially in a factory.

Let's look at an example and then work through it.

'You've Been Mugged' make branded cups and crockery. This extract from their Trial Balance was prepared on 30 September 2009. Prepare a Manufacturing Account, indicating clearly the subtotal for direct costs.

Trial Balance extract – You've Been Mugged – 30 September 2009

	Dr £	*Cr* £
Stock 1 October 2008		
Raw materials	36,500	
Work in progress	2,300	
Finished goods	57,200	
Purchases	218,900	
Purchase returns		1,400
Direct wages	184,000	
Indirect wages	35,000	
Sales salaries	102,000	
Royalties	7,000	
Sales		985,000
Sales returns	2,100	
Power and other expenses	39,000	
Machinery at cost	141,000	
Machinery depreciation (1.10.08)		28,200
Carriage in	4,000	
Carriage out	3,600	

Notes:

1 Stock at 30/09/09 was valued as follows: raw materials: £35,900, work in progress: £3,300, finished goods: £68,200.

2 General expenses are apportioned as 70% to the factory, 30% to the office.

3 Depreciation is 10% per annum on a straight line basis.

Answer:

Manufacturing Account – You've Been Mugged – 30 September 2009

	£	£
Opening stock raw materials		36,500
Purchases		218,900
Carriage in		4,000
Less Purchase returns		(1,400)
		258,000
Less Closing stock raw materials		(35,900)
Total cost of material consumed		222,100
Direct wages		184,000
Royalties		7,000
Prime Cost		413,100
Indirect manufacturing costs		
Indirect wages	35,000	
Power and other expenses (39,000 × 70%)	27,300	
Machinery depreciation (141,000 × 10%)	14,100	
		76,400
		489,500
Add Opening stock – work in progress		2,300
		491,800
Less Closing stock – work in progress		3,300
Production cost		488,500

If you look at this example you should be able to figure out what's going on. Present your answer as clearly as this and you'll pick up the marks. But let's see what's really happening.

You remember that we're just adding up the manufacturing expenses. However, there are two types of manufacturing expense, and they need to be calculated separately.

3.4.1 DIRECT MANUFACTURING EXPENSES

These can be matched exactly to the items that have been made. Learn them:

- Raw materials
  - Purchases
  - Opening stock
  - Closing stock
  - Carriage inwards
  - Returns outwards
- Direct labour
- **Royalties**

royalties
Costs, like paying a designer, or image rights if you sell an official Elvis Presley T-shirt.

Note how Carriage Inwards applies to purchases of raw materials and goes in the Manufacturing Account, not the Trading Account. The same applies to Returns Outwards. Returns In, meanwhile, are finished goods we've sold, so they still go in the Trading Account. The firm in your exam is unlikely to both manufacture and purchase saleable goods, but watch out for this sort of thing if they do. Direct wages could be called direct labour, or just manufacturing wages.

Direct expenses are added in the outer of two columns, and their total is called the 'Prime Cost'. Don't forget to label it. In this example you were specifically asked to identify it.

3.4.2 INDIRECT MANUFACTURING EXPENSES

Also called 'factory overheads', these are just general expenses that can't be matched directly against output. Learn these too, and understand the difference:

- Indirect labour
  - Cleaning or security staff
  - Supervisors

- Utilities
  - Electricity
  - Water
- Rent
- Depreciation of machinery

These items are added in the inner of the two columns, and their total entered in the outer column. It can now be added to the Prime Cost.

A few things to note:

- Expenses outside the factory don't count. If you're offered something like Administration Expenses in your Trial Balance, leave it. That's why the sales salaries and carriage outwards aren't in the answer. They go in the Profit and Loss Account as normal.
- Indirect labour would include cleaners, security, warehouse staff, supervisors etc. These people work in the factory, but their work can't be measured in terms of units produced.
- Your firm may pay one rent or electricity bill, which applies to the offices as well as the factory. You have to divide the expense between the Manufacturing Account and Profit and Loss Account. If you're told, for example, that 75% of a £4,000 bill is for the factory and 25% for administration, then put £3,000 in the Manufacturing Account. Don't forget the other £1,000 when you do the Profit and Loss Account.
- Depreciation. We looked at this in the section on adjustments and provisions. If the depreciation applies to a factory item, then it's a manufacturing expense and goes in the Manufacturing Account.

3.4.3 STOCK

Stock is a funny item in Manufacturing Accounts. You learned in Unit 1 how to add Opening Stock to Purchases and deduct Closing Stock. Now we have to do it three times. When you're manufacturing, you have to consider

- Stock of raw materials
- Stock of finished goods ready to sell
- Stock of goods that aren't finished, but aren't just raw materials any more

Stock of raw materials is added and subtracted right at the start of the Manufacturing Account. Stock of unfinished goods, or 'work in progress', is added and subtracted at the end of the manufacturing account, after you've subtotalled the prime cost and the indirect costs. Have a look at the example to see this working.

Stock of finished goods, meanwhile, goes in the Trading Account as usual.

3.4.4 THE TRADING ACCOUNT

We've calculated the bottom line figure in our Manufacturing Account. You may see it called Production Cost of Goods Completed, or just Production Cost, or something similar, but recognisable. In our example the figure was £488,500. This bottom line figure replaces 'Purchases' in the Trading Account. In fact, it's the reason for making the Manufacturing Account. We haven't bought goods to sell, we've made them and used this figure in the same place.

Let's see how the Trading Account would look for our example.

Trading Account – You've Been Mugged – 30 September 2009

	£	£
Sales		985,000
Less Sales returns		(2,100)
		982,900
Less cost of sales		
Opening stock of finished goods	57,200	
Cost of goods completed	**488,500**	
	545,700	
Less Closing stock of finished goods	(68,200)	
		(477,500)
Gross Profit		505,400

Note how the stock figures are for completed goods. There's no Purchases figure, or Purchase Returns, as these were purchases of raw materials and they've already been dealt with in the Manufacturing Account.

You're now ready to put sales salaries and carriage out in the Profit and Loss Account as usual.

3.4.5 FACTORY PROFIT AND UNREALISED PROFIT [A]

Now you really are being tested. A-grade students should try to understand this.

If you measure the manufacture and sale of your product as all one thing, then you can move the cost of goods completed to the Trading Account at cost price with no problem. But what if you treat manufacturing as a separate operation? Perhaps you want to measure how your factory is performing compared with, say, another supplier. Perhaps you've found that you can produce your goods for less than you'd pay an outside supplier, and reckon that the difference is factory profit. Alternatively, it's common to add a percentage to the cost of goods completed as a factory profit margin.

Let's assume that we'll add 10% to the production cost in our example, and also that the value we're given for the stocks of finished goods have had this manufacturing profit included.

The accounts now look like this:

Manufacturing Account (extract) – You've Been Mugged – 30 September 2009

	£	£
Production cost		488,500
Manufacturing Profit (10%)		48,850
Transfer value to Trading account		537,350

Trading Account – You've Been Mugged – 30 September 2009

	£	£
Sales		985,000
Less Sales returns		(2,100)
		982,900
Less cost of sales		
Opening stock of finished goods	57,200	
Transfer value of goods completed	**537,350**	
	594,550	
Less closing stock of finished goods	(68,200)	
		(526,350)
Gross profit on trading		456,550
Add profit on manufacturing		**48,850**
Total Gross Profit		505,400

See how the factory profit as part of Transfer Value makes the Cost of Sales larger, and so reduces the trading Gross Profit. See also that it can be added on to show the full profit. Note that some systems add the factory profit to the Net Profit instead.

Provision for unrealised profit

When we include transfer value and opening and closing stocks in the Trading Account, they're valued with the factory profit included. However, since we haven't actually sold the closing stock yet, we haven't made the profit on it yet.

Do you remember from the section on valuation of stock, that we have to choose the lower of 'cost price' or 'net realisable value'? For a similar reason we have to take the factory profit out of the Closing Stock of Finished Goods when we make our final accounts. It's the cost value we need to find our Net Profit, and the factory profit we remove is called unrealised profit.

To calculate the unrealised profit, use the same process that you used to extract the VAT from cash sales in section 1.3.2.

If you're told that stock is transferred at cost plus z%, then find

z /(100+z) × closing stock

Similarly, if you're told that you can manufacture Who-ja-ma-flops at £80,000, or buy them in at £100,000, then your unrealised profit is £20,000. This is 20% of the final value. Now you can apply this percentage to your closing stock.

In general, that's

[(purchase cost – production cost) / purchase cost] × closing stock

In this example we've added 10% factory profit, to reach a figure of £68,200. The unrealised profit is:

10%/110% × 68,200 = 6,200

Now you've found your unrealised profit you have to account for it. Provision for unrealised profit works rather like provision for doubtful debt (see section 3.2.2). It's a rolling buffer, and any increase in provision is an expense in the Profit and Loss Account.

In our example, the provision for last year was 10%/110% × 57,200 = £5,200. The new provision is £6,200, so the expense of increased provision is £1,000. This expense features in the Profit and Loss account and reduces the Net Profit.

In the Balance Sheet we deduct the provision from the Stock of Finished Goods in the Current Assets section. Make sure you show the cost value for your finished goods.

Balance Sheet (extract) – You've Been Mugged – 30 September 2009

	£	£	£
Current Assets			
Stock of raw materials		35,900	
Stock of work in progress		3,300	
Stock of finished goods	**68,200**		
Less provision for unrealised profit	**(6,200)**		
		62,000	

FURTHER READING

Frank Wood and Alan Sangster, *Business Accounting 1*, Chapter 37
David Cox and Michael Fardon, *A/S Accounting for AQA*, Chapter 28
Ian Harrison, *Introducing Accounting for A/S*, Chapter 23

USEFUL WEB SITES

www.aqa.org.uk/qual/gceasa/acc_assess.html This is always your most useful web site. Download as many exam papers as your printer will allow.

www.bized.ac.uk Choose 'accounting' as your subject. Have a look at the balloon company section.

www.google.co.uk

SAMPLE QUESTIONS

3.4.1 (E)

Noriv plc is a manufacturing business. The following figures have been extracted from the company's ledgers as at 31 May 2003.

		£
Stocks as at 1 June 2002:	Raw materials	21 450
	Work in progress	14 780
	Finished goods	58 620
Sales		657 000
Purchases of raw materials		234 090
Direct labour costs		260 000
Indirect labour costs		82 800
Factory overheads (excluding labour costs)		138 000
Manufacturing royalties		6 560
Returns inwards		1 000
Returns outwards		980
Carriage inwards		750
Carriage outwards		1 340

Additional information

(1) At 31 May 2003 stocks were valued as follows:

	£
Raw materials	22 170
Work in progress	13 750
Finished goods	60 650

(2) At 31 May 2003 factory wages accrued and unpaid amounted to £8000. One quarter of this was for indirect labour and the remainder was for direct labour.
(3) Provision for depreciation of factory machinery for the year was £25 000.

Required

(a) Selecting from the information given, prepare an extract from the manufacturing account for the year ended 31 May 2003 to show prime cost.

....

(16 marks)

(b) Explain what is meant by 'work in progress'.

....

(3 marks)

Total 19%

Source: Assessment and Qualifications Alliance, June 2003

3.4.2 (E)

Cathy Yow manufactures garden furniture. The following balances have been extracted from her books of account as at 31 December 2001.

		£
Stocks as at 1 January 2001:	Raw materials at cost	9 000
	Work in progress at cost	3 000
	Finished goods at cost plus 25%	8 750
Purchases of raw materials		63 600
Direct labour costs		146 800
Factory overhead costs		106 790
Administrative expenses		140 500
Manufacturing royalties		8 140
Sales		568 720
Plant and machinery at cost		400 000
Provision for depreciation of plant and machinery 1 January 2001		160 000
Office equipment at cost		115 000
Provision for depreciation of office equipment 1 January 2001		75 000
Provision for unrealised profit 1 January 2001		1 750

Additional information

Factory output is transferred to the trading account at factory cost plus 25%.

Stocks at 31 December 2001 were valued as follows:

	£
Raw materials at cost	9400
Work in progress at cost	3100
Finished goods at cost plus 25%	9250

Direct labour costs accrued at 31 December 2001 amounted to £3450.

Required

(a) Prepare the prime cost section only of the manufacturing account for the year ended 31 December 2001 for Cathy Yow, selecting from the information given.

Cathy Yow
Manufacturing account extract for the year ended 31 December 2001

(8 marks)

(b) Calculate the amount to be charged to the profit and loss account for the adjustment to the provision for unrealised gross profit.

The adjustment is £..

Workings ....

(3 marks)

(c) Explain why Cathy needs to make provision for unrealised profit in her final accounts.

(4 marks)

Total 15%

Source: Assessment and Qualifications Alliance, May 2002

3.4.3 (E)

Jacqui King plc is a manufacturing business. The following figures have been extracted from the company's books of account as at 30 November 2001.

		£
Stocks as at 1 December 2000:	Raw materials	47 600
	Work in progress	23 000
	Finished goods	76 400
Sales		3 780 000
Purchases of raw materials		498 000
Factory overheads (excluding labour costs)		548 000
Factory labour costs		959 400
Office salaries		365 000
Royalties		17 000
Provisions for depreciation:	Factory machinery	48 000
	Delivery vehicles	56 000
	Office equipment	11 000

Additional information

(i) At 30 November 2001 Stocks were valued as follows:

	£
Raw materials at cost	50 900
Work in progress at cost	24 100
Finished goods at cost	79 200

(ii) Factory labour costs are apportioned:
2/3 to direct labour and
1/3 to indirect labour

Required

(a) Prepare the manufacturing account for the year ended 30 November 2001 for Jacqui King plc, selecting from the information given.

The account should show clearly the totals for raw materials consumed, prime cost and total production cost.

Jacqui King plc
Manufacturing Account for the year ended 30 November 2001

(17 marks)

(b) Explain the term 'royalties'.

(3 marks)

Total 20%

Source: Assessment and Qualifications Alliance, January 2002

3.4.4 (E)

On 31 May 2001 the following balances were extracted from the books of Victor Norrios Ltd, a manufacturer of CD, DVD and video storage systems. Finished goods are transferred from the factory to the trading account at cost plus 20%.

	£	£
Stocks as at 1 June 2000:		
Raw materials at cost	38 460	
Work in progress at cost	18 420	
Finished goods at cost plus 20%	118 380	
Purchases of raw materials	178 940	
Factory wages	460 000	
Office salaries	155 000	
Sales		1 170 390
Indirect factory expenses	61 350	
Rent and rates	52 000	
General administrative expenses	58 400	
Provision for unrealised profit as at 1 June 2000		19 730
Machinery at cost	340 000	
Vehicles at cost	600 000	
Office equipment at cost	424 000	
Provisions for depreciation as at 1 June 2000:		
Machinery		175 000
Vehicles		400 000
Office equipment		169 600

Additional information as at 31 May 2001

(1) Stock valuations were as follows:

	£
Raw materials at cost	40 120
Work in progress at cost	21 300
Finished goods at cost plus 20%	123 780

(2) The company had paid £12 000 rates for the period 1 April 2001 to 30 September 2001. Rates are apportioned 3/4 to the factory and 1/4 to the offices of the company.

(3) The company owed its factory workers £5000 wages. 80% of factory wages are direct wages; the remainder are indirect.

(4) The company makes provision for depreciation of fixed assets at the following rates using the straight line method:
Machinery 10% per annum
Vehicles 25% per annum
Office equipment 15% per annum

Required

(a) Prepare a manufacturing account for the year ended 31 May 2001 for Victor Norrios Ltd
(i)

Victor Norrios Ltd
Manufacturing account for the year ended 31 May 2001

(15 marks)

(ii) Prepare a trading account for the year ended 31 May 2001 for Victor Norrios Ltd

(5 marks)

(b) Using figures from the books of Victor Norrios Ltd, explain how unrealised profit should be treated in the company's

(i) Profit and loss account for the year ended 31 May 2001;

....

(3 marks)

(ii) Balance sheet as at 31 May 2001.

....

(3 marks)

Total 26%

Source: Assessment and Qualifications Alliance, June 2001

3.4.5 (E)

Dewray plc manufactures bedroom furniture.

All completed furniture is transferred to the trading account at cost plus 20%.

The following figures have been extracted from the trial balance of the company as at 31 December 2002 after calculating prime cost.

		Dr	Cr
		£000	**£000**
Prime cost		1207	
Factory overheads		915	
Factory machinery at cost		150	
Office equipment at cost		60	
Provision for depreciation	– factory equipment		90
	– office equipment		18
Provision for unrealised profit			26
Stocks as at 1 January 2002			
work in progress at cost		34	
finished goods at cost plus 20%		156	
Sales			3 460

Additional information

(1) All fixed assets are depreciated at 10% per annum on cost.

		£000
(2) Stocks as at 31 December 2002	– raw materials at cost	75
	– work in progress at cost	36
	– finished goods at cost plus 20%	192

Required

(a) Prepare a summarised manufacturing account for the year ended 31 December 2002.

Dewray plc
Summarised manufacturing account for the year ended 31 December 2002

	£000
Prime cost	1207

(7 marks)

(b) Prepare a trading account for the year ended 31 December 2002.

Dewray plc
Trading account for the year ended 31 December 2002

£000

(6 marks)

(c) Calculate the amount of the adjustment to the provision for unrealised profit to be shown in the profit and loss account for the year ended 31 December 2002.

The amount of the adjustment to the provision for unrealised profit to be shown in the profit and loss account is:

£..

Workings ....

(4 marks)

(d) Explain how the amount calculated in (c) should be shown in the profit and loss account.

(2 marks)

(e) Complete the following extract from the balance sheet.

Dewray plc
Balance sheet extract as at 31 December 2002

Current assets
Stock – raw materials..
– work in progress..
– finished goods ....

(4 marks)

Total 23%

Source: Assessment and Qualifications Alliance, January 2003

3.4.6 (E)[A]

Tecyl Products is a manufacturing business. It transfers all goods manufactured to the trading account at production cost plus 20%.

The following figures relate to stocks held by the business.

	As at 1 December 2002	As at 30 November 2003
	£	£
Stocks of Raw materials	27 000	28 000
Work in progress	9 000	8 500
Finished goods	22 200	23 400
Provision for unrealised profit	3 700	3 900

Required

(a) Calculate the amount of provision for unrealised profit to be entered in the profit and loss account for the year ended 30 November 2003.
What effect will the change have on the gross profit?

The profit and loss entry is £..

The effect will be ....

(3 marks)

(b) Show in detail how the information relating to **all** stocks should be shown on the balance sheet as at 30 November 2003.

Tecyl Products
Balance sheet extract as at 30 November 2003

Current assets – Stocks	**£**

(5 marks)

(c) Explain why it is necessary for Tecyl Products to provide for unrealised profit.

(4 marks)

Total 12%

Source: Assessment and Qualifications Alliance, January 2004

Concepts

3.5

Concepts are rules for accounting. They make sure everybody makes up their accounts in a way that makes sense, and seems fair when talking to a prospective business partner, or a bank manager, or the tax man.

POINTS TO CONSIDER

- How do the concepts make adjustments for stock necessary?
- How do the concepts make depreciation necessary?
- How do the concepts make provision for doubtful debt necessary?
- How do the concepts make net realisable value for stock necessary?

In business, everybody should play by the same rules so that they can deal with each other effectively.

Allow me to illustrate. The England football team visit the tiny nation of Nosuchthingasaneasy-gamistan. When the game starts, it soon becomes clear that the Nosuchi team play with 12 men not 11, they have throw-ons instead of corners, and their version of the off-side rule is just plain crazy. How can both teams play? Fortunately, FIFA makes the rules for everyone to play football by.

In accounting there are similar rules for everyone. These rules are called **SSAPs** and **FRSs**, although they all support the basic principles called Concepts.

SSAPs and FRSs

SSAPs are the Statements of Standard Accounting Practice, while the FRSs are the Financial Reporting Standards. These parallel sets of rules overlap, with the FRSs superceding the SSAPs. For example, the set of rules for accounting for tax used to be SSAP 8, but they've been replaced by FRS 16. These rules are governed by the ASB, or Accounting Standards Board. From 2005, accounts must also comply with the IFRSs, or International Financial Reporting Standards.

You may be asked some quite sophisticated questions about how 'Concepts' relate to your accounts. Learn these, and practise applying them to the practicalities you've learned so far. Understanding the concepts will help you to make sense of things like depreciation. If you're asked to discuss why it's important to provide for depreciation or unrealised profit etc, you will get marks if you refer to the relevant concepts.

Arguably the four most important concepts are accruals, prudence, consistency and going concern.

3.5.1 GOING CONCERN

The going concern concept states that the Financial Statements (e.g. Balance Sheet) should assume that the business will still be running next year.

Going concern and fixed assets

At your factory on a remote island near Zanzibar, you've been depreciating a custom-built asparagus-slicing machine at 10% per year. After three years your books say it's dropped from £10,000 to £7,000. But wait – if your business stopped tomorrow there's no way you could sell such an item for £7,000. Although you've been making a good profit from the asparagus, the machine would be practically worthless to anyone else. However, by assuming you'll still be using it for years to come you can use your current method of valuation. This rather extreme case illustrates a general situation faced by most businesses who own machines and vehicles.

Cost, or historical cost concept

Similarly you're likely to see a building still listed at cost price, even if it's the £50,000 your father paid for it in 1987. Since the original cost is the only value you can be sure of, it's the one you continue to use.

3.5.2 CONSISTENCY

The consistency concept states that if you have adopted a method for producing your accounts in one year, you should continue to use that method for future years. This allows you to compare figures from consecutive years. Any changes in method should be stated clearly and allowed for.

Consistency and depreciation (see prudence and accruals)

Say you've been depreciating an item at 10% on cost for three years (a custom-built asparagus-slicing machine, for instance), and say after three years it's now worth £7,000. Each year your Net Profit has been reduced by £1,000. Supposing you now switch to the reducing balance method. Next year's drop in value will be just £700, and your net profit will be £300 higher. This is inconsistent and shouldn't happen.

Consistency and the manufacturing account

If you've been allocating 80% of your electricity bill to your factory operation, then this overhead adds to your cost of production and reduces your Gross Profit (Net Profit is unaffected). You would not be allowed to make your Gross Profit look better by reducing the allocation, say, to 60%.

3.5.3 PRUDENCE

The prudence concept states that profits should not be overstated (nor understated). In plain English, this concept stops you making your business look better than it actually is (or, technically, worse than it is). Prudence also means you should ensure that losses are provided for as soon as they are anticipated, but not provide for profits until they are realised (see realisation below). Prudence is the concept that gives accountants their reputation for caution.

Prudence and the valuation of stock

You should not allow your stock to appear more valuable than it is. This is why the lower figure of purchase cost and net realisable value is chosen for stock valuation.

Prudence and doubtful debt (see accruals)

Some debtors just won't pay you, and your figure for total debtors as an asset is almost certainly over-optimistic. This is why we're obliged by the prudence concept to deduct doubtful debt from the debtors in the Balance Sheet.

Prudence and unrealised profit

We can't assume that we'll get the factory profit on our unsold finished stock, so it's deducted in a similar way to doubtful debt.

Prudence and depreciation (see consistency and accruals)

You're not allowed to nudge up your Net Profit by failing to allow for depreciation on your delivery van in your Profit and Loss Account.

The realisation concept

The realisation concept states that sales, and hence profits, can only be allowed for when they've actually been made. This essentially means that you can only count a sale when the customer has actually taken possession of goods, or at least formally undertaken to pay for them.

For example, if you're sitting on ten West End theatre tickets when the accounts are drawn up, and an agent tells you over the phone that he'll come in tomorrow to buy them, you may not count this as a sale. You must wait until he actually buys them. Note that if an agent has bought the tickets on credit, but simply hasn't paid for them yet, the sale does count.

Since the realisation concept refers to the time when a sale is made, it is related to the accruals concept as well as the prudence concept.

3.5.4 ACCRUALS

The accruals concept states that revenues must be matched against the expenses incurred to generate them. This concept is vital. There's a bit of double vision that takes some getting used to, but understanding accruals is the key to understanding almost everything that's confusing in accounting.

Accruals refers, essentially, to the time period in which activity takes place. If your accounting year runs from January to December, then we want to know about every transaction that took place between 9 a.m. on 2 of January until 5.30 p.m. on New Year's Eve. Now, if all transactions were for cash, there would be no problem. But they're not. Credit transactions mean there's a time difference between the revenue being generated and cash being received, and also between expenses being incurred and cash being spent.

- Revenue, or income, is generated when a sale is made (see 'The realisation concept' above). Receiving the payment does not necessarily happen in the same accounting period.
- Expense, meanwhile, is incurred when a purchase is made, not when it is paid for.

The accruals concept means that profit depends on revenue and expense, not the receipts and payments of cash.

Let's illustrate this with some examples.

Accruals and depreciation (see consistency and prudence)

If you buy a delivery moped in 2011, and expect it to last for 5 years, then the expense of having a moped must be spread over those five years. The bundle of cash you handed over at the start does not affect your profit. The depreciation, however, does, for each year.

Accruals and doubtful debt (see prudence)

Some debtors won't pay you. The trouble is, you don't know who or by how much. Since bad debt has to be matched against the sales they apply to, we make a provision – an estimate of which debts for this time period will be found to be bad in the next one.

Accruals and prepayments (see section 3.2.3)

If your staff have worked for you through the last month of the accounting year, but for whatever reason you haven't paid them yet, their labour is still an expense for this year. The account for Wages shows the figure for payments made, but you must add the figure for wages due – or wages accrued. The same goes for prepayments – if you've already paid a service charge for next year, deduct it until next year. It's not an expense for this year.

Accruals and stock (see prudence)

Opening stock may have been bought last year, but it was used to make sales for this year. Matching expenses against this year's revenues means we add it on to Purchases for this year. Closing stock may have been bought this year, but it will be used to make sales for next year. Matching expenses against next year's revenues means we can't count it with the Purchases for this year. Take it away now and count it next year.

3.5.5 OTHER CONCEPTS

Apart from these four important concepts, you may find yourself juggling with some of the others.

Business entity

The business entity concept states that accounts measure the money of the business, not the owner. Expenses should be business expenses, not the proprietor's private expenses. Assets are not capital, and vice versa.

Materiality

The materiality concept states that if a long-term asset is inexpensive enough to be of no material interest, it should be counted as an expense: e.g. stationery.

Objectivity

The objectivity concept states that an accountant should not allow subjective feelings to affect the neutrality of the accounts.

Dual aspect

The dual aspect concept states that every transaction in the books should feature a debit entry and a corresponding credit entry. This is the concept behind the Accounting Equation: **assets = liabilities + capital**, and it ensures that the assets of a company exactly equal the claims against them by both the owners and any other creditors.

FURTHER READING

Frank Wood and Alan Sangster, *Business Accounting 1*, Chapter 10
David Cox and Michael Fardon, *A/S Accounting for AQA*, Chapter 26
Ian Harrison *Introducing Accounting for A/S*, Chapter 22

USEFUL WEB SITES

www.aqa.org.uk/qual/gceasa/acc_assess.html This is always your most useful web site. Download as many exam papers as your printer will allow.

www.bized.ac.uk Choose 'accounting' as your subject. There are BAIT interactive tests on concepts.

www.frc.org.uk This site provides you with lots of lovely detail.

www.google.co.uk

SAMPLE QUESTIONS

3.5.1

Required
(a) Identify two concepts that apply to the valuation of stock.

(2 marks)

(b) Explain why each concept applies.

(4 marks)

3.5.2

Required
(a) What is the accruals concept?

(3 marks)

(b) Describe **two** examples of the accruals concept affecting the accounts.

(2 marks)

3.5.3

Required
Assets can sometimes appear in the books at value either higher or lower than that which they would fetch if sold.

Explain how this might be the case because of:

(i) The going concern concept
(ii) The cost, or historical cost, concept.

(2 marks each)

3.5.4

Required
Explain how depreciation is affected by at least two accounting concepts.

(3 marks each)

3.5.5

Required
Explain, with examples, how the accounts are affected by

(i) The accruals concept
(ii) The prudence concept
(iii) Both

(6 marks)

3.5.6

Cliff's Theatricals are preparing their final accounts as at 30 September 2005. They have been advised that some of their procedures need to be corrected.

Required

Complete the following to show one concept that affects each procedure, why it applies, and what action, if any, should be taken. The first item is completed for you.

(i) Cliff bought a new vehicle last year. He wants to record its current value at its full purchase price.
Concept: *prudence*
Reason: *figures should not be made to look unrealistically optimistic*
Action: *Choose a realistic rate of depreciation.*

(ii) Cliff has been depreciating his hire costumes at 15% on cost. This year he only wants to allow for 10% depreciation so that he has lower expenses.
Concept:
Reason:
Action:

(4 marks)

(iii) Cliff has recorded the full figure for debtors as a current asset.
Concept:
Reason:
Action:

(4 marks)

(iv) Since he bought it a few years ago, Cliff's shop has been recorded as £75 000 in his fixed assets section. This year he wants to record it at a new higher value, similar to that fetched by properties sold in his road in the last year.
Concept:
Reason:
Action:

(4 marks)

(v) Cliff has some lighting which wasn't selling because it was damaged, so he's fixed it and reduced the sale price. The new price, less repair costs, is lower than the purchase price used in the trading account.
Concept:
Reason:
Action:

(4 marks)

(vi) Cliff has bought a film-set used in a confectionery commercial, although he's waiting until he pays for it before he records the purchase in the books.
Concept:
Reason:
Action:

(4 marks)

(vii) Cliff has paid a cheque to cover his business insurance for October as well as for August and September. He has included the full sum paid as an expense for this year.
Concept:
Reason:
Action:

(4 marks)

(viii) Cliff took some props home for a party, and has since decided to keep them for himself. Because he owns the business he wants to call this a business expense.
Concept:
Reason:
Action:

(4 marks)

(ix) Cliff is a big fan of Judy Charlston, an obscure B-movie actress from the sixties. He bought the boots she wore in 'Space Scouts' for £7 in auction, but wants to record them as an asset worth £50 to reflect their sentimental value.
Concept:
Reason:
Action:

(4 marks)

(x) Cliff has bought a new hole-punch for £9.90. His old one lasted for six years, so he's planning to depreciate the new one at £1.65 per year.
Concept:
Reason:
Action:

(4 marks)

3.5.7 (E)

Given below are three **unconnected** proposals for three **different** businesses.

(1) Ben Chan has always depreciated his fixed assets at the rate of 20% on cost. He thinks that he may sell his business next year so he has proposed changing the rate of deprecation to 5% this year as this will increase his profits.
(2) Lotte Betz's drawings have increased this year to £36 000. Lotte's drawings normally average £18 000 per annum. She is proposing to charge the usual £18 000 to drawings and include £18 000 as business expenses.
(3) Harry Jones has his financial year end on 30 June 2001. He has been negotiating to supply ski jackets to Pierre Duval in August 2001. Pierre will sign the contract on 5 July 2001 when he returns from a business trip to Austria. Harry proposes to include the selling price of the jackets, £9700, in his sales figure for the year ending 30 June 2001.

Required
Identify which generally accepted accounting concepts should have been applied and the correct treatment for each proposal. Proposal 1 has been answered for you.

Proposal	Concept	Action
(1)	Consistency	Continue to depreciate at 20%
(2)		
(3)		

(6 marks)

Total 6%

Source: Assessment and Qualifications Alliance, June 2001

Limited Liability Companies 3.6

So far we've been accounting for 'sole traders' – businesses with one owner who owns all the capital and keeps all the profit.

Many companies are owned by more than one person – sometimes lots of people – each of whom own 'shares' of the company. The good news for you is that the basic Trading Account and Profit and Loss Account and Balance Sheet are essentially the same. The not so good news is that you're likely to be tested on the differences.

POINTS TO CONSIDER

- How is profit shared out when there may be thousands of owners of a business?
- What is a Capital Reserve?
- How does the Balance Sheet for a Limited Liability Company differ from that of a sole trader?
- What are the benefits and drawbacks of becoming a Limited Liability Company?
- Are all Limited Liability Companies traded on the Stock Exchange?
- How does risk affect the investment you make in a company?
- If Reserve Capital belongs to the shareholders, can they withdraw Capital Reserves as cash?

3.6.1 THE APPROPRIATION ACCOUNT

Lots of owners means lots of people wanting a share of the profit. You can think of appropriation as 'who gets what'. The Appropriation Account is (mostly) a list of people who want a share of the net profit, and it goes straight after the Profit and Loss Account to show who gets what.

Here's a Trial Balance extract for a Limited Liability Company as it stands after the Trading and Profit and Loss Accounts have been drawn up. Let's look at how the Appropriation section works.

Silly Lilly Ltd – Trial Balance (extract) – 31 October 2009

	Dr £	*Cr* £
Ordinary Share Capital (£1)		800,000
Preference Share Capital (6%)		200,000
Profit and Loss Account (1.11.08)		350,000
Share Premium Account		120,000
General Reserve		250,000
Debenture Stock (8% – repayable 2016)		150,000
Director's remuneration	40,000	
Interim ordinary dividend paid	80,000	
Debenture Interest Paid (½ year to 30.04.09)	6,000	

Notes:

- Net Profit was calculated as £840,000
- The director proposes:
  - To allow corporation tax of £120,000
  - To allow for the preference dividend, and a final ordinary dividend of 7p
  - To transfer £110,000 to the General Reserve

Silly Lilly Ltd – Profit and Loss Appropriation Account – 31 October 2009

	£	£
		840,000
Director's remuneration[1]	40,000	
Debenture Interest Paid (150,000 × 8%)[2]	12,000	(52,000)
Net Profit[3]		788,000
Corporation tax[4]		(120,000)
Profit after tax[5]		668,000
Preference Share dividend (200,000 × 6%)[6]	12,000	
Ordinary Share dividend (interim)[7]	80,000	
Ordinary Share dividend (800,000 × 7/100)[8]	56,000	(148,000)
		420,000
Transfer to General Reserve[9]		(110,000)
Retained Profit for the year[10]		310,000
Profit and Loss Account (1.11.08)		350,000
Profit and Loss Account balance c/d		660,000

So what's happening?

1 **Director's remuneration** is paying the director. Because you don't have one owner who runs the business, a director is employed (a director may well be a shareholder). Paying him or her is an expense – it should have gone in the Profit and Loss Account. If you're asked to prepare the Profit and Loss Account, do include this.

2 A **debenture** is a kind of loan (see section 3.6.3.3). Interest is an expense. This also should have gone in the Profit and Loss Account. But be careful – it's quite common to see that you've only paid half of your debenture interest. The expense should always be a percentage on the full amount. If you have unpaid interest, it's an accrual in exactly the same way as if you had a note telling you that 'interest unpaid amounts to £6,000'. Your expense is the full £12,000.

3 We put these expenses together and recalculate the Net Profit. Now we're ready to share this profit. The order in which you do this is important.

4 The tax man always gets his share first. You should label the after-tax profit.

5 You should be aware that some examples of an Appropriation section would add last year's Profit and Loss balance at this point. However, your AQA examiner probably isn't expecting it so we'll leave it out.

6 Now we pay the shareholders – the people who own shares of the business – their share of the profit. This payment is called a **dividend**. There are two types of shareholder. We'll learn more about them in Section 3.6.3.

Preference shareholders get a fixed percentage, and they get paid before Ordinary shareholders.

7 Ordinary shareholders get paid what the directors say they get paid. It depends on how well the business is doing and how much profit the directors want to keep for investment. Here they get a final dividend of 7p per share. Since share capital is valued at £800,000, and the shares are £1 each, there must be 800,000 shares. The dividend, then, is 800,000 × 7p.

An **interim dividend** is an extra payment made early. Just add it on.

8 We deduct all of the dividends from the after-tax profits.

9 There's still a lot of profit left over. The directors might want to keep this profit in the company, since profit adds to capital, and the more capital you have in the company the more assets you can own. Here we put some in a reserve.

10 And there's still some profit left unused. This can be called **Retained Profit** or **Undistributed Profit** since it hasn't been distributed yet. You must say that this is the 'Retained profit for the year'.

Finally we can add the Profit and Loss Account balance from last year to find a new Profit and Loss Account balance for this year. Use this figure in the Balance Sheet in the Capital section. Don't use the figure for Net Profit – that's all been shared out.

For Sole Trader businesses we've just moved the profit into a capital account. As you can see, the job of doing that has become more complex, which is why we use the Appropriation Account.

The Share Premium Account is another type of capital, and we'll see it in the Balance Sheet.

3.6.2 THE BALANCE SHEET

You've already learned how to make the Fixed Asset and Current Asset sections in a Balance Sheet, and these sections are not very different for a Limited Liability Company. We'll just summarise them in our example. However, you've just calculated a lot of payments to share out in the Appropriation section, and you still owe this money. These items will make the Current Liabilities section much bigger. Also, we now have different kinds of capital to deal with in the Financed By section.

Here's how your Balance Sheet might look.

Balance Sheet (extract) – Silly Lilly Ltd – 31 October 2009

	£	£	£
Fixed Assets			2,000,000
Current Assets		562,700	
Creditors: amounts falling due within one year			
Creditors	77,000		
Debenture Interest due (150,000 × 8% – 6,000)[1]	6,000		
Other accruals[2]	1,700		
Corporation tax[3]	120,000		
Preference Share dividend	12,000		
Ordinary Share dividend	56,000		
		(272,700)	
Net Current Assets			290,000
Creditors: amounts falling due after more than one year			
Debenture Stock (8% – repayable 2016)[4]			(150,000)
			2,140,000
Financed by:			
Ordinary Share Capital (£1)[5]	800,000		
Preference Share Capital (6%)	200,000		
Share Premium Account	120,000		
General Reserve[6]	360,000		
Profit and Loss Account (31.10.09)[7]	660,000		
	2,140,000		

1 Remember, we still owe a half year's interest. Here we've calculated what should have been paid less what has been paid. The difference is a liability.

2 The other accruals would be of the kind you've already learned.

3 You still owe the tax and dividends you calculated in the Appropriation section. Put them here. Don't include the interim dividend – you've already paid that.

4 You should put a subheading 'Creditors: amounts falling due after more than one year' and then list your debentures and mortgages. There will be

marks available for labels and layouts. Your examiner may insist, for example, that you use the terms 'Creditors: amounts falling ...' and 'Net current assets', which are standard for Limited Liability accounts.

5 Look at all this capital – and none of it is Drawings. The Ordinary and Preference share capital is the money put in by the owners when they bought their share of the business. Sometimes when you buy shares you have to pay a premium (we'll look at this in more detail in section 3.6.3.5). This is recorded in a Share Premium Account and is a form of capital.

6 See how the General Reserve now shows the old balance plus the new amount transferred to it in the Appropriation section (see also section 3.6.3.5).

7 See also how the Profit and Loss Account balance is the bottom line, not Net Profit.

3.6.3 FINANCING LIMITED LIABILITY COMPANIES

A Limited Liability Company isn't just a large company with lots of owners. It could be a small company with one owner. There are rules and laws to say what a Limited Liability Company actually is.

A Limited Liability Company is, legally, a separate legal thing from its owners. If a sole trader's business owes lots of money, then so does the sole trader. With a Limited Liability Company, however, the liability is limited to the money that the owners have paid for their shares.

When a business becomes a Limited Liability Company:

1 The owner protects his or her private assets.
   - If the business collapses, each shareholder can only lose the value of their shares.
   - The 'veil of incorporation' separates the business from its owners, to the extent that the business and owners can owe each other money and sue each other.

2 It appoints one or more Directors, who:
   - Run the business
   - Are often major share holders
   - Are appointed by the shareholders, and removed by them
   - Report every year at the AGM (Annual General Meeting) of the company

3 Shares are sold to bring more money into the business without borrowing money and hence paying interest.
   - The value of these shares can be of any value, but are often £1 in an exam

- One shareholder can buy any number of shares. In 2005, Malcolm Glazer bought most of the shares in Manchester United Football Club. This, effectively, meant that he owned the club. Supporters were unhappy because he borrowed the money to buy the shares, so losing the advantage of not paying interest, and incurring a massive expense for the club.

4 There are more legal duties and obligations.

- You have to send to the government (Companies House).
  - (i) A memorandum of association: this states your company name, registered address and nature of business.
  - (ii) Articles of association: these are the rules for how your company will run.
  - (iii) Any other documents required by law: currently these are Form 10 and Form 12, concerning the directors of the company and other legal requirements.
- Your accounts must be published.
  - (i) They must be checked by an independent referee called an Auditor.
  - (ii) A copy must be sent to Companies House.
  - (iii) A copy must be sent to every shareholder.
  - (iv) Any member of the public can see your accounts.

5 It can be a Private or Public Limited Liability Company.

- Private Limited Companies:
  - (i) Have 'Ltd' or 'Limited' on the end of the company name.
  - (ii) Can have one or more members.
  - (iii) Can have any amount of share capital.
  - (iv) Can only sell shares privately. There are lots of private limited liability companies in the UK, often formed by small groups of people who know each other.
- Public Limited Companies:
  - (i) Have 'PLC' on the end of the company name.
  - (ii) Must have two or more members.
  - (iii) Must have at least £50,000 of authorised share capital.
  - (iv) May sell shares publicly on the stock exchange. This gives PLCs access to lots of possible shareholders, and allows them to raise larger amounts of capital.

Ordinary and preference shares

The shares most often bought are called ordinary shares. It's the ordinary shareholders that attend the AGM and vote in (or out) the directors. In 2004, for example, Eurotunnel shareholders voted not to renew the seats of the Chief Executive and Chairman on the Board of Directors. AGMs are usually less dramatic than this.

Preference shareholders:

- Are paid a fixed percentage dividend on their capital – like interest on a loan.
- Are not allowed to vote at the AGM.
- Get preference on recovering their capital over ordinary shareholders in the event of the business winding up (finishing).
  - Note that Debenture holders get their original loan back even before Preference Shareholders – low risk.
- Get preference on the payment of dividends over ordinary shareholders, i.e. if there's not enough to go around, the preference shareholders get their dividends first.
  - If you hold **Cumulative Preference Shares** and there's not enough profit to pay all of your dividend during one year, then you're still owed your dividend the following year.
  - If you hold **Non-cumulative Preference Shares** and there's not enough profit to pay all of your dividend one year, then you lose the difference.
  - Compare this with a secured loan (i.e. a debenture) where you get your interest whether there's a profit or not.

Ordinary shareholders:

- Are paid a dividend decided by the directors. They may vote to decrease this dividend but not to increase it.
- Are allowed to vote at the AGM.
- Are the last to get their share of their capital if the business winds up.
- Are the last to get their share of the profit (after holders of loan stock and preference shareholders). This means they'll get nothing in a bad year, but a bumper return in a good year. Ordinary shares are a relatively risky investment with a chance of big returns.
- In practice, as we've seen, the directors can chose to keep some profit in the company to allow for investment and the purchase of assets. It's all about whether the ordinary shareholders' money is kept in the business where it can grow, or dished out so they can go on a nice holiday.

Authorised and issued share capital

The company must state in its Memorandum of Association a figure for its **Authorised** or **Nominal** share capital. This is the maximum amount of capital it can have. You'll remember that a PLC must have a minimum of £50,000 authorised share capital. If they need more money than their maximum they have to vote for it at the AGM.

However, the directors may choose only to sell enough shares to raise the finance they need. These shares are issued, and the money raised is **Issued**

Share Capital. It can issue more shares at a later date if it needs to raise more money.

Sometimes you may see **Called Up** capital, where only some of the value of each share has been asked for. The amount of capital actually paid is called **Paid Up** capital. If the business has a problem, the shareholder is still liable for the unpaid portion of their share.

Debenture stock (loan capital)

You'll know what a mortgage is. You borrow a frightening amount of money and buy a house. If your house rockets in value, then you don't mind paying the interest. If things go badly for your finances, however, the mortgage lender can sell your home to get their money back.

A **Debenture** (a secured loan certificate) works in a similar way. We've talked about it as a loan before, but let's look more closely.

A company can choose to issue Debenture certificates instead of shares. They stay fixed in value and offer a fixed rate of interest every year. The expense of interest is paid before the sharing of profit. Also, like a mortgage, the certificates will be 'secured', so that the lender gets first shot at the assets of the company (specified assets or not) if the business folds. Unsecured debentures are called 'simple' or 'naked' debentures.

The rate of interest payable will show up in the information you're given in your exam. You'll see a date as well, telling you when you have to pay back the value of the loan (a 'redeemable debenture'). This is normally a confirmation that the stock comes under 'Creditors: amounts falling due after more than one year', not 'Creditors: amounts falling due within one year'. Debentures are a typical example of what's called Loan Capital.

Share capital and loan capital compared

The investors and directors will choose how money is invested in the company depending on risk.

Investors:

- Those who invest by buying shares can make a lot of money if the company is successful and more people want to buy in. The value of the shares goes up and they can be sold at a profit. This is what the major shareholders in Manchester United did in 2005. However, if the business does badly the value of the shares will drop. The success of the business also affects **Earnings Per Share** (profit after tax per share), and hence dividends. Buying shares has a risk involved.

- Those who lend money by buying debentures will always get a predictable return in the form of interest. They'll also get paid first if the business closes. However, they will miss out on piles of cash if the business does well. Debentures are a less risky investment.

Businesses:
- Those who issue more shares instead of debentures are relatively safe if the business doesn't do well. There are fewer creditors expecting interest, and shareholders just have to shrug their shoulders if it's a thin year. If business booms, however, there will be lots of shareholders wanting a cut, and profit will be spread more thinly for everyone – including the original shareholders. Shareholders are also happy with a dividend that's lower than interest rates if their shares are increasing in value. This low risk approach by businesses is called low gearing.
- Those who issue debentures instead of more shares could face problems if there are not enough profits to pay the interest. However, if the business booms, then a relatively comfortable interest payment is made, and the relatively few shareholders get a nice big dividend. This comparatively risky approach is called high gearing.

The Share Premium Account and other reserves

When we looked at the Balance Sheet in Unit 1 the capital was easy: the proprietor invested some money, and the profit was added to it. The total was one nice, neat figure.

As we've seen in the Limited Liability Company, however, capital is less clear-cut. As well as the Issued Capital, there are different types of Reserve Capital:
- Profit and Loss Account balance
- General Reserve Account
- Share Premium Account

Let's look again at Silly Lilly Ltd.

Say Silly Lilly starts by issuing 400,000 Ordinary £1 shares, and £200,000 worth of Preference shares. We'll assume that the Capital is fully paid up. This £600,000, at the beginning, represents the capital in the company.

The Profit and Loss Account balance

The business does well, and profit is made. Some of this profit is distributed as dividends, and some is kept in the company for investment.

This '**Retained Profit**' (Profit and Loss Account balance carried forward) is one form of reserve capital. It belongs to the Ordinary shareholders as a reward for their risk. The original value of the capital is still listed, and the

Profit and Loss Account balance carried forward represents the added profit that hasn't been 'withdrawn' as dividends.

The General Reserve Account

The directors may decide to make a formal account for some of this extra profit. A General Reserve is common, although a Buildings Reserve may be opened, for example, to finance a new office. These named Reserve accounts are still just overflow profits, but they're kept in a bucket with their name on it.

Note that the profit kept in the company exists in the form of assets (e.g. money in the bank) which can be used to grow the business even bigger, instead of being taken out and spent privately. You'll see the relationship between profit and cash examined in Unit 4.

The Share Premium Account

Now let's say Silly Lilly Ltd wants to raise more money by issuing another 400,000 Ordinary £1 shares (assuming this is still within their Authorised Capital limit). The shares issued originally have increased in value as the company has grown, and are now selling for £1.30 (even though there's still £1 written on the share certificate). Please note that this rise in value has no effect on the accounts of a company. The share is like a lost Rembrandt, sold at a car boot sale for £10, and later sold on for £10 million – providing no benefit for the poor stallholder.

To reflect their market value, the new £1 shares are sold at £1.30, raising a total of £520,000. This is put in the Bank (debit entry) and adds to the company's assets. The £400,000 nominal value is lumped in with the original Ordinary Share Capital, while the extra £120,000 is put into a reserve called a Share Premium Account (these are both credit entries).

Now every shareholder has an equal claim on dividends, and an equal claim on the various Reserve Capital accounts.

Capital Reserves and Revenue Reserves

Now that we've got everything straight, let's confuse matters. Some of this 'Reserve Capital' is also called a 'Capital Reserve'. And some of it isn't.

- Capital Reserves:
  - Share Premium Account
  - Revaluation Reserve: if your company owns buildings etc. which have appreciated in value, it may record the increase in Fixed Assets, and record a corresponding increase in Capital as a Revaluation Reserve. This

fair reflection makes the company stronger if another company tries to take it over.

These Capital Reserves represent growth in the value of the company. They are separate from the profit the business makes, and are not available for distribution as dividends. They do, however, belong to the Ordinary Shareholders, but are only available when a revalued asset is sold, or the company is wound up.

- Revenue Reserves:
  - General Reserve
  - Profit and Loss Account balance

These Reserves were kept back from the profit the business made (i.e. the revenue generated) and may be released as dividends if the directors wish to do this.

FURTHER READING

Frank Wood and Alan Sangster, *Business Accounting 1*, Chapter 45
David Cox and Michael Fardon, *A/S Accounting for AQA*, Chapter 27
Ian Harrison, *Introducing Accounting for A/S*, Chapter 24

USEFUL WEB SITES

www.aqa.org.uk/qual/gceasa/acc_assess.html This is always your most useful web site. Download as many exam papers as your printer will allow.

http://news.bbc.co.uk/1/hi/business/3606431.stm
A report on the Eurotunnel AGM

www.companieshouse.gov.uk Straight from the horse's mouth. A drop-down menu offers you 'Information and guidance on...'

www.fastlinksolutions.co.uk/limitedc.htm This page outlines the pros and cons of becoming a limited liability company.

www.bullbearings.co.uk Visit the Student Centre and click on Share Dealing for a comprehensive guide.

www.bigbubbleweb.co.uk Go to Resources and Guides for more information on stocks and shares.

www.unisys.com/common/investors/glossary/

www.google.co.uk

SAMPLE QUESTIONS

3.6.1

Below is the capital section from the Balance Sheet of Zanchetta RDL Ltd as at 30 April 2008.

Financed by:	
Ordinary Share Capital (£ 1 shares)	900 000
7% Preference Share Capital	200 000
Buildings reserve	280 000
General Reserve	170 000
Share Premium Account	270 000
Retained profit (30.04.08)	130 000
	1 950 000

Required

(a) Explain **one** difference between Ordinary and Preference shares, identifying the advantages and disadvantages of each from the point of view of the company.

(5 marks)

(b) The figures for Zanchetta RDL Ltd's authorised ordinary share capital and issued ordinary share capital are different. Which of these figures is listed in the Balance Sheet?

(1 mark)

(c) Which items in the Balance Sheet were generated directly by trading profit?

(3 marks)

Carl Hunter currently holds 20 000 ordinary shares in Zanchetta RDL Ltd. He's concerned that any undistributed profit not paid out in dividends has been lost.

Required

(d) Advise Carl on whether or not he has been deprived of his money.

(3 marks)

Carl is considering buying a new issue of ordinary £1 shares, but is dismayed that he will have to pay £1.60 per share.

Required

(e) Explain the situation to Carl by showing how the new capital will be recorded in the balance sheet.

(4 marks)

3.6.2

Required
Discuss ordinary share capital, preference share capital and debenture stock as different means of raising finances, explaining the differences in terms of the risk involved to both the company and the investor.

(9 marks)

3.6.3 (E)

The draft profit for the year ended 31 May 2003 of Srian plc is £12 000 000. The following information for the year has not been taken into account.

	£
Ordinary dividends – paid	800 000
– proposed	1 300 000
Directors' fees	1 500 000
Provision for corporation tax	2 600 000
Debenture interest	1 200 000
Transfer to general reserve	1 000 000

Required
(a) Prepare the profit and loss appropriation account for the year ended 31 May 2003.

Srian plc
Profit and loss appropriation account for the year ended 31 May 2003

(9 marks)

The following has been extracted from the balance sheet of Srian plc as at 31 May 2003.

	£
Ordinary shares of £1 each fully paid	25 000 000
6% debentures	20 000 000

The directors have seen an opportunity to expand the company's operation. They need to raise £30 000 000.

The directors are considering raising the whole amount by
Either an issue of 20 000 000 ordinary shares at £1.50 each
Or an issue of £30 000 000 6% debentures.

Required
(b) Evaluate the two methods of raising finance being considered by the directors of the company.

(12 marks)

Total 21%

Source: Assessment and Qualifications Alliance, June 2003

3.6.4 (E)
The following balances have been extracted from the books of account of Pafftol Ltd **after** a draft trading and profit and loss account was prepared for the year ended 31 March 2004.

	£
Issued share capital:	
Ordinary shares £1 each fully paid	500 000
7% debentures (2015–2018)	400 000
Plant and machinery at cost	1 420 000
Vehicles at cost	710 000
Provisions for depreciation:	
plant and machinery	192 000
vehicles	150 000
Net profit for the year	676 000
Profit and loss account 1 April 2003	439 000
Bank Balance (debit)	113 600
General reserve	250 000
Share premium account	100 000
Stock 31 March 2004	211 000
Debtors	24 900
Creditors	16 500
Interim ordinary dividend paid	30 000

Additional information and instructions

The following have not been included in the balances shown above:

(1) directors' fees £200 000;
(2) debenture interest paid £14 000;
(3) debenture interest accrued £14 000;
(4) proposed ordinary dividend £60 000;
(5) corporation tax payable £102 000;
(6) transfer to general reserve £50 000.

Required
(a) Prepare a profit and loss appropriation account for the year ended 31 March 2004.

(8 marks)

(b) Prepare a balance sheet as at 31 March 2004.

(23 marks)

The directors of Pafftol Ltd wish to raise £600 000 additional capital. They are unsure whether to:

(1) Issue a further 200 000 ordinary shares with a nominal value of £1 each at a premium of £2 each:

or

(2) Issue 6% debentures.

Required

(c) Advise the directors which of the two options would be the most beneficial to the company.

(8 marks)

Total 39%

Source: Assessment and Qualifications Alliance, June 2004

3.6.5 (E)

The following is the summarised draft balance sheet as at 31 December 2002 for David Mark Ltd.

	£	£
Fixed Assets		700 000
Current Assets		
Stock	85 000	
Debtors	60 000	
Bank	17 000	
	162 000	
Less current liabilities		
Trade creditors	37 000	125 000
		825 000
Share capital and reserves		
Ordinary shares of 50 pence each		250 000
8% preference shares of £1 each		100 000
Profit and loss account		400 000
General reserves		75 000
		825 000

The company's retained profit for the year, before appropriations, was £150 000, which has been included in the profit and loss account figure shown in the balance sheet above.

Additional information

The following have **not** yet been taken into consideration:

(1) Transfer from profit and loss account to the general reserve £45 000
(2) A proposed final dividend on preference shares of £4000.
(3) A proposed final dividend on ordinary shares of 7 pence per share.
(4) An issue of 200 000 ordinary shares of 50 pence each at 75 pence per share.

(**Note** these shares are not eligible for dividend in the year ended 31 December 2002.)

Required

(a) Calculate the retained profit for the year ended 31 December 2002 after appropriations.

£

Retained profit for the year as per draft final accounts	150 000
Corrected retained profit for the year	

(4 marks)

(b) Prepare the summarised balance sheet as at 31 December 2002 as it would appear after taking into account the additional information listed above.

David Mark Ltd
Summarised Balance Sheet as at 31 December 2002

(10 marks)

(c) State the type of business ownership that would have 'Ltd' as part of its name.

(2 marks)

(d) Assess the importance of the term 'Ltd' to an ordinary shareholder in David Mark Ltd.

(5 marks)

Total 21%

Source: Assessment and Qualifications Alliance, January 2003

3.6.6 (E)

The following draft balance sheet has been prepared from a correct trial balance by an inexperienced clerk.

Grift Ltd
Balance Sheet as at 28 February 2002

	£		£
Premises	270 000	Debtors	8 500
Stock 28 February 2002	17 000	Stock 1 March 2001	21 000
Bank Balance (dr)	1 500	Vehicles	170 000
Trade creditors	6 000	Authorised ordinary shares	1 000 000
Proposed ordinary dividend	18 000	Retained earnings	93 000
Issued ordinary shares	500 000	Machinery	150 000
'Balancing figure'	630 000		
	1 442 500		1 442 500

Required

(a) Explain the difference between the authorised share capital and the issued share capital of a limited company.

(3 marks)

(b) Prepare a redrafted balance sheet for the company presented in good form.

(10 marks)

Roger Grift had been in business as a sole trader for many years. On 1 January 2000 he turned his business into Grift Ltd, a limited company.

Required

(c) Discuss **one** factor that Roger Grift should have considered before changing his business into a limited company.

(6 marks)

Total 19%

Source: Assessment and Qualifications Alliance, May 2002

3.6.7 (E)

The following information has been extracted from the books of account of Leroy McDade plc as at 31 December 2001.

	£
Issued share capital:	
Ordinary shares of 50p each fully paid	1 600 000
7% debentures (2020–2025)	200 000
Share premium account	800 000
Profit and loss account balance 1 January 2001	612 000
General reserve	150 000
Interim ordinary dividend paid 4 August 2001	40 000
Trade creditors	78 200
Directors' fees	117 000
Provision for corporation tax due	180 000

Additional information

(i) Net profit for the year after interest but before taxation was £546 000.

(ii) Debenture interest is payable half-yearly to 30 June and 31 December. It is paid to debenture holders on 27 July and 27 January each year.

(iii) The directors propose a transfer to general reserve of £50 000 and a final ordinary dividend of 5p per share.

Required

(a) Prepare the profit and loss appropriation account for the year ended 31 December 2001 of Leroy McDade plc.

(10 marks)

(b) Prepare balance sheet extracts as at 31 December 2001 for Leroy McDade plc showing the sections for:

(i) the capital and reserves, and (5 marks)

(ii) creditors falling due within one year (ie current liabilities). (4 marks)

(Headings: 1 mark)

(c) Discuss the advantages and disadvantages that an investor should consider when deciding whether to invest in debentures or ordinary shares.

(15 marks)

Total 35%

Source: Assessment and Qualifications Alliance, January 2002

Unit 4

INTRODUCTION TO MANAGEMENT ACCOUNTING:
accounting for management and decision making

Costs

4.1

Unit 4 is slightly different from the work you've done so far. It deals not with recording and adding up the money that's been moved around, but with understanding what it means, and planning what's going to happen in the future.

You can get a long way toward the mark you need just by learning some formulae and applying them intelligently. Interpreting the implications will take more work, and will get you a better grade.

We'll start with the costs. Costs means money you have to pay for things. It's similar (though different) to the work we've done on assets, profit and so on. Payments are no respecters of the accruals concept. Even if you depreciate a machine over five years, you may have to pay cash in one lump when you buy it. That's a cost. Remember, profit is revenue less expenses. Expenses are very slightly different from costs, in terms of when the money moves out.

POINTS TO CONSIDER

- How do you define fixed costs? Can you give examples?
- How do you define variable costs? Can you give examples?
- How about semi-variable costs?
- marginal cost is another name for what?
- Why do accountants do marginal costing?
- How do you make a marginal costing statement?
- What are overheads?

There may not be a question just on costs, but you will surely be tested on costs in one question or another. For example, to tackle break-even, we first have to understand two different types of cost: fixed and variable.

Fixed costs

> **output**
> What you produce, or the number of things you make.

Fixed costs don't change (or 'vary') with output. They stay fixed for a given period, and can be called 'period costs'. If you rent a cake shop, for example, it costs you £300 per month whether you sell one cake or a thousand, so rent is a fixed cost. Interest on a loan is another regular outlay that doesn't change if you have a busy month or a quiet one.

Fixed costs include:

- Fixtures and fittings
- Vehicles
- Advertising campaigns
- Rent
- Interest
- Buying an automatic packing machine

Variable costs

Variable costs, meanwhile, do change with output.

- Raw material is a perfect example. Make one cake and you only have to pay for 1 kg of flour, 1 kg of sugar and so on.
- Labour is another variable cost. In all but the smallest businesses you can hire labour and lay it off as demand rises and falls.
- Power and fuel would also be variable costs.

Marginal cost

Variable costs can sometimes be called marginal cost, which is the cost of making one more unit. Be careful with this one, as marginal cost when used in economics includes an element for fixed costs.

Marginal costing, meanwhile, involves measuring the cost of production just in terms of its variable costs (ignoring fixed costs). It's a useful tool for management accounting, letting you chase new revenue using your existing fixed cost resources. This, as we shall see, leads us to break-even analysis.

A **Marginal costing statement**, meanwhile, is a column of figures that goes from Sales to Net Profit – much like a Trading and Profit and Loss Account – but breaks your expenses down into variable costs and fixed costs. This lets you see how the balance lies between these two types of cost. If you're asked for one it could look like this:

Marginal Costing Statement

	£	£
Sales		1,000,000
Variable Cost 1	350,000	
Variable Cost 2	200,000	
		(550,000)
Total contribution		450,0000
Fixed Cost 1	150,000	
Fixed cost 2	50,000	
		(200,000)
Net Profit		250,000

You'll notice that total revenue less total variable costs is called **Total Contribution**. We'll learn more about contribution in section 4.2 on Break-even.

Semi-variable costs

These are part fixed, part variable. A telephone service involves a fixed line rental plus variable call costs. Some labour, meanwhile, is regarded as semi-variable, if a sales force works for a salary plus commission, for example.

Direct costs and indirect costs / overheads

You may also encounter direct and indirect costs. You'll remember these from the manufacturing account in Unit 3. Direct costs can be matched against what you are producing (for example, raw materials or someone actually making something), while indirect costs are just generally incurred (like electricity, or someone sweeping up). Indirect costs can be called overheads – which means any general business expense.

As you might guess, direct costs are usually variable costs, although the definitions are different, and indirect costs can be either fixed or variable.

FURTHER READING

Frank Wood and Alan Sangster *Business Accounting 1*, Chapters 37 and 48
David Cox and Michael Fardon, *A/S Accounting for AQA*, Chapter 30
Ian Harrison, *Introducing Accounting for A/S*, Chapters 27 and 28

USEFUL WEB SITES

www.bized.ac.uk Choose 'economics' as your subject, and have a search round 'firms'. You should find this page:

www.bized.ac.uk/learn/economics/firms/costrevenue/notes.htm

www.google.co.uk

SAMPLE QUESTIONS

4.1.1

Required

(a) Explain the key difference between fixed costs and variable costs, identifying two examples of each.

(5 marks)

(b) What is a semi-variable cost?

(1 mark)

(c) What does the term 'marginal cost' mean?

(1 mark)

(d) K & S Moss Ltd produces shoes. The directors are planning to increase production next month by 10%. Which of the above types of cost should be most closely considered?

(1 mark)

4.1.2 (E)

Which Direction Ltd produces compasses that sell for £20 each.

The following costs relate to the six months ended 31 December 2003, when 5000 compasses were produced and sold.

	£
Direct labour	23 000
Direct materials	35 000
Other direct costs	21 000

Of the other direct costs £12 000 are fixed costs.

Required

(a) Distinguish between direct and indirect costs.

(2 marks)

(b) Calculate the marginal cost of one compass.

(5 marks)

(c) Prepare a marginal costing statement for the six months ended 31 December 2003. Show the total contribution and the profit for the period.

(5 marks)

(d) Explain one advantage of producing a marginal costing statement.

(2 marks)

Total 14%

Source: Assessment and Qualifications Alliance, January 2004

Break-even 4.2

It's quite common to have a straightforward question on break-even.

Break-even means making enough money not to make a loss – although you haven't quite made a profit yet. Break-even means just covering all of your costs. Questions on Break-even can also include calculating the profit you might make.

POINTS TO CONSIDER

- What is Contribution, and the formula for Contribution?
- What is the Break-even volume, and what are the formulae for Break-even?
- What is the formula for Profit?
- How do changes in costs affect Break-even, profit etc.?
- What are the limitations of Break-even analysis?
- How can Break-even be represented on a graph?

4.2.1 CONTRIBUTION AND CALCULATION

When we calculate break-even, we have to calculate how many units we need to sell, allowing for all of our variable costs, to just pay off all of our fixed costs. For this, we need the contribution.

Contribution is the selling price (per unit) minus the variable costs (per unit). We can use 'price' to mean 'selling price', but it's a good idea to use the full name, as you may get confused with 'purchase price'.

If the selling price of a cake is 99p, and your variable costs are 40p, then the contribution is 99–40 = 59p. This is the money available to pay off your fixed costs. When you've sold enough cakes to pay them all off, you've broken even. After that, the contribution becomes the profit you can keep on each item.

You may need to calculate the contribution from total figures. For example, if total variable costs are £3,000, and total production is 1,000 units, then variable cost per unit must be £3. So the break-even quantity (or break-even volume) is the number of units you must sell to pay all your costs. Volume always refers to the things you make, not the money you take. The break-even value, meanwhile, is the money you'll take from these sales. Just multiply the volume by the price.

Here are the formulae. Learn them all perfectly, and you'll get some straightforward marks. Understand them if you can – 'p.u.' is a reminder to you that this figure is 'per unit'.

Contribution (p.u.)	= price p.u. – variable costs p.u.
Break-even (quantity)	= fixed costs / contribution p.u.
	= fixed costs / (price – variable costs)
Break-even value	= break-even quantity × price p.u.
	= fixed costs × price / (price – variable costs)
Profit	= sales volume × contribution p.u. – fixed costs
	= sales volume × (price – variable cost) – fixed costs
or	= total revenue – total cost
	= price × volume – (fixed cost + volume × variable cost)

If you are confident and fluent with the formulae for any part of Unit 4, you can pick up many of the marks you need to pass the exam.

How to tackle a big calculation

When you get a break-even question, you may be given some information (like price, variable costs, expected sales etc.) and asked to calculate the break-even volume, profit etc. Your teacher may have his or her own way to coach you on this, but I recommend a systematic approach.

- Start by writing what you know in a nice smart list.
- Write down the formulae you need.
- Write out the formulae with the numbers substituted in. Calculate and pick up the marks.

Example

Kikijo Ltd makes and sells microphones.

Their costs are:

• Materials per unit	£17
• Labour per unit	£14
• Variable overheads per unit	£8
• Fixed overheads per month	£1,200

They sell their microphones for £79, and expect to sell 80 microphones each month.

i) Calculate the break-even volume
ii) Calculate the break-even value
iii) Calculate the expected profit

Answer:

Variable = 17 + 14 + 8 = 39
Fixed = 1,200
Price = 79
Contribution = price – variable
= 79 – 39 = 40

i) Break-even volume = 1,200 / 40 = 30 units
ii) Break-even value = 30 × 79 = £2,370
iii) Profit = sales × contribution – fixed
= 80 × 40 –£1,200 = £2,000

You may be asked to evaluate the effect of changing a factor, like raising the price, or using cheaper materials and reducing variable costs.

For every new calculation, write out the known information again. Don't bodge with what you wrote for the first example – or you'll make mistakes and lose marks. Just take 15 seconds to frame the new calculation clearly again.

Example

Kikijo Ltd is considering switching to a new product. It would use cheaper materials costing £13 per unit and would sell for £69. Kikijo anticipates 90 sales per month. Calculate the new break-even volume and profit they can expect, and recommend whether or not to launch the new product.

Variable = 13 + 14 + 8 = 35
Fixed = 1,200
Price = 69
Contribution = price – variable
= 69 – 35 = 34
Break-even volume = 1,200 / 34 = 36 units
Profit = sales × contribution – fixed
= 90 × 34 –£1,200 = £1,860

Stay with the original product, as the new product has higher break-even and lower profit despite higher sales. Also, Kikijo's reputation might be affected by producing a lower quality product.

The break-even volume calculation here actually reveals a figure of 35.29 units. You can't sell 35.29 microphones, so use a whole number. And don't be tempted to round down. If you sell 35 units you haven't broken even. You must sell 36 units to cover all of your fixed costs.

4.2.2 CHANGES AND LIMITATIONS

If you're asked about the effect of changing a factor, use some common sense and don't be afraid to state the obvious. Here are some examples – see how many of them can be deduced from the formulae themselves:

- Raising the price
  - Increases the contribution
  - Reduces the break-even volume
  - May reduce sales
  - Competitors may need to be watched
- Cheaper materials
  - Reduces variable costs
  - Increases contribution
  - Reduces break-even volume
  - Allows a price reduction
  - May damage reputation
- Spend more on advertising
  - Increases the fixed costs
  - Increases sales volume
  - May require a rise in price
  - May allow a rise in price without damaging sales volume
- To increase contribution
  - Raise price
  - Reduce variable costs
- To reduce break-even volume
  - Raise price
  - Reduce variable costs
  - Reduce fixed costs

You may also be asked about the limitations of break-even analysis. These should make sense. Try to make sentences in the exam without losing the facts from the bullet points:

- Assumes all stock is sold
  - i.e. unsold stock incurs costs but does not produce revenue
    - Which affects the result
- Assumes fixed costs remain unchanged
  - e.g. charges may change during the year
  - Purchases of fixed assets may become necessary
- Assumes variable cost per unit remains unchanged with volume
  - Variable costs can rise in the short run
  - Economies of scale can reduce costs in the long run (if you produce more, you can buy in bulk, qualify for discounts and so on)
- Assumes no semi-variable costs (a combination of fixed and variable)
  - These would need to be separated
- Assumes one product and one selling price
  - Averages over a product range introduce extra uncertainty
- Is dependent on predicted figures
  - Sales volume is particularly difficult to predict accurately
- Excludes external factors
  - Anything from new competitors to government legislation can affect a plan

4.2.3 GRAPHS

You may be asked to draw or read a break-even graph. They're not too hard. Let's have a look at the graph for Kikijo's original plan.

You can see that we're plotting the money (both costs and revenue) on the y-axis against the volume of units sold on the x-axis.

1 Fixed costs are just fixed – they make a horizontal line at £1,200.
2 Variable costs, meanwhile, rise as the volume rises. They are added to the fixed cost to give a Total Cost curve (the function of this line in this case can be expressed as $y = 39x + 1{,}200$).
3 The Revenue curve is found by multiplying the volume by the price ($y = 79x$).
4 While the Revenue curve is lower than the Total Cost curve, Kikijo is making a loss. While the Revenue curve is above the Total Cost curve, Kikijo is making a profit. Break-even volume and value can be found where the Revenue curve crosses the Total Cost curve.
5 The vertical distance between the Revenue curve and the Total Cost curve gives the profit or loss for any given volume. The projected profit is the difference between the two lines at the projected sales volume.
6 The horizontal distance from the break-even volume to the projected sales

volume, meanwhile, is the Margin of Safety. If you sell fewer units than you expect, this shows how far short of projected sales you can fall before you make a loss.

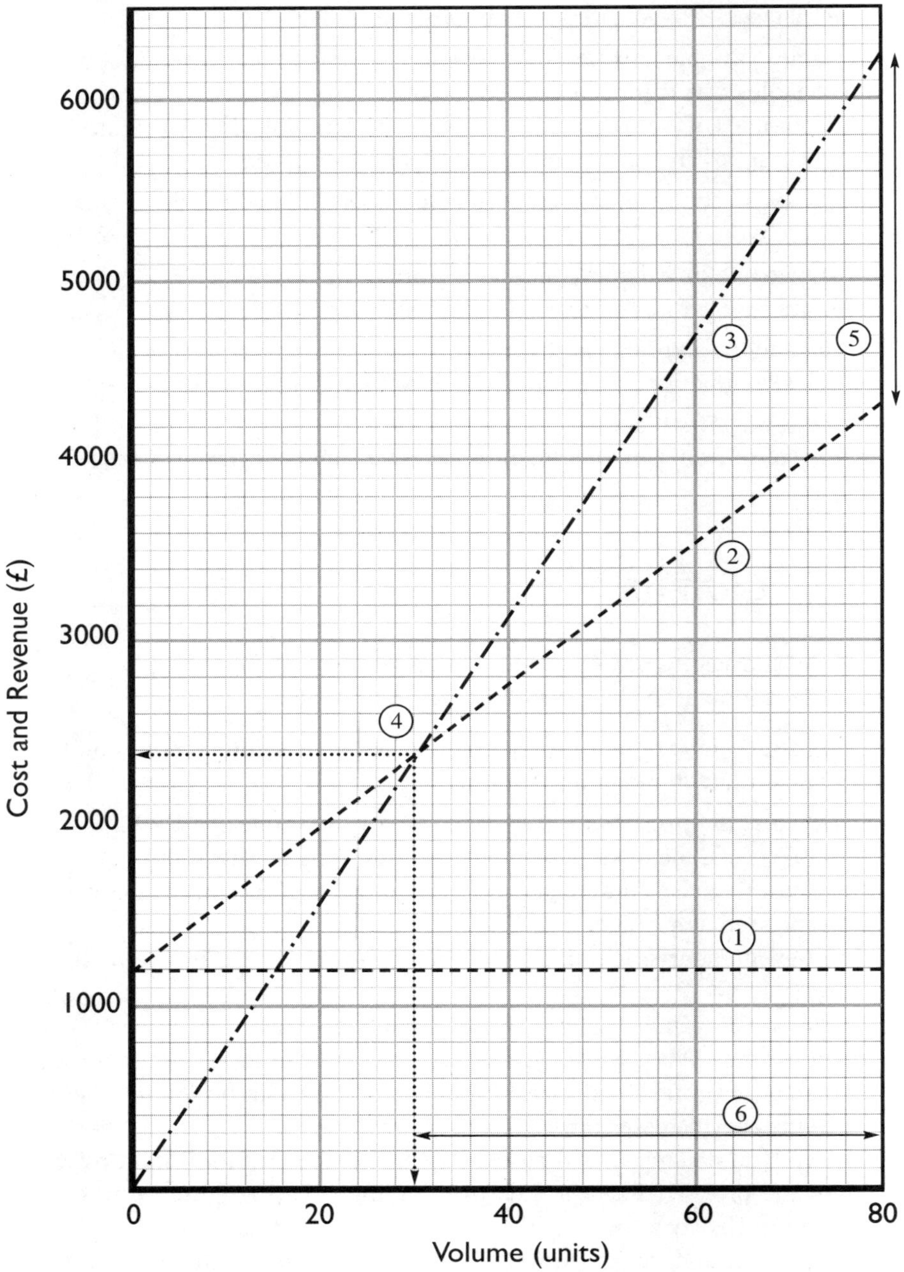

The graph has the advantage that the information can be seen clearly – as long as it is large, evenly scaled and well labelled. Plot it carefully.

FURTHER READING

David Cox and Michael Fardon, *A/S Accounting for AQA*, Chapter 31
Ian Harrison, *Introducing Accounting for A/S*, Chapter 28

USEFUL WEB SITES

www.aqa.org.uk/qual/gceasa/acc_assess.html This is always your most useful web site. Download as many exam papers as your printer will allow.

www.bizhelp24.com/accounting/breakeven_accounts.shtml

www.revisionguru.co.uk/ Go to Business Studies, and click on the Text Book (not AQA) to find a section on accounts.

www.google.co.uk

SAMPLE QUESTIONS

4.2.1

Madobie Ltd produces ornamental figurines. The company's costs and revenues are as follows:

	£
Variable costs per unit	19
Price per unit	39
Fixed costs for the month	3 800

Last month Madobie sold 350 figurines, and expects to sell the same this month.

Required

(a) State the formula for contribution and calculate it.

(2 marks)

(b) State the formula for breakeven volume and calculate it.

(2 marks)

(c) State the formula for breakeven value and calculate it.

(2 marks)

(d) State the formula for profit and calculate it.

(2 marks)

(e) State the formula for margin of safety and calculate it.

(2 marks)

(f) If fixed costs rise by 20%, calculate the price rise required to give the same breakeven volume.

(4 marks)

4.2.2

Vicky Faversham Ltd makes miniature steam engines. Vicky has estimated the following figures for the month of July 2009:

	£
Factory wages	3 200
Materials	700
Rent of factory	900
Miscellaneous fixed expenses	600
Advertising	700
Power and fuel	100
Price per unit	190

She expects to produce and sell 50 steam engines.

Required

Complete the following table:

	£
Total fixed costs	
Total variable costs	
Variable costs per unit	
Contribution per unit	
Breakeven quantity	
Expected profit	

(6 marks)

4.2.3 (E)

Newman Electronics Ltd manufactures one product which sells for 32 per unit.

The company plans to manufacture 40 000 units.

Annual costs are expected to be:

	£
Variable costs	360 000
Semi-variable costs of which £80 000 are fixed	280 000
Other fixed costs	340 000

In the year ended 31 March 2003 46 000 units were produced and sold.

Required

(a) Define the following:

(i) fixed costs;

(1 mark)

(ii) variable costs;

(1 mark)

(iii) semi-variable costs;

(1 mark)

(b) Calculate the expected contribution *per unit*. State the formula used.

Formula ....

(1 mark)

Contribution per unit ....

(7 marks)

(c) Prepare a statement for Newman Electronics Ltd for the year ended 31 March 2003 to show clearly the *total* contribution and *total* profit for the year.

(7 marks)

Total 18%

Source: Assessment and Qualifications Alliance, June 2003

4.2.4 (E)

Pinder Ltd manufactures parachutes.

The cost of producing one parachute is

	£
Materials (£4 per metre)	10
Labour (£8 per hour)	16
Other variable costs	8

Total fixed costs for the year are expected to be £134 000.

Each parachute sells for £44. The company expects to sell 22 000 parachutes each year.

The production manager intends to purchase new advanced machinery, which will reduce the time taken to produce one parachute by 25%.

In order to operate the machinery the workforce must be retrained for two months at a cost of £32 000. If the retraining is completed satisfactorily the workforce will receive a 12.5% pay rise.

It is expected that not all of the workforce will wish to be retrained.

Required

(a) Define the term 'contribution'

(2 marks)

(b) Calculate the contribution per unit:

(i) **before** the proposed purchase of the machinery;

(2 marks)

(ii) **after** the proposed purchase of the machinery;

(3 marks)

(c) Assess the effect the proposed purchase of machinery will have on the profitability of Pinder Ltd.

(8 marks)

Total 15%

Source: Assessment and Qualifications Alliance, May 2002

4.2.5 (E)

Suddley Ltd manufactures a single product.
For the year ending 31 March 2002 each unit is expected to sell for £50.
The expected costs per unit for the year ended 31 March 2002 are:

	£
Materials	12
Labour	16
Variable overheads	7

The annual fixed overheads are expected to be £450 000.

Suddley Ltd has a maximum annual production capacity of 37 500 units.

Required

(a) Define and calculate:

(i) The contribution per unit;

(ii) The break-even point in £s and units.

State the formula used in each case.

(i) Formula:..

Definition: ....

Calculation:..

(5 marks)

(ii) Formula:..

Definition: ....

Calculation:..

(9 marks)

(b) In the graph shown, the letters **A**, **B**, **C** and **D** have been used to identify particular lines or terms used in accounting.

In the table below, match each line or term against the correct letter.

Line or term	**A, B, C, or D**
Fixed costs	
Total Sales Revenue	
Break-even Point	
Margin of Safety	

(4 marks)

(c) From the graph, calculate the profit made from the sale of 35 000 units.

(3 marks)

(d) Explain **two** possible consequences for Suddley Ltd if the selling price is reduced to £47 per unit.

(4 marks)

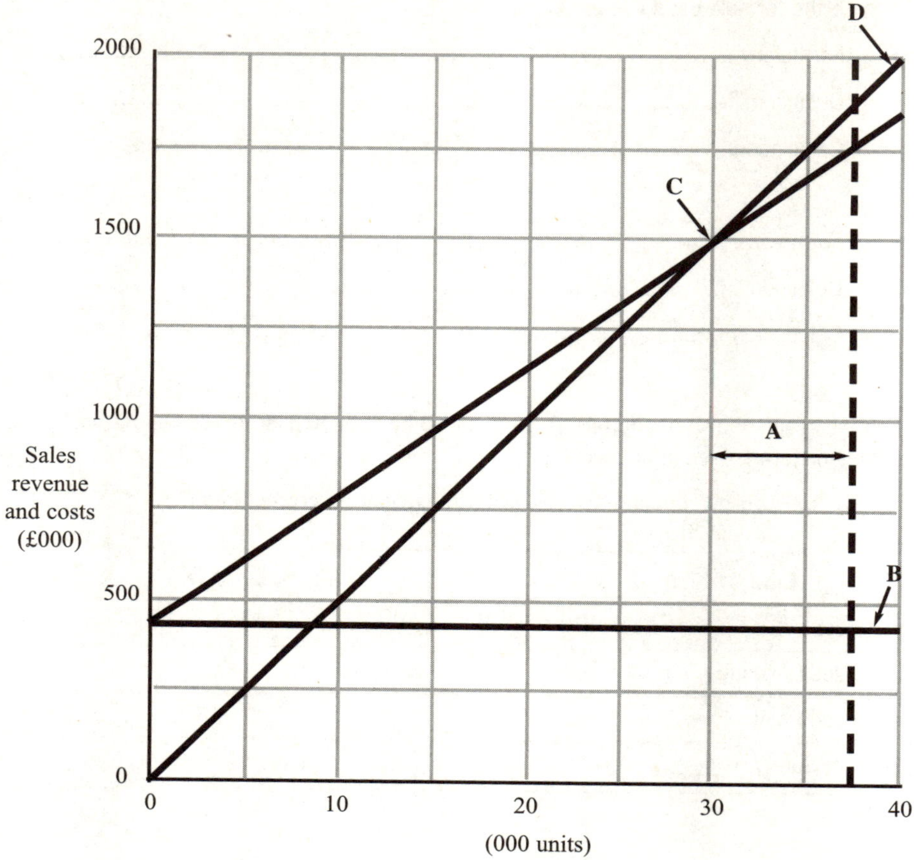

Total 25%

Source: Assessment and Qualifications Alliance, June 2001

Ratios and business performance

4.3

Calculating your current assets, profit and so on are all very well, but do they tell you if you're doing well or badly? There's always a section on ratios and performance, and if you learn this well you could mop up some big marks. More good news: the question should mostly be straightforward.

POINTS TO CONSIDER

- What is liquidity and what are the liquidity ratios?
- What are the different ways of measuring profit?
- What is the difference between Profit and Cash?
- How do you measure how efficiently your stock is sold and payments are made?
- How do you compare figures to show how performance is changing over time?

Remember all those assets, liabilities and capital? You'll probably be given some typical information from your Trading and Profit and Loss Account and Balance Sheet and asked to state and calculate certain ratios.

There are three types of ratio you may be tested on:

- Liquidity ratios
- Profit ratios
- Efficiency ratios

We'll use an example to show how the ratios work.

Lilibelle Ltd has the following figures:

	£
Sales/Turnover	310,000
Opening stock	12,000
Purchases	245,000
Closing stock	9,000
Cost of sales	248,000
Gross profit	62,000
Net Profit	38,000
Debtors	19,000
Current assets	31,000
Creditors	17,000
Current liabilities	24,000
Capital employed	205,000

Use the ratios to find how the business is doing.

4.3.1 LIQUIDITY RATIOS

It's no good making a million in profit if you've no cash in the bank to pay your electricity bill. **Liquid** means easy to spend, or easy to move around, and **liquidity** refers to the current assets and current liabilities in your balance sheet, and your ability to pay bills. Poor liquidity is as dangerous for a business as small profits.

Current ratio

current assets / current liabilities = current ratio

e.g.

Current assets:	31,000
Current liabilities:	24,000

Current ratio:
31,000/24,000 = 1.29

If your current liabilities are bigger than your current assets then the ratio will be less than one. If your assets are bigger than liabilities then the ratio will be greater than one.

If your liabilities are much bigger than your assets you could have trouble paying your creditors (e.g. ratio < 0.8). If your assets are much bigger than your liabilities (e.g. ratio > 3) then you're very safe when the bills come in, but are your assets working as hard as they could be? Do you have lots of debtors who should be paying you? Lots of unsold stock? Money in the bank, perhaps, which could be invested in assets or advertising?

Acid test ratio

Since stock is regarded as difficult to liquidate, the acid test ratio (or quick ratio) is a better indication of liquidity.

(current assets – stock) / current liabilities = acid test ratio

This, of course, is the same as 'current assets without stock' divided by current liabilities.

e.g.

Closing stock:	9,000
Debtors, bank etc.:	22,000
Current assets:	31,000
Current liabilities:	24,000

Current ratio:
22,000/24,000 = 0.92

4.3.2 PROFIT RATIOS

£40,000 profit in a year is pretty good if you run a market stall. However, if you're a multinational corporation it's pretty poor. When you find your bottom-line profit you need to measure what it means.

Return on Capital Employed (ROCE)

Net Profit / capital employed (× 100%) = Return on Capital Employed

e.g.

Net Profit:	£38,000
Capital employed:	£205,000

ROCE:
38,000/205,000 × 100% = 18.54%

A '**Return**' is what you get back from an investment. Capital employed is the money that's been invested in your business, and Net Profit is your return on that investment. ROCE can also be called **Net Profit on Capital Employed**.

Are you investing your capital wisely? If your return is lower then 3% you'd do better to walk to the high street and put your money in a regular savings account. Certainly, since there's a risk in business, your return should be higher than that of a guaranteed investment like a debenture (say 10%). Many businesses would consider a 15% return worthwhile and a 20% return good, but they'd like to see it rising year on year.

ROCE is usually expressed as a percentage, so multiply your fraction by 100, or hit [inv/shift] before you hit [=] on your calculator.

Net Profit margin

Net Profit / Sales (× 100%) = Net Profit margin

e.g.

Net Profit:	£38,000
Sales:	310,000

Net Profit margin:
38,000/310,000 × 100% = 12.26%

Net Profit margin, or Net Profit on Sales, varies greatly from business to business, as does Gross Profit on Sales. Be aware that Sales can also be called turnover, which refers to the total revenue flowing through the business.

Mark up

Another figure you may be asked about is mark-up, or Gross Profit mark-up. Some resellers set their price by adding a percentage of the cost price – for example buying chocolate bars at 30p and adding 33% to sell them at 40p. Any business, however, might be interested in finding the mark-up, and you may be asked to find what the mark-up was on a given selling price.

Gross Profit/cost of sales (× 100%) = Mark-up

e.g.

Gross Profit:	£62,000
Cost of sales:	£248,000

Mark-up:
62,000/248,000 × 100% = 25%

Don't get mark-up confused with profit margin. Your profit margin is the percentage of selling price that you keep. Mark-up is the percentage you add to the cost to get the selling price. It's typically 20–30%, but could be 100%, depending on the type of business.

Profit and cash

It's easy to think that making a big profit leads directly to big piles of cash in the bank. It's not that simple. If your business buys a car for £100 and sells it for £200, then you'll probably take your £200 and buy two more cars. There you are with two cars and no cash, but £100 profit on paper and the prospect of another £200 profit and £400 cash to come. Because cash is constantly being reinvested in the business, you can't say that profit is just cash.

- **Profit.** This is the difference between the revenues you make from trading and the expenses you incur generating those revenues. In other words it's money-in take away money-out, usually over a period like a year. Also, profit is adjusted to allow for accruals, depreciation and so on. Profit is added to capital on paper, although it exists in your business as the assets that are held against that capital.

- **Cash.** This is money actually in the bank, or in your little grey cash tin. It is the portion of the assets held against your capital that exist in liquid form. Cash can be seen, if you like, as the profit that hasn't been reinvested into other assets or withdrawn.

4.3.3 EFFICIENCY RATIOS

There are three important efficiency ratios, concerning how quickly you're getting paid, how quickly you're paying your bills, and how quickly you're selling on your stock.

Debtor collection period

debtors / credit sales (× 365 days) = Debtor collection period

e.g.

Debtors:	19,000
Sales:	310,000

Debtor collection:
19,000 / 310,000 × 365 = 22 days

The period is normally shown in days, so calculate debtors / sales (to find the fraction of a year taken to get paid), and multiply by 365. Obviously you can use × 12 or × 52 for the period in months or weeks if required. Credit terms are often 30 days, so anything around or under this number means that your debtors are under control. Much higher, and some debtors are having a laugh and need to be encouraged to pay up. Some debts could be bad.

Three more points:

- If you're asked for a 'per year' figure, just find the reciprocal (i.e. 1 / answer), or calculate credit sales / debtors (i.e. up-side down).
- This ratio applies only to credit sales – if you only have one sales figure then assume that all sales are on credit. Ignore cash sales.
- Getting your money quickly helps your liquidity.

Creditor payment period

A similar formula applies for creditors:

creditors / credit purchases (× 365 days) = Creditor payment period

e.g.

Creditors:	17,000
Purchases:	245,000

Creditor payment:
17,000 / 245,000 × 365 = 25 days

For cash-flow purposes, the creditor payment period wants to be as long as possible. Certainly you should try to keep it longer than your debtor collection period – otherwise your money's going out quicker than it's coming in. If this happens, you may be making a profit, but you'll run out of cash before you can enjoy it.

If you're asked to compare debtor collection with creditor payment, don't be afraid to state the obvious, e.g. 'the debtor collection period is shorter than the creditor payment period'. You could also suggest, for example, that your creditor payment period should be longer than your debtor collection period to ensure liquidity. You may also be asked to compare periods for consecutive years.

Stock turnover period (stockturn)

average stock / cost of sales = stock turnover period

or (opening + closing stock) ÷ 2 / cost of sales (× 365 days)

e.g.

Opening stock:	12,000
Closing stock:	9,000
Average stock:	10,500
Cost of sales:	248,000

Stockturn:
10,500 / 248,000 × 365 = 15 days

Again, this period is normally shown in days, so find the fraction of a year that the stock is being kept and multiply by 365. A shorter period is better for business – the stock you sell is more current, and storing stock costs money. Long stockturn means that stock is not such a liquid asset.

Again, these periods vary from business to business. If Lilibelle is just trading in cut flowers, then 15 days typical stock turnover is pretty awful. What are they doing with £10,000 worth of wilting Pussytoes in the van? Many businesses dealing in non-perishable goods, however, would consider a stockturn of 15 days to be very acceptable.

Comparing two sets of figures

For any ratio, an exam question is likely to ask you to make two sets of figures, for example for consecutive years, and compare and comment on them. You can pick up points just for making an intelligent assessment of the figures available – especially the ratios.

Your answer is in **bold** type.

For example:

Shrayesh Patel supplies dentures. He has collected the following information for his last two trading years.

	Year ended 31 Jan 2010 £	*Year ended 31 Jan 2011* £
Sales	401,000	336,000
Opening stock	35,000	34,000
Closing stock	34,000	37,000
Cost of sales	284,000	199,000
Net profit	31,000	43,000
Current assets	49,000	52,000
Current liabilities	48,000	43,000
Debtors	13,000	12,000
Capital (end of year)	265,000	288,000

Find for each year his:

	2010	*2011*
Acid test ratio	**(49–34) / 48 = 0.31**	**(52–37) / 43 = 0.35**
ROCE	**31/265 = 11.7%**	**43/288 = 14.9%**
Net Profit Margin	**31/401 = 7.73%**	**43/336 = 12.80%**
Debtor Collection period	**13/401 × 365 = 11.8 days**	**12/336 × 365 = 13.04 days**
Stockturn	**34.5/284 × 365 = 44.3 days**	**35.5/199 × 365 = 65.1 days**

Comment on the performance of Shrayesh's business, and make suggestions on how it could be improved.

Answer:

Although sales are down for the year ended 2011, the business has generally improved, with the capital reserves and profit both up. The acid test ratio has improved, although it is perilously low in both years. There are very few current assets to pay the liabilities in both years, putting the business in danger.

The return is fair and improving, and the profit margin has improved. This means that more money is being made on the capital and kept from each sale. The debtor payment period is very good and improving, which suggests that customers are encouraged to settle bills quickly. However

the stockturn is slipping, so stock is being kept for longer which costs money and is bad for liquidity.

The most urgent improvement to be made is the liquidity. Shrayesh is keeping a lot of stock which needs to be paid for. His cost of sales is lower in 2011, although his stock is higher.

Don't be afraid to start your comparison by stating the obvious, e.g. 'the acid test ratio is smaller in 2009 than in 2008'. Then try to make a point for each mark available, for example by making a further comment on how it affects the business, e.g. 'which means that less money is available to pay each debtor'.

Saying something in two ways when one would do also clarifies your claim for all marks available; e.g. 'reduce collection period and increase payment period' will nail down 2 marks, when 'bring the collection and payment periods closer together' might not be so obvious.

Be sure to consider how the liquidity, profit and efficiency are affected by the change. Are things getting better or worse?

FURTHER READING

Frank Wood and Alan Sangster *Business Accounting 1*, Chapter 47
David Cox and Michael Fardon, *A/S Accounting for AQA* Chapter 29
Ian Harrison, *Introducing Accounting for A/S*, Chapter 26

USEFUL WEB SITES

www.aqa.org.uk/qual/gceasa/acc_assess.html This is always your most useful web site. Download as many exam papers as your printer will allow.

www.revisionguru.co.uk/business/ratios.htm Well worth a look.

www.findoutinfo.com Click on Knowledge and then the Meaning of Ratios, and you'll find a whole list of ratios you never new existed. Lots of opinion offered about performance.

Try putting **8thLecture(2).pdf** into a search engine. These notes from Birkbeck College are very comprehensive.

www.unisys.com/common/investors/glossary/

www.google.co.uk

SAMPLE QUESTIONS

4.3.1

The following figures have been taken from the financial statements of Sarah Brazil Films Ltd at the end of consecutive trading periods.

	Year ended 30 September 2007	**Year ended 30 September 2008**
	£	£
Turnover	300 000	380 000
Purchases	220 000	270 000
Opening Stock	16 000	18 000
Closing Stock	18 000	17 000
Net Profit	24 000	38 000
Current Assets	42 000	43 000
Debtors	24 000	26 000
Current Liabilities/creditors	36 000	41 000
Capital	190 000	228 000

Required

(a) For each of the following, state the formula and calculate the figure for each year.

(i) Current ratio

(3 marks)

(ii) Acid test ratio

(3 marks)

(iii) Creditor payment period (in days)

(3 marks)

(iv) Debtor collection period (in days)

(3 marks)

(v) Stockturn period (in days)

(5 marks)

(vi) ROCE

(3 marks)

(vii) Net Profit on Sales

(3 marks)

(viii) Mark-up

(4 marks)

(b) Comment on the liquidity, efficiency and profitability of Sarah Brazil Films Ltd over the two years.

(5 marks)

4.3.2 (E)

Ali Ahmet's books show the following information for the past two years.

	For the year ended 31 October 2002	**For the year ended 31 October 2003**
	£	£
Sales	12 000	18 000
Opening stock	1 700	2 400
Purchases	6 100	9 460
Closing stock	(2 400)	(3 300)
Gross profit	6 600	9 440
Overheads	(1 200)	(2 600)
Net profit	5 400	6 840

Required

(a) Calculate the net profit margin for **each** of the two years. State the formula used.

Formula ....

(1 mark)

Calculation as at 31 October 2002 ....

(1 mark)

Calculation as at 31 October 2003 ....

(1 mark)

(b) Calculate the mark up for **each** of the two years. State the formula used.

Formula ....

(1 mark)

Calculation as at 31 October 2002 ....

(1 mark)

Calculation as at 31 October 2003 ....

(1 mark)

(c) Calculate the rate of stock turnover for **each** of the two years. State the formula used.

Formula ....

(1 mark)

Calculation as at 31 October 2002 ....

(1 mark)

Calculation as at 31 October 2003 ....

(1 mark)

(d) Comment on the results obtained in parts (a), (b) and (c) above.

(6 marks)

Total 15%

Source: Assessment and Qualifications Alliance, January 2004

4.3.3 (E)

Season Suppliers Ltd sell Christmas gifts. The following information is available for the last two years.

	As at 31 October 2001	**As at 31 October 2002**
	£	£
Trade debtors	43 000	32 550
Trade creditors	28 500	38 500
	For the year ended 31 October 2001	**For the year ended 31 October 2002**
Credit sales	680 000	660 000
Credit purchases	520 000	540 000

Required

(a) State the formula for the debtor collection period.

....

(1 mark)

(b) State the formula for the creditor payment period.

....

(1 mark)

(c) Calculate the debtor collection periods in days for the years ended 31 October 2001 **and** 31 October 2002. Show your workings.

Year ended 31 October 2001	**Year ended 31 October 2002**

....

(4 marks)

(d) Calculate the creditor payment periods in days for the years ended 31 October 2001 **and** 31 October 2002. Show your workings.

Year ended 31 October 2001	**Year ended 31 October 2002**

....

(4 marks)

(e) Briefly evaluate Seasons Suppliers Ltd's management of credit control. Base your answers on your calculations from (c) and (d).

....

(4 marks)

Total 14%

Source: Assessment and Qualifications Alliance, January 2003

4.3.4 (E)

The following is an extract from the trial balance of Williamson Ltd as at 30 November 2001.

	Dr	Cr
	£	£
Stock as at 1 December 2000	22 000	
Debtors	50 080	
Bank		2 000
Trade creditors		48 000
Credit sales		356 705
Credit purchases	350 400	

Additional information:

(i) Stock as at 30 November 2001 was valued as £33 000.

(ii) A trade debtor has notified Williamson Ltd that they have gone into liquidation. This debtor does not expect to be able to pay any of the outstanding debt of £7080. No adjustment has been made for this.

Required

(a) Define the term 'working capital'.

....

(3 marks)

(b) Calculate the following, clearly showing your workings. State the formula used:

(i) The working capital ratio;

....

(2 marks)

(ii) The acid test ratio;

....

(2 marks)

(iii) The debtor collection period;

....

(2 marks)

(iv) The creditor payment period;

....

(2 marks)

(c) Analyse the effect on Williamson Ltd's liquidity and its liquidity ratios caused by:

(i) Writing off the bad debt:

....

(4 marks)

(ii) Increasing the value of stock over the year.

....

(5 marks)

Total 20%

Source: Assessment and Qualifications Alliance, January 2002

Budgetary control

4.4

Expect to rely on your wits for this one, though the principle is pretty easy. Using formulae to measure efficiency is relatively straightforward, but questions on budgets take many forms. If you have a head for numbers and systems then there are lots of easy marks here for some routine maths. If you don't, then you should practise a lot.

POINTS TO CONSIDER

- How do payments in advance and in arrears affect the cash flow for a month?
- How do your **outlay** and **income** for a month affect your Net Cash Flow?
- Why might you use '£,000' to head the columns of a budget?
- How do you make a Production Budget? A Purchases Budget? A Debtors Budget?

Budgets are plans or **forecasts** for cash flow, sales, purchases and so on. This isn't about profit, it's just the money moving in and out, or units being made. You can expect to have to put a lot of numbers in a lot of correct places – with some tricky calculations thrown in, too.

income/inflow
Money coming in.

outlay/outflow
Money going out – could be called 'costs' or similar.

projected/forecast
What you think will happen, like the weather forecast.

Here's an easy one:

Cash Budget for Laomi & Tiffany Ltd for three months ending 30 April 2008

	February £	*March* £	*April* £
Income	500	600	300
Outlay	300	400	700
Net Cash Flow	200	1,000	(400)
Opening Balance	700	900	1,900
Closing Balance	900	1,900	1,500

4.4.1 PREPARING A CASH BUDGET

You're likely to be given a budget to prepare. This will involve a grid, with
- Income and outlay in rows, and
- Time periods (usually months) in columns

Typically you'll be given some starting information, like first month's sales or current bank balance, and some trends, like costs will increase by 5% per month. There's often some fiddly stuff to get right, like 'purchases are 60% of next month's predicted sales, and are paid two months in arrears'.

Your job is to calculate what will be happening to the money in the business, and to fill in the grid. Bear in mind that budgets are about the cash coming and going, not about sales being made or profit being earned.

Let's look at an example and model answer for a cash budget, since that's as tricky as it's likely to get. In fact, since there's more than one way to do this, let's suggest variations so you can choose one that makes sense to you.

> **in arrears**
> After the event. Wages are usually paid in arrears, e.g. on the last day of the month you work. Debts settled 'two months in arrears' will be paid two months after the sale was made.
>
> **in advance**
> Before the event. Rent is usually paid in advance, e.g. on the last day before the month you use a space.

Nic-nax Ltd buys and sells sophisticated garden ornaments for rock stars. The manager wants you to prepare a cash flow budget for the autumn season using the following information:

1. **Actual sales for August were £57,000, and forecast sales are as follows:**
   - **September £55,000**
   - **October £57,000**
   - **November £53,000**
   - **December £61,000**
2. **75% of sales will be cash, and the remaining 25% will be to credit customers, payable one month in arrears.**

3 **Purchases will be 60% of the following month's forecast sales, and will be payable two months in arrears.**

4 **The following costs will be paid in the month in which they are incurred:**
(a) Wages: £10,000 per month, except October which will be £10,500.
(b) Fixed costs will be £4,000 for September, and are expected to rise by 5% per month.
(c) Variable costs are 12% of forecast sales.

5 **The bank balance on 31 August was £14,300.**

Prepare a cash budget for the three months ending November 2009.

You may be given a blank grid with the months in each column, but how you label the rows is probably down to you. The following answer is acceptable. See if you can follow it. Label each row as you go. In an exam, it is not enough to have the knowledge – you need to demonstrate it.

Answer:

Cash Budget for Nic-nax Ltd for three months ending 30 November 2009

	September	*October*	*November*
Inflow	£	£	£
[1]Cash Sales	41,250	42,750	39,750
[2]Credit Sales	14,250	13,750	14,250
	55,500	56,500	54,000
Outflow			
[3]Purchases	34,200	33,000	34,200
[4]Wages	10,000	10,500	10,000
[5]Fixed costs	4,000	4,200	4,410
Variable costs	6,600	6,840	6,360
	54,800	54,540	54,970
[6]Opening Balance	14,300	15,000	16,960
[7]Net Cash Flow	700	1,960	(970)
Closing Balance	15,000	16,960	15,990

1 If sales for September are expected to be £55,000, and 75% of that is cash, the £55,000 × 75% will be money coming in. I make that £41,250. The same goes for the next two months.

2 Get your calculator out. If these figures don't make sense, then are you calculating for the right month? If credit sales are paid a month **in arrears**, then the credit payments coming in during September are for sales in August. You want 25% of the August figure of £57,000 to show this stream of cash flow.

3 Oh dear, what's this? We're anticipating sales for the following month, and buying in at 60% of the selling price. But since this is payable two months in arrears, then the money actually goes out one month after the sales figures in question. So, start with September's payment, which will be 60% of August's sales, and continue for subsequent months.

4 Wages are straightforward – just put the figure in the box.
5 For fixed costs, use your calculator to find £4,000 + 5% for the October figure, and add 5% to this answer for each month after that. Check it with your calculator now to be sure. The variable costs aren't difficult.

> To add 5% on your calculator, I recommend you multiply by 1.05 or 105%.
>
> Either use:
> '4000 × 1.05 =' **or** '4000 × 105 [inv/shift] ='
>
> If you need to keep increasing the value for the next period, don't cancel the answer. Just hit '× 105 [inv/shift] =' again for the November figure, and repeat for each subsequent month.
>
> If you have to reduce something by 5%, use 0.95 or 95%.

6 Now we look at how much money is in the bank. We're told that the closing balance for August is £14,300. This means that September's opening balance will be the same.
7 Now, if £55,500 has come in, and £54,800 has gone out, then you're going to be better off by the difference – £700. This can be called Net Cash Flow. Add this on to find the closing balance, which you carry over to be the opening balance for the next month. The closing balance should always be the bottom line. That's the figure that tells you the state of your bank account at the end of any given month.

Note that you don't need a column for August or December, even though you have figures for those months. You're only asked to present figures for September to November; the grid in the exam should guide you on this one. There may be cases where you need to include extra information: here, for example, the credit payments figure for September comes from the August sales figure. It's uncommon but possible that you'll be given extra information which can be ignored, like the December figure here.

Here's an alternative presentation. All we've done is to work in thousands – note the £,000 at the head of each column. This will make the numbers clearer, save you time hitting the '0' button on your calculator, and reduce the chance of silly slips.

Cash Budget for Nic-nax Ltd for three months ending 30 November 2009

	September	*October*	*November*
	£,000	£,000	£,000
Income			
Cash Sales	41.25	42.75	39.75
Credit Sales	14.25	13.75	14.25
	55.50	56.50	54.00
Outlay			
Purchases	34,20	33.00	34.20
Wages	10.00	10,50	10.00
Fixed costs	4.00	4.20	4.41
Variable costs	6.60	6.84	6.36
	54.80	54.54	54.97
Opening Balance	14.30	15.00	16.96
Net Cash Flow	0.70	1.96	(0.97)
Closing Balance	15.00	16.96	15.99

Alternative 2

You may, however, choose to calculate the net cash flow balance for each month first, then the opening and closing balances (Alternative 3).

Net Cash Flow	0.70	1.96	(0.97)
Opening Balance	14.30	15.00	16.96
Closing Balance	15.00	16.96	15.99

Alternative 3

Or, you could put the opening balance at the very top with income as part of a 'plus' section, which means you don't need to show the monthly cash flow balance (Alternative 4). This is a recognised system, and an acceptable exam answer, but since monthly cash flow can be a useful indicator you may prefer alternatives 1 or 2.

Cash Budget for Nic-nax Ltd for three months ending 30 November 2009

	September	*October*	*November*
	£,000	£,000	£,000
Opening Balance	**14.30**	**15.00**	**16.96**
Cash Sales	41.25	42.75	39.75
Credit Sales	14.25	13.75	14.25
	69.80	71.50	70.96
Outlay			
Purchases	34.20	33.00	34.20
Wages	10.00	10.50	10.00
Fixed costs	4.00	4.20	4.41
Variable costs	6.60	6.84	6.36
	54.80	54.54	54.97
Closing Balance	15.00	16.96	15.99

Alternative 4

Try some exercises with purchase budgets and production budgets, for example. They look alarming, and scary, but you just have to be careful about putting the right number in the right box. Hopefully a cash budget in your exam will be simpler than this one.

This cash flow is looking good, but watch out in the exam for budgets that go way **into the red** (negative balances). Perhaps there's a big outlay on a vehicle or machine that sends the bank balance decidedly the wrong side of zero. Maybe your regular overheads are just too much to handle. If you're asked for advice, you could suggest that:

- Big capital outlays are spread over monthly payments.
- Debtors are encouraged to pay quickly (like Nic-nax).
- Creditors are asked for long payment terms (like Nic-nax).

4.4.2 OTHER BUDGETS

You may be asked to name one or more budgets or to prepare a budget other than a cash budget.

Apart from the Cash (flow) budget, here are some important ones. They're generally less difficult than a cash budget, although the AQA exam doesn't shy away from finding ways to challenge your ability. Be ready for anything – including a very simple one – but always make sure you're using the right figures.

Sales budget

This helps you see what sales levels to expect, and the revenues you can get from them. Since any business operates within the limits of the marketplace, they're important guides for preparing other budgets (like cash budgets). However, sales budgets are notoriously difficult projections to make in business, and so are an area of uncertainty in the budgets that depend on them.

Production budget

A production budget lets you plan how many units to make in any given month (if you're a manufacturer). It will be based on a sales budget, or may include one. Typically, a factory will have an idea of projected sales and a policy for stock levels ready for the next month. Your task is to calculate the number of units needed to

- Satisfy sales for the month and
- Meet the required closing stock level

For example:

> **Lenhi Ltd makes designer hubcaps. Sales have been rising by 100 sets per month and this is expected to continue. Opening stock is 200 sets, and closing stock will now be maintained at 25% of the following month's projected sales. Prepare a production budget for the three months to March 2011.**

Your writing is in **bold**.

Answer:

Lenhi Ltd – production budget to March 2011

	January	*February*	*March*
Sales	1,400	1,500	1,600
Opening Stock	**200**	**375**	**400**
Closing Stock	**375**	**400**	**425**
Production	**1,575**	**1,525**	**1,625**

See how the closing stock in the first month will be 375 sets (1,500 × 25%). Lenhi needs to produce 1,400 sets that month to sell, less the 200 sets they opened with, plus the 375 sets to keep in stock. That's 1,575 sets. Alternatively, you can simply subtract opening stock from your calculated closing stock, and add the difference to that month's sales. Practice one to make sure you understand it.

Production budget – even-flow production

If your factory prefers it can produce a regular quantity every month. For this you'll need to find the quantity required for the whole period and divide it into equal portions to use as your bottom line each month; e.g.

$$1{,}575 + 1{,}525 + 1{,}625 = 4{,}725$$

$$4{,}725 \div 3 = 1{,}575 \text{ per month}$$

Now you can make a similar table work by jiggling the closing stock figures.

	January	*February*	*March*
Sales	1,400	1,500	1,600
Opening Stock	**200**	**375**	**450**
Closing Stock	**375**	**450**	**425**
Production	**1,575**	**1,575**	**1,575**

When you know how many units you'll produce, you can plan to buy raw materials.

Purchases budget

This allows you to plan how much raw material to buy in for production, or how much stock to buy in for the sales you expect to make. Perhaps you want to make sure your suppliers won't let you down, or maybe you need to make sure you'll be able to pay for what you buy.

If you follow a closing stock level policy, then you should, of course, start by making a budget like the production budget. If finance is an issue, meanwhile, you'll want an extra row for the cash outlay required. You may be working on a mark-up system, or a gross profit margin system. Look again at section 4.3.2 if you're not sure about these. Let's look at how this might work with the production budget in the last example. You can assume that all costs are purchase costs.

Lenhi Ltd sells hubcap sets for £80 per set. Their margin is 60%. Prepare a purchases budget.

Lenhi Ltd – purchases budget to March 2011

	January	*February*	*March*
Production	1,575	1,525	1,625
Purchases	**£50,400**	**£48,800**	**£52,000**

We know that the sets will sell at £80 each, and that 60% of that is profit margin. That means that 40% is cost. £80 × 40% = £32 per set in costs, giving us a required outlay in January of 1,575 × £32 = £50,400.

Compare this carefully with this alternative:

Lenhi Ltd sells hubcap sets for £80 per set. Their mark up is 60%. Prepare a purchases budget.

Lenhi Ltd – purchases budget to March 2011

	January	*February*	*March*
Production	1,575	1,525	1,625
Purchases	**£78,750**	**£76,250**	**£81,250**

What's the difference?

Well, we're talking about mark-up not margin. £80 is cost plus 60% – that's 60% of the cost, not 60% of price as before. Put another way, £80 = 160% of the cost.

Getting the figure for cost from the total is like extracting the VAT from cash sales or the Unrealised profit from a Manufacturer's Trading Account:

$$100\% / 160\% \times £80 = £50 \text{ per set}$$

We can double-check this figure: what's £50 + 60% of £50? I think it's £80.

Finally we use 1,575 units × £50 = £78,750 for our January purchases budget.

Debtors' budget

This allows you to forecast how much money will be owed on credit sales for any month. Ignore any information on cash sales.

Let's look at a tricky example. If you're good at logic you'll have an advantage in the exam.

Lenhi Ltd sells stock on credit, and has £125,000 of debtors at the start of the year. 50% of customers pay in the following month and claim a 5% discount. The other 50% pay after two months. Remembering that sales have risen by 100 sets per month, calculate the closing debtors for the three months to March.

Lenhi Ltd – debtors budget to March 2011

	January	*February*	*March*
	£	£	£
Opening debtors	**125,000**	**139,600**	**154,400**
Sales revenue	[1]**112,000**	**120,000**	**128,000**
	237,000	**259,600**	**282,400**
Credit payments (1 month)	[2]49,400	53,200	57,000
Credit payments (2 months)	[3]**48,000**	**52,000**	**56,000**
	97,400	**105,200**	**113,000**
Closing Debtors	**139,600**	**154,400**	**169,400**

1 We find the sales revenue for each month by multiplying the sales volume (1,400, 1,500 and 1,600 sets) by £80. Take care not to use the production figure – debtors come from sales. This sales figure represents increased debtors. Add it to your opening debtors.

2 Now we need to find the money coming in from December, when sales would have been 1,300. This will be:

$$1{,}300 \text{ sets} \times £80 \times 50\% \times 95\%$$

That's the money coming in from the half of the people that pay quickly and get a discount.

3 Next we calculate the income from November's sales. That'll be 1,200 × £80 × 50% (no discount). We can add these payments to find the total income for the month, and calculate the balance of debtors. Carry the balance forward.

Practise and find a system for completing budgets like this – you'll get in a mess otherwise.

Creditors' budget

This allows you to forecast how much money you will owe for credit purchases for any month. The principle will be similar to that of the debtors' budget.

4.4.3 BENEFITS AND LIMITATIONS

You may be asked to explain the benefits or limitations of the budgets you've calculated. Some of these points will apply to more than one budget, so they're arranged here for you to learn.

Some examples of benefits:

1. Helps with planning
   (a) e.g. banking instructions
   (b) Staffing levels
   (c) Purchase or production levels
2. Allows preparation
   (a) e.g. negotiate an overdraft for temporary cash flow problems
   (b) Negotiate credit terms with suppliers
   (c) Predict and overcome potential limitations
3. Gives opportunity to make changes for permanent problems
   (a) e.g. raise prices
   (b) Change supplier
   (c) Buy fixed assets
4. Motivates employees to meet targets
5. Lets you see problems before they become problems

Some examples of limitations:

1. Depends on the accuracy of your information
2. Does not account for external factors
   (a) Suppliers
   (b) Economy
   (c) Market
   (d) Unexpected expenses
3. Doesn't solve problems, just identifies them

These will only stick ready for the exam if you try using them for practice questions. Learn by doing so now.

FURTHER READING

David Cox and Michael Fardon, *A/S Accounting for AQA*, Chapter 32
Ian Harrison, *Introducing Accounting for A/S*, Chapter 29

USEFUL WEB SITES

www.aqa.org.uk/qual/gceasa/acc_assess.html This is always your most useful web site. Download as many exam papers as your printer will allow.

www.bizhelp24.com Click on Business Accounting, and then An Introduction to Small Business Budgeting. Here you'll find a guide that's very comprehensive as you click through each section.

www.google.co.uk

SAMPLE QUESTIONS

4.4.1 (E)
Martin runs a fruit stall in a market which is open each day.

The following information is available.

	May 2004 (Actual)	**June 2004 and July 2004 (Expected changes on May's figures)**	**August 2004 (Expected changes on May's figures)**
	£	**£**	**£**
Sales	5000	An increase of 5%	An increase of 25%
Purchases	3000	To stay the same	An increase of 15%
Delivery costs	1000	An increase of 10%	An increase of 25%
Packaging	100	To stay the same	An increase of 20%

Each month Martin withdraws £500 for his personal use and pays £200 rent.

On 1 June 2004 Martin has £100 in the bank.

Required
(a) Prepare a cash budget for the three months ending 31 August 2004.

(11 marks)

Source: Assessment and Qualifications Alliance, June 2004

Parts (b), (c) and (d) of this question can be found in Chapter 4.5.

4.4.2 (E)
Lee's Landscapes Ltd supplies plants for residential gardens.

The results for the year ended 31 March 2003 are:

	£000
Sales	150
Purchases	110
Trade debtors	12
Trade creditors	11

All sales and purchases are on credit terms.

Total sales for the year ending 31 March 2004 are expected to be:

April–June	£20 000 per month
July–October	£15 000 per month
November–March	£5 000 per month

As at 31 March 2004 trade debtors and trade creditors are expected to be £14 000 and £10 000 respectively.

There is no closing stock. The profit margin is 25%.

The business prepares budgets on a two-monthly basis.

Required
(a) Prepare a purchases budget for the year ending 31 March 2004.

	April and May £000	June and July £000	August and September £000	October and November £000	December and January £000	February and March £000
Sales						
Margin						
Purchases						

(12 marks)

(b)
(i) Calculate the debtors' collection period for **each** of the last two years. State the formula used.

Formula..

(1 mark)

Year ended 31 March 2003	**Year ending 31 March 2004**
....	....
....	....

(6 marks)

(ii) Calculate the creditors payment period for **each** of the last two years. State the formula used.

Formula ....

(1 mark)

Year ended 31 March 2003	**Year ending 31 March 2004**
....	....
....	....

(6 marks)

(c) Comment on the results from (b). Give **one** recommendation to improve the credit control at Lee Landscapes Ltd.

Debtors' collection period ....

Creditors payment period ....

Recommendation ....

(5 marks)

31%

Source: Assessment and Qualifications Alliance, June 2003

4.4.3 (E)

N Kayali, the assistant accountant, at Strudwick Stationers Ltd, has obtained the following information for the seven months ending 30 September 2002. This information is to be used to prepare a cash budget for the four months ending 31 August 2002.

(1) Actual sales were £44 000 and £46 000 for March and April 2002 respectively.

(2) Totals forecast sales at the end of each of the next five months are expected to be:

2002				
May	June	July	Aug	Sept
£	£	£	£	£
44 000	46 000	42 000	44 000	48 000

80% of each month's total forecast sales are expected to be for cash. The debtors are expected to pay one month in arrears.

(3) Purchases are expected to be 70% of the following month's total forecast sales value and are paid for two months in arrears.

(4) The following costs are expected to be paid for in the month in which they occur:
Wages £9000 per month to 31 July 2002 and £9500 per month thereafter
Fixed Costs £3000 per month
Variable costs being 10% of each month's total forecast sales.

(5) The bank balance as at 1 May 2002 was £12 100.

Required

(a) Prepare a cash budget for each of the four months ending 31 August 2002.

Strudwick Stationers Ltd
Cash budget for four months ending 31 August 2002

Details	**May** £000	**June** £000	**July** £000	**Aug** £000

(20 marks)

(b) N Kayali is unsure of the benefits of producing a cash budget for a four-month period. Explain **one** benefit to Strudwick Stationers Ltd of completing a four-month cash budget.

....

(3 marks)

23%

Source: Assessment and Qualifications Alliance, May 2002

4.4.4 (E)

Peversal Papers Ltd manufactures reams of paper. Each ream is sold for £22 and costs £12 to manufacture.

The company's policy is to maintain stock levels at the end of each month at 20% of the next month's expected sales.

Sales for 2002 are expected to be:

Feb	March	April	May	June
£88 000	£99 000	£110 000	£121 000	£110 000

Customers are allowed one month's credit. Only 5% pay immediately and receive a 2% discount for prompt payment.

Stock as at 1 March 2002 is expected to be 900 units.

Administration and distribution costs which are paid in the month in which they occur are expected to be:

Feb	March	April	May	June
£26 000	£28 000	£34 000	£38 000	£36 000

The bank balance on 1 March 2002 is expected to be £6000.

Production costs are paid in the month in which they occur.

Required

(a)

(i) Complete the following cash budget for the 3 months ending 31 May 2002.

Cash budget for Peversal Papers Ltd
For the three months ending 31 May 2002

	March £000	**April £000**	**May £000**
Sales – cash			
– credit			
Production costs			
Admin/distribution			
Net inflow/outflow			
Opening balance			
Closing balance			

(6 marks)

(ii) Complete the following production budget for the 3 months ending 31 May 2002.

	Production budget for Peversal Papers Ltd For the three months ending 31 May 2002		
	March Units	**April Units**	**May Units**
Sales			
Opening stock			
Closing stock			
Production			

(8 marks)

(b) The Managing Director of Peversal Papers Ltd believes that a cash budget is all that is required, however the Production Manager disagrees. He believes that the production budget is vital too. Assess **three** advantages to Peversal Papers Ltd of using both a cash budget **and** a production budget.

(9 marks)

23%

Source: Assessment and Qualifications Alliance, January 2002

4.4.5 (E)

Sunshine Ltd sells beach buckets and spades. The forecast information for the six months ending 31 October 2002 is:

	May	June	July	August	September	October
	£000	£000	£000	£000	£000	£000
Sales	16	20	26	28	24	20
Purchases	12	16	18	14	12	10
Overheads	4	8	8	8	8	4

Additional information

(1) On average 20% of each month's sales are expected to be for cash. A further 60% will be given one month's credit. The rest will be given two months' credit. All monies should be received when due.

(2) The increase in overheads arises from the employment of casual staff. The overheads are paid in the month in which they occur.

(3) Suppliers are expected to allow one month's credit.

(4) The cash at the bank balance as at 1 July 2002 is £7200 overdrawn.

Required

(a) Prepare a detailed forecast month-by-month cash budget for the four months ending 31 October 2002

Sunshine Ltd
Cash budget for four months ending 31 October 2002

	July £000	Aug £000	Sept £000	Oct £000
Sales – cash				
– 1 month				
– 2 months				
Purchases				
Overheads				
Net inflow/outflow				
Opening balance				
Closing balance				

(11 marks)

(b) (i) Assess the cash position of Sunshine Ltd as at 31 October 2002.

....

(6 marks)

(ii) Recommend **one** way the company could improve its cash position.

....

(2 marks)

19%

Source: Assessment and Qualifications Alliance, June 2001

4.5 Social accounting

Accounting is all about money, but the business decisions you make will affect more than just money. Staff, other businesses, the environment; all of these can be affected by your choices in business.

POINTS TO CONSIDER

- What sorts of business decisions affect real lives?
- How might reducing your business activity cause stress to employees, their family and their community?
- What business decisions might influence global warming, for example?
- What instances can you think of where a business decision has had a bad effect on people or wildlife?
- What decisions for short-term financial gain might lead to long-term costs?
- What decisions that incur short-term costs might lead to long-term gains?

Thousands of people were left unemployed when Rover's Longbridge car plant closed in 2005, with hundreds more businesses affected by the reduced economic activity. Tens of thousands were killed and injured in the Indian city of Bhopal in 1984, when a deadly gas was released from a Union Carbide industrial plant which had cut costs on safety.

These high-profile events were the result of business decisions based on management accounting. The Rover decision was probably tough but inevitable. The Union Carbide decision was disastrous.

Every day, in businesses on every scale, managers are using accounts, plans and budgets to make decisions that affect real lives. They have to weigh up the costs and benefits of business policy, and their decisions can bring prosperity, or leave people and animals poisoned, families struggling with the stress of debt, and whole communities feeling the knock-on effects.

When you eventually go into business, you may have to make decisions that affect real lives, and there will be a question in your exam which asks you to look at choices faced by the owner of a business. This is asking you to consider issues beyond the balance sheet: for example, how closing a branch of a shop would affect the local economy. It may also ask you to consider how these issues might, in turn, affect the profitability of the business.

These issues might include

- Closing an unprofitable business
- Making staff **redundant** due to new technology
- Using non-renewable resources or environmentally dangerous materials
- Trading **unethically**, e.g. buying from a country with a poor record on human rights
- Cutting corners on health and safety

redundant
Not needed any more

ethical
Responsible, moral, behaving well – doing the right thing for other people

morale
How happy people are feeling

You'll need to think about the exact situation they give you, but keep these useful ideas in mind. A bullet-point list will get you marks, but you should be able to use the points in a well-written answer to do well. Learn and understand this list.

- Technology
  - involves set up costs
    - could affect cash flow in the short term
    - could require price rises
  - can save money in the long term
  - can make you more productive
  - could make some workers redundant
  - requires retraining
- Redundancies
  - cause stress to the people who are laid off
  - affect the local economy/other businesses/local taxes
  - cost a lot in redundancy pay-offs
  - save money in the long term
  - affect **morale** of remaining workforce
  - cause insecurity
    - could consider retraining or using workers for another job
- Retraining
  - is expensive in the short term
  - gives a more productive workforce
  - adds value
  - boosts morale
  - is an investment – improves reputation

- Unethical practices/environmentally damaging practices/economising on health and safety
  - can be the most economically effective option
    - lower costs
    - bigger profit
    - more competitive prices
  - can be harmful to overseas workers/wildlife/employees
  - can cause bad publicity, e.g. campaigns, strikes
  - can damage reputation
  - could affect sales in the long term
  - can affect morale of workforce/increase turnover of employees
  - may be illegal
    - police and courts may get involved
    - business could close
  - should look into facts
  - could look at alternatives

This is an area where you might want to read more widely, to develop a sense of how business affects real lives, and about why a business might make decisions that look like mistakes – or turn out to be mistakes. However, there will be a limit to the amount you can write in the exam, and the list above is a versatile place to start.

Look out for marks available for examples, recommendations or chances to develop an idea – and make sure you use the information given in the question. Remember to talk about the choices both in terms of cost and profit, and in terms of non-financial effects. Businesses do affect real lives.

FURTHER READING

David Cox and Michael Fardon, *A/S Accounting for AQA*, Chapter 33
Ian Harrison, *Introducing Accounting for A/S*, Chapter 30

USEFUL WEB SITES

www.aqa.org.uk/qual/gceasa/acc_assess.html This is always your most useful web site. Download as many exam papers as your printer will allow.

www.cbs-network.org.uk/socacaud.html This talks about Social Auditing – acting to consider issues beyond short-term profit.

news.bbc.co.uk/1/hi/england/west_midlands/4468513.stm en.wikipedia.org/wiki/Bhopal_Disaster

www.neweconomics.org A whole site that campaigns for responsible business practice.

www.google.co.uk

SAMPLE QUESTIONS

4.5.1

Jesper Hansen produces golf clubs. His facility is currently making a small loss, with staff wages running at £240 000 per year. He is considering three five-year options.

For the first option he will change nothing.

For the second, he will need to buy new machinery for £180 000, which will allow him to make one third of his staff redundant at a cost of £30 000. The remaining staff will need to be trained to use the new machinery, at a cost of £20 000.

For the third option, he will sell his current factory for £300 000, making all of his present staff redundant at a cost of £90,000, and open a new factory in China, similar to his current facility, at a cost of £350 000. Labour in China is half the cost of labour at home, although it will cost him £8 000 per year to import the golf clubs.

Required

(a) Calculate the five-year cost of adopting:

(i) option one

(1 mark)

(ii) option two

(1 mark)

(iii) option three

(1 mark)

(b) Write a report to Jesper, discussing the financial and social consequences of each option.

(5 marks)

4.5.2

Abercrombie Davis and Briggs Ltd produce medical equipment. They want to increase their profit, and have identified three areas where they can reduce costs: quality control, health and safety, and waste management.

Required

(a) Write a report to the directors of Abercrombie Davis and Briggs Ltd, advising them of the consequences of these courses of action to:

(i) The shareholders
(ii) Employees
(iii) Customers
(iv) The environment

(8 marks)

(b) How might the suggested courses of action affect the profitability of the company in the long term.

(5 marks)

4.5.3

Doug Green exports sports-car seat covers to the USA. He has been offered some exotic animal skins by a dealer from an African country recovering from civil war. Some of the animals are protected species, but the dealer insists the country needs the income.

Required

Advise Doug of the ethical issues he faces, and the business consequences of buying in the exotic seat covers.

(5 marks)

4.5.4 (E)

Jack Smart is the manager of a factory which produces cardboard boxes from recycled paper. The current production process needs to be replaced. Jack has the following two options:

Option 1. Invest in new recycling machinery at a cost of £450 000. In order to finance this purchase a loan of £600 000 will need to be taken out. This will be repayable at the end of five years. Interest is paid annually at 10%. Also, 15% of the staff will no longer be needed and will have to be made redundant or take early retirement in the first year at a cost of £160 000. Most of the remaining staff will need to be retrained to use the new machinery, which is expected to cost £60 000 and is payable over 2 years.

Option 2. To make cardboard boxes from paper which has not been recycled. This will involve investing in new machinery at a cost of £250 000. This will be financed by a loan of £300 000 repayable at the end of five years. Interest is paid annually at 10%. No staff will need to be made redundant. The retraining costs are expected to be £80 000 and are payable in the first year. Jack is unsure how customers will react to boxes which are not made from recycled paper. However, he believes that this is the better option as it will have less of an effect on cash resources and therefore profitability.

Both machines will be depreciated using the straight-line method over 10 years.

Required

(a) Explain the difference between profit and cash.

....

(4 marks)

(b) Calculate the effect of **each** option on profit and cash for the next financial year.

OPTION 1

PROFIT	**CASH**
....	....

(8 marks)

OPTION 2

PROFIT	**CASH**
....	....

(7 marks)

(c) State which option you would recommend. Justify your choice.

(7 marks)

Total 26%

Source: Assessment and Qualifications Alliance, January 2003

4.5.5 (E)

Martin runs a fruit stall in a market which is open each day.

On 1 September 2004 a supermarket is due to open near to the market. After this, Martin expects there to be a resulting loss in his trade of 30% based on the sales for May.

Martin is considering replacing his stock with organic produce. This would increase purchase costs by 60%. He believes that, if he increases his selling prices by the same amount, he will lose many regular customers.

Required

(b) Assess the financial implications for September if Martin does **not** replace his stock with organic produce.

(4 marks)

Martin proposes to change the packaging on his current produce and pass the produce off as organic. The new packaging will cost 10% more than the May prices but all other costs will remain the same as in May. The produce labelled as organic will then be sold at a 10% increase on the price in May. Martin does not expect to lose many customers this way.

Required

(c) Assess the financial implications for September if Martin changes the packaging and replaces his stock with produce which will be sold as if it were organic.

(6 marks)

(d) Discuss whether Martin should introduce produce passed off as if it were organic. Consider the ethical implications and make alternative recommendations.

(9 marks)

Source: Assessment and Qualifications Alliance, June 2004

Part (a) of this question can be found in Chapter 4.4.

Super-question: Hubble Bubble

Accounting isn't just one thing – it's a process. From buying stock to calculating your profit, there are many steps between the first purchase and the bottom line. Your A/S level exam won't test you on the whole process, although finding that you can follow it will help you feel you have the measure of accounting, and give you confidence when you're tested.

Try this super-question from a course at the same level as A/S. It takes you from a purchase invoice to a profit ratio, and grills you on layouts and adjustments in between. Then it tests your understanding on some items outside the accounting process.

The exam covers material from all of the units in the A/S exam, but is suitable for students taking just Units 1, 3 and 4. If you're a good student, you should be able to tackle it, and be ready for most of the things an A/S exam can throw at you.

Good luck!

Oxford Business College

The Oxford International Diploma

Accounting

Mock Exam – June 2004

1. Answer all of the questions:
   - questions 1 – 3 on this question sheet
   - questions 4 – 10 on the paper provided.
2. The total marks available: 80%
3. Time allowed: Three hours
4. This exam paper has 4 printed pages.
5. Paper dictionaries are allowed, but electronic dictionaries are not.
6. A calculator and a pencil are recommended.

Hubble Bubble make and sell fish tank accessories.

You are required to complete their end of year accounts for May 31st 2004.

1. The following information has been entered into the Purchases account and the Bank account, but not into the account for the supplier, Pump-O-Max Ltd.

Enter the information into their account and balance it off.

Purchase Invoice: 26 May 2004	£270
Cheque Counterfoil: 15 May 2004	£490

Pump-O-Max Ltd

Dr	£		Cr	£
		1 May	**Balance b/d**	**540**

Marks available: [5]

2. The balance for creditors without Pump-O-Max is £31,680.

Using your answer for question 1, calculate the new balance for Creditors.

Creditors' balance without Pump-O-Max	31,680
Balance for Pump-O-Max c/d	
New Creditors balance 31 May 2004	

Marks available: [1]

3. Insert your new Creditors' balance from question 2, and total the credit balances, to complete the Trial Balance for Hubble Bubble.

Marks available: [2]

	Dr £	Cr £
Buildings at cost	300,000	
Equipment at cost (factory)	20,000	
Equipment at cost (office)	5,000	
Delivery vehicles at cost	40,000	
Provision for depreciation (1/6/2003)		
Equipment (factory)		4,000
Equipment (office)		2,000
Delivery vehicles		10,000
Provision for doubtful debt (1/6/2003)		1,000
Stock of raw materials (1/6/2003)	21,000	
Work in progress (1/6/2003)	10,000	

(continued)	Dr £	Cr £
Stock of finished goods (1/6/2003)	17,000	
Purchases (raw materials)	160,000	
Carriage inwards	3,000	
Royalties	7,000	
Wages (direct)	54,000	
Wages (indirect)	12,000	
Wages (sales and administration)	32,000	
Miscellaneous income		2,000
Motor expenses	8,000	
Rates and insurance	30,000	
Communication expenses	14,000	
Debenture interest paid (1/2 year)	2,500	
Debtors	38,000	....
Creditors		
Bank	3,000	
Sales		410,000
Ordinary share capital (@ £1)		200,000
6% Preference share capital (@ £1)		40,000
10% Debenture stock (due 2009)		50,000
Profit & Loss account balance b/d (1/6/2003)		25,500
	776,500	

Notes

- Closing stock was valued as follows:
  - Raw materials 18,000
  - Work in progress 3,000
  - Finished goods 11,000
- Rates and insurance are apportioned as:
  - Factory 80%
  - Office 20%
- Depreciation is calculated as follows:
  - Factory equipment 20% on cost
  - Office equipment 40% reducing balance
  - Vehicles 25% reducing balance
- Sales wages owing amounts to £3,000, and communications expenses of £700 are prepaid for 2004/5.
- Provision for doubtful debt is to increase to £2,000
- The directors are allowing £9,500 tax and an ordinary dividend of 7p per share.

4. Prepare the Manufacturing account for Hubble Bubble for the year ended 31st May 2004.

Marks available: [14]

5. Prepare the Trading and Profit and Loss account for Hubble Bubble, with appropriation section, for the year ended 31st May 2004.

Marks available: [16]

6. Prepare the Balance sheet for Hubble Bubble for the year ended 31st May 2004.

Marks available: [18]

7. (i) Calculate the
- Acid test ratio
- ROCE
- Gross profit on sales ratio
- Debtor payment period

Marks available: [8]

(ii) Comment briefly on the performance of Hubble Bubble.

Marks available: [4]

8. Explain how day books are used for cash sales and credit sales.

Marks available: [4]

9. Explain how the accruals concept affects the treatment of depreciation in accounting.

Marks available: [4]

10. Outline the main differences between ordinary and preference shares.

Marks available: [4]

Total marks available [80]

Source: The Oxford International Diploma – Oxford Business College – Mock Exam – June 2004

SUPER-QUESTION: MODEL ANSWER

1.

Pump-O-Max

Dr					Cr
15th May	Bank	490	1st May	Balance b/d	540
31st May	Balance c/d	320	26th May	Purchases	270
		810			810
			1st June	Balance b/d	320

2.	Creditors without Pump-O-Max	31,680
	Balance from Pump-O-Max c/d	320
	New creditors balance	32,000

3.	Creditors	32,000
	Credit column total	776,500

4.

Hubble Bubble Ltd – Manufacturing Account – May 31st 2004

	£	£
Opening stock (raw materials)		21,000
Purchases (raw materials)		160,000
Carriage inwards		3,000
		184,000
less closing stock		(18,000)
Cost of raw materials		166,000
Direct labour		54,000
Royalties		7,000
Prime cost		227,000
Indirect expenses		
Labour	12,000	
Insurance (30,000 × 80%)	24,000	
Depreciation (20,000 × 20%)	4,000	
		40,000
		267,000
Add work in progress (1/6/2003)		10,000
Less work in progress (31/5/2004)		(3,000)
Cost of production c/d		274,000

5.

Hubble Bubble Ltd – Trading and Profit and Loss Account – May 31st 2004

	£	£
Sales		410,000
Less cost of sales		
Opening stock	17,000	
Cost of production	274,000	
	291,000	
less closing stock	(11,000)	(280,000)
Gross profit		130,000
Miscellaneous income		2,000
		132,000
Expenses		
Depreciation: equipment ((5,000 – 2,000) × 40%)	1,200	
Depreciation: vehicles ((40,000 – 10,000) × 25%)	7,500	
Wages (32,000 + 3,000)	35,000	
Motor	8,000	
Rates + insurance (30,000 × 20%)	6,000	
Communications (14,000 – 700)	13,300	
Debenture interest (50,000 × 10%)	5,000	
Provision for doubtful debt (2,000 – 1,000)	1,000	(77,000)
Net Profit		55,000
Less Tax		(9,500)
		45,500
Preference dividend	2,400	
Ordinary dividend	14,000	(16,400)
		29,100
Profit and loss balance (1.6.03) b/d		25,500
Profit and loss balance c/d		54,600

6.

Hubble Bubble Ltd – Balance Sheet – May 31st 2004

	£	£	£
Fixed Assets			
Buildings	300,000	0	300,000
Equipment (factory)	20,000	8,000	12,000
Equipment (office)	5,000	3,200	1,800
Vehicles	40,000	17,500	22,500
			336,300
Current Assets			
Stock	32,000		
Debtors	38,000		
Provision for doubtful debt	(2,000)		
Prepayments	700		
Bank	3,000	71,700	
Current Liabilities			
Creditors	32,000		
Tax	9,500		
Preference Dividend	2,400		
Ordinary Dividend	14,000		
Accruals (2,500 + 3,000)	5,500	(63,400)	
Working Capital			8,300
Debenture			(50,000)
Capital Employed			294,600
Financed By			
Ordinary Share Capital	200,000		
Preference Share Capital	40,000		
P/L balance b/d	54,600		
	294,600		

7.

(i)

Acid Test Ratio	0.63
ROCE	18.7%
Gross profit on sales	31.7%
Debtor payment period	33.8 days

(ii) Hubble Bubble's liquidity is very tight. They have very few liquid assets and some big bills to pay.

However, their return ratios are good, indicating a healthy, effective business, and their debtor payment period is under control.

8.

Cash sales are not recorded in day books.

When a credit sale is made, however, an invoice is given to the customer. Copies of these invoices are collected and the important details are recorded in the Sales Day Book.

Details include customer, name, sale value and VAT, an invoice number to refer back to the original document, and a folio reference to the customer's account in the Sales Ledger.

At the end of a period, the accountant will move totals from the Sales Day Book to the customers' accounts.

9.

The accruals concept says that net profit is the difference between revenues and the expenses incurred in generating those revenues. Revenues and expenses must be matched up. This is different from considerations of receipt and expenditure. The time period will always consider the time when the expense is incurred.

In the case of depreciation, an item paid for in full in one year can have a useful life over many years. The expense of having an asset exists throughout this useful life, and so must be accounted for in each year that it is in use.

The result is that a prediction is made regarding the expected lifetime of an asset, and its cost is spread over each year of that lifetime.

An expense, appropriately calculated, is included in the Profit and Loss Account, and the sum of all depreciation so far deducted from the item's original value in the Balance Sheet.

10.

Shares are just a share of a company. The owner of a share of the company is entitled to a share of the profits.

Ordinary shares are bought by people hoping to make a big profit, as the dividend is variable and will be larger if the company is successful. Ordinary shares give holders the right to vote at the AGM.

Preference shares are bought by people hoping to make a steady profit at lower risk, as the dividend is fixed like interest. Preference shares do not give holders the right to vote at the AGM, but holders do claim dividends before ordinary shareholders, and assets before ordinary holders if the company closes.

Answers

Note: questions marked (E) are genuine past AQA exam questions. Only short or partial answers for papers from 2001 and 2002, as provided by the author, are shown here. Answers for papers from 2003 and 2004 can be found by downloading the relevant mark sheet from the AQA web site: **www.aqa.org.uk/qual/gceasa/acc assess.html**.

1.2.1 Ian Heritage Ltd

Transaction	**Subsidiary Book**	**Account to be debited**	**Account to be credited**
Cheque sent to settle account with World Cups Ltd	Cash Book	World Cups Ltd	Bank
Cash discount given to Ainsley Ltd	Cash Book	Discounts allowed	Ainsley Ltd
Goods returned to World Cups Ltd	Returns out / purchase returns day book	World Cups Ltd	Returns out / purchase returns

1.2.2 Boris's Balalaikas

(a) Trade Discounts: offered because a customer buys from you regularly, e.g. they are 'in the trade'. You can make more money by keeping a regular customer with a discount. The discount is not recorded in the books as the selling price is reduced. Cash Discounts: given for paying your bill quickly. Getting paid quickly makes cash available to a business and you don't lose out on interest. Record it in the Cash Book.

(b)

4×55	£220
Less 15%	£33
	£187
Plus VAT at 17.5% × 90%	£29.45
	£216.45

1.2.3

Below are two possibilities. You could choose any three examples from the table in this chapter.

Subsidiary Book	**Source document**
Cash Book	Cheque counterfoil
Sales day book	Sales invoice

1.2.4

Document	**Subsidiary Book**	**Account to receive debit entry**	**Account to receive credit entry**
Invoice sent with goods to Zitaz Ltd	Sales day book	Zitaz Ltd	Sales / VAT
Invoice for new computer system received from Bishop's Ltd	Journal	Computers or machinery	Bishop's Ltd
Paying in slip	Cash Book	Bank	The account of the debtor

1.2.5 Gracetune Ltd

Invoice

$4 \times$ flute @ £170	£680
$2 \times$ tuba @ £190	£380
Subtotal	£1060
Less 20% trade discount	£212
Subtotal	£848
Plus VAT at 17.5% × 95%	£140.98
Total	£988.98

1.2.6

Transaction	Document	Book of Prime Entry
Giving a cash discount	Sales invoice	Cash book
Paying a small expense	Petty cash voucher or a receipt	Petty cash book
Returning goods to a supplier	Debit note	Returns out day book
Getting a cash discount	Purchase invoice	Cash book

1.2.7 (E) B E Jones (Wholesale)

(a) Total: £1041.23
(b) (i) purchase day book
(ii) sales day book
(c) See notes in this section.

Note: The full answer to this question, including suggested content for answers, should be found by downloading the relevant mark sheet from the AQA web site:
www.aqa.org.uk/qual/geeasa/acc_assess.html

1.2.8 (E) Wholesale Car Spares
(a) Credit note
(b) £905.30
(c) Returns out day book. 776.25, 129.05 = 905.30

1.3.1 The Iccing Bike Co.

(a)

VAT on credit sales		£402.50
VAT on cash sales (£822.50 × 17.5/117.5)		£122.50
		£525.00
Less VAT on credit purchases	£315.00	
Less VAT on new racks purchased (£423 × 17.5/117.5)	£63.00	(£378.00)
Balance due to HM Customs and Excise		£147.00

(b) Credit side

1.3.2

Lynne's Cane Furniture

Dr					Cr
Date		£	Date		£
01.01.10	Balance b/d	1,100	31.01.10	Returns Inwards	220
31.01.10	Sales	1,720	31.01.10	Bank	950
			31.01.10	Balance c/d	1,650
		2,820			2,820
01.02.10	Balance b/d	1,650			

1.3.3 Hayley's Comics

(a)

VAT Account

Dr					Cr
		£			£
31.10.12	Purchases	756.00	31.10.12	Returns out	56.00
"	Returns in	22.75	"	Credit Sales	1,256.50
"	Expenses	164.50	"	Cash Sales	353.50
	Balance c/d	722.75			
		1,666.00			1,666.00
				Balance b/d	722.75

(b) £ 722.75

1.3.4 (E) R Masters

(a) Cash sales VAT = 1 291.56, total = 4 965.01, balance c/d = 1 880.90

(b) It is the amount to be paid to HM Customs and Excise. It is in the current liabilities.

1.4.1 (E) J A Summerfield

(a) Column subtotals: Dr: 4.67; 517.23; 904.66.
Cr: 7.96; 517.23; 904.66.
Balances b/d: 50.00 (cash); 30.33 (bank).

(b) (i) Count the money.
(ii) Bank reconciliation.

(c) See notes in this section.

1.5.1

(a)

	Dr	*Cr*
General expenses	✓	
Sales		✓
Returns outwards		✓
Carriage inwards	✓	
Discounts received		✓
Interest paid	✓	
Carriage outwards	✓	
Drawings	✓	
Creditors		✓
Capital		✓
Last year's closing stock	✓	

1.5.2

(a) It can show up certain kinds of error in the books, i.e. those affecting one side or other of the Trial Balance.

(b) Limitation: If an error affects both sides, or neither, it will not be found.
Example 1: errors of omission, where a transaction has been left out of the books completely. The balance is unaffected.
Example 2: errors of commission, where a transaction has been entered in the correct side of the wrong account. The balance is unaffected.
Example 3: choose any of the examples in the chapter.

1.5.3

(a)

Chris'n'Jack Trial Balance – 31 March 2009

	Dr £	Cr £	
Sales		512,000	✔
Returns inwards		2,800	✘
Purchases	242,000		✔
Debtors	93,000		✔
Creditors		49,000	✔
Discounts allowed	1,700		✔
Discounts received	1,100		✘
Bank overdraft		23,000	✔
Cash		1,700	✘
Premises	120,000		✔
Electricity etc	800		✔
Carriage inwards		700	✘
Carriage outwards	600		✔
Returns outwards	2,100		✘
Stock (01.04.08)	17,000		✔
Capital	180,000		✘
Drawings	22,000		✔

1.5.4

(a) It is a list of balances in the accounts.

(b) Single entry/undercasting or overcasting of an account/entry of the wrong figure as one half of a double entry.

(c) Choose any of the examples in the chapter, e.g. error of omission, error of principle etc.

1.6.1

Trading Account for Francine and Debbie for the year ended 31.12.11

	£	£
Sales		48,000
Less returns inwards		(3,000)
		45,000
Less cost of sales		
Opening stock	9,000	
Purchases	22,000	
Carriage inwards	600	
Less Returns outwards	(2,000)	
	29,600	
Less closing stock	(5,000)	(24,600)
Gross Profit		20,400

1.6.2

Profit and Loss Account for Francine and Debbie for the year ended 31.12.11

	£	£
Gross profit		20,400
Discounts received		1,000
		21,400
Less Expenses		
Discounts allowed	1,500	
Power	900	
Bank charges	800	
General expenses	1,600	
Carriage outwards	500	
Motor expenses	1,100	(6,400)
Net Profit		15,000

1.6.3

Balance Sheet for Francine and Debbie at 31.12.11

	£	£	£
Fixed Assets			
Building	140,000	0	140,000
Vehicles	19,000	0	19,000
Equipment etc.	11,000	0	11,000
			170,000
Current assets			
Stock	5,000		
Debtors	8,000		
Bank	2,000		
Cash	1,000	16,000	
Less current liabilities			
Creditors		(7,000)	
Working capital			9,000
Less mortgage			(110,000)
			69,000
Financed by:			
Capital		70,000	
Add Net Profit		15,000	
		85,000	
Less drawings		(16,000)	
		69,000	

1.6.4

Trading and Profit and Loss Account for Hurle and Pennington
for the year ended 31.08.08

	£	£
Sales		390,000
Less returns inwards		(12,000)
		378,000
Less cost of sales		
Opening stock	28,000	
Purchases	140,000	
Carriage inwards	1,000	
Less returns outwards	(11,000)	
	158,000	
Less closing stock	(21,000)	(137,000)
Gross Profit		241,000
Discounts received		6,000
		247,000
Less expenses		
Carriage outwards	6,000	
Discounts allowed	5,000	
Electricity	4,000	
Gas	3,000	
General expenses	5,000	
Motor expenses	7,000	(30,000)
Net Profit		217,000

Balance Sheet for Hurle and Pennington at 31.08.08

	£	£	£
Fixed assets			
Premises	1,250,000	0	1,250,000
Vehicles	89,000	0	89,000
Equipment	224,000	0	224,000
			1,563,000
Current assets			
Stock	21,000		
Debtors	61,000		
Bank	14,000		
Cash	2,000	98,000	
Less current liabilities			
Creditors		(82,000)	
Working capital			16,000
Less mortgage			(800,000)
			779,000
Financed by:			
Capital		600,000	
Add Net Profit		217,000	
		817,000	
Less drawings		(38,000)	
		779,000	

1.6.5

Trading Account for Sandra Warden for the year ended 30.04.10

	£	£
Sales		692,000
Less returns inwards		(3,000)
		689,000
Less cost of sales		
Opening stock	48,000	
Purchases	354,000	
Carriage inwards	900	
Less returns outwards	(2,000)	
	400,900	
Less closing stock	(51,000)	(349,900)
Gross profit		339,100

1.6.6

(a)

Trading and Profit and Loss Account for DWR Productions for the year ended 30.11.07

	£	£
Sales		61,000
Less returns inwards		(1,000)
		60,000
Less cost of sales		
Opening stock	1,300	
Purchases	23,000	
Carriage inwards	800	
Less returns outwards	(1,100)	
	24,000	
Less closing stock	(1,260)	(22,740)
Gross profit		37,260
Discounts received		90
		37,350
Less expenses		
Electricity	640	
Carriage outwards	1,900	
General expenses	2,200	
Motor expenses	850	
Discounts allowed	140	(5,730)
Net Profit		31,620

(b)

(i) Drawings: capital/financed by
(ii) Cash: current assets
(iii) Premises: fixed assets
(iv) Bank overdraft: current liabilities

1.6.7

(i) Fixed assets: anything belonging to the business to use rather than sell on, that generally remains on the books from year to year.
Example: machinery

(ii) Current assets: anything belonging to or due to the business which is likely to vary from year to year.
Example: bank balance

(iii) Current liabilities: money the business owes which they expect to pay within a year
Example: money due to creditors

(iv) Long-term liabilities: money the business owes which they do not expect to pay within a year
Example: mortgage

(v) Capital/financed by: money due to the owner of the business, because it has been invested or because profit has been made.
Example: net profit

1.6.12 (E) R Masters

(a) (i) 56 581 less 32 530 = 24 051. See notes in this section.
(ii) Totals: 60 841, Credit balance b/d: 48 341.

(b) Net profit/loss, invest more capital, drawings.

1.6.13 (E) Amaryllis Trading

(a) Sales Cr: 16 493.27 and 4 560.30. Returns In Dr: 1 269.43 and 236.91. Purchases Dr: 10 276.41 and 2 769.56. Returns Out Cr: 1 039.41 and 127.50.

(b) 19 547.23 less 12 670.23 = 6 877.00.

(c) (i) 12 670.23, (ii) 15 311.19, (iii) 19 547.23

1.6.14 (E) Joe Kinsworth

(a) Profit Cr side. Drawings Dr side, Capital Cr side, totals = 202 973.

(b) 147 600, add 43 373 less 38 600 = 4 773, less 46 000 = 106 373. 94 373 add 24 000 less 12 000 = 106 373.

1.6.15 (E) Wholesale Car Spares

(a) Capital = 109 566, totals = 225 741

(b) 97 795 less 55 561 = 42 234

1.7.1 Tony and Lucy

(a) A bank reconciliation statement is used to make sure that the account for Bank shows the same figures as the bank's account for the business.

(b) The purchases ledger (total creditors) and sales ledger (total debtors) are verified by Control Accounts.

(c) A Suspense account is used as a temporary store for errors affecting the trial balance.

1.7.2 The Little Octopus Café

(a)

Suspense

Dr	£		Cr £
Sales	620	Balance	890
Returns out	180		
Discounts received	80		
Balance c/d	10		
	890		890
		Balance b/d	10

(b) Error of omission, where a transaction is not recorded in the books e.g. a purchase is made but no entry is made in the creditor's account or the purchases account. etc. Allow any three from the list in Chapter 1.5.

(c) The suspense account is only used for errors that affect the balance. Other errors only need to be recoded in the Journal.

1.7.3
(a)

Purchase Ledger Control Account

Dr 2007		£	2007		*Cr* £
1/7	Balance b/d	20	1/7	Balance b/d	12,390
31/7	Purchase returns	1,800	31/7	Purchases	72,900
31/7	Discounts received	60	31/7	Refunds for overpayment	30
31/7	Bank	69,150	31/7	Debit Balance	30
31/7	Contra set-off	70			
31/7	Credit Balance	14,250			
		85,350			85,350
1/8	Debit Balance	30	1/8	Credit Balance	14,250

(b) The closing credit balance represents money owed to creditors.

1.7.7 (E) A Smith and Co.
(a) (i) credited; (ii) credited; (iii) debited (see notes in this section).
(b) Credit side: 378 + 230 + 420 + 46 = 1 074.
Debit side: 540 + balance c/d 534 = 1 074.
(c) –600 (balance on statement) add 265, less 469, add 270 = –534 (balance on Bank account).

1.7.8 (E) R Masters
(a) Trial balance, control account, bank reconciliation
(b) Sales/suspense 270
returns in/suspense 800
suspense/discount received 400
J. Jones/A. Jones 350

1.7.10 (E) Wholesale Car Spares
(a) Can check the adding up in the sales or purchases ledger / shows up errors / guards against fraud by junior staff.
(b) Dr: 25 800 add 540 add 100 = 26 440.
Cr: 37 add 720 add balance c/d 25 683 = 26 440.
(c) See notes in this section.

1.8.1
Quiller's could adopt a spreadsheet package like Excel, to display plans and results in table form, or to calculate tax, interest and statistics easily. Or they could go further and adopt Sage Instant Accounting, a widely used package specifically for accounting, which will help them to integrate all of their accounting functions. Or they could go further still and adopt an AIS (accounting information system), which can be linked to stock control using a bar code scanner.

They can choose an 'off-the-shelf' package – a general system that fits most businesses, which is less expensive, but also less adaptable. Or they could choose a bespoke or customised package. This can be designed to work exactly the way the business wants, but could be expensive, so is probably only suited to a larger enterprise.

A computerised accounting system will also help Quiller's to produce reports automatically, with a more professional appearance, which would be important to a publishing company, especially when sending out invoices or customer statements. It would also help with error detection and exception reporting, like credit limits, stock levels and delivery times.

1.8.2

To: Mayglyn Motorbikes
From: *your name here*
Date: *today's date*
Subject: Uses, issues and advantages regarding upgrading a computer system

A new computerised system can be used to connect many different shop functions automatically, saving time and money and reducing mistakes. It produces reports quickly and automatically, with a more professional appearance, e.g. customer statements, financial statements, cash-flow analysis, pay rolls and stock reports.

Mayglyn needs to choose between an 'off-the-shelf' package – a general system that fits most businesses, which is less expensive but less adaptable, or a bespoke or customised package that can be designed to work exactly for the way your business wants.

Mayglyn also needs to consider that any change brings stress and needs management, that staff will need new training, although accounting skills are still more important than computing skills. The new system must comply with Data Protection Act 1998, and care must still be taken when inputting data.

He also needs to think whether the new computer system should replicate the old paper system, or be redesigned. Could he, for example, adapt an off-the-shelf package? He then needs to think about time scales, development, testing and how to introduce the new system.

Computerisation has the advantage that inputting information is only necessary once, as it can be done via EPOS (laser scanning) or document scanning, and moved around automatically. This increases speed, accuracy (since more automation reduces the opportunity for error), efficiency and consistency.

It could also help with error detection and exception reporting (it automatically flags problems), like credit limits, budget control, stock levels and other performance targets.

1.8.3

To: Rhys's Teapot Shop
Subject: options and problems when expanding a computer system

Rhys could consider:
Sage Instant Accounting

- A widely used package specifically for accounting

AIS (accounting information systems)
- Can be linked to EPOS (electronic point of sale) and stock control

Management Information System (MIS) which helps decision-making
- More job satisfaction
- Information can be
  - Stored in a smaller space
  - Accessed and cross referenced easily
  - Copied/backed up easily in case of accident

He should also choose between:

An 'off-the-shelf' package – a general system that fits most businesses
- Less expensive
- But is it exactly what he wants?

A bespoke/customised package
- Can be designed to work exactly for the way his business wants
- Could be expensive

A computerised system does the same job, but better:

Input is only necessary once
- Can be done via
  - EPOS – laser scanning
  - Document scanning

Calculations are made automatically
Passwords can improve security
Skilled staff are more productive

Increases
- Speed (saves time)
- Accuracy (more automation reduces the opportunity for error)
- Efficiency
- Consistency

Produces reports automatically
- Quicker, more reliable, more professional appearance
- Customer statements
- Financial statements
- Cash-flow analysis
- Pay rolls
- Stock reports

Error detection / Exception reporting (automatically flags problems)
Credit limits – are your customers buying more than they can pay for?
Budget control – are limits being broken?
Low levels of stock – is it time to re-order?
Delivery times – are we meeting all of our performance targets?

There may, however, be problems. Any change brings stress and needs management

- Staff will need new training
- Must comply with Data Protection Act 1998
- Increased reporting efficiency can bring information overload
- Will better efficiency mean that redundancies are necessary?

1.8.4 Wrod's Quads
See notes in this section.

1.8.5 Legs By Liz
See notes in this section.

2.3.1

Sheng Motors want to revalue their premises, which were bought for £130,000 several years ago, but are now valued at £180,000.

(a) Fixed assets
(b) It would increase by £50,000
(c) It would need to add £50,000 to a revaluation reserve in the capital section.

2.3.2

Isabel & Owen Ltd

(a) Start with profit of £107,000. Discounts received should have been added not deducted. Replace £1,000 and then add it again. Deduct the motor expense of £2,500. The error of principle with the computer doesn't affect the trial balance, but it will affect the profit. Add £21,000 back on. Deduct the remaining balance for business rates of £9,000. We deducted £4,500 and added £3,000 when it should have been the other way around. Add £1,500 twice to compensate.

	107 000
add 2 000	= 109 000
less 2 500	= 106 500
add 21 000	= 127 500
less 9 000	= 118 500
add 3 000	= <u>£121 500</u>

(b) The computer will need to appear in the fixed assets section. The capital will need to be adjusted to account for the new net profit.

2.4.1

Profit and cash flow are different. A Cash Flow Statement will show movements of cash that can't be seen in profit statements, and shows the differences between a firm's profit levels and cash levels.

Cash is the liquid assets actually available to be spent by the business. Profit is the difference on the books between revenue and the expenses incurred in generating that revenue.

It is compulsory for all but the smallest businesses to make a statement under FRS1, one of the rules of accounting.

Poor cash flow is more dangerous to a business than poor profit. For this reason, everyone involved in a business will be interested in seeing how it is doing.

2.4.2
The Directors' Report will generally include the financial performance for the last year, e.g. revenue, profit, debt, share prices and dividends. It will also advise about transfers to reserves, assets that have been acquired or disposed of, the names and shareholdings of directors active in the last year, and other business activities that will be of interest to stakeholders.

It may also cover the firm's policies on employment, training, welfare, creditor payment or corporate responsibility. Any other significant activity, like donations to charity, will also be included, along with prospects for the coming year.

The directors should announce the AGM (annual general meeting), when shareholders can vote on aspects like electing directors and accepting the ordinary dividend.

The Auditors' Report should describe their responsibilities and those of the directors, describe the basis of their assessment of the financial statements, and confirm that the financial statements have been prepared in accordance with the Companies Act 1985, and that they give a true and fair picture of the company's affairs

2.4.3
Intangible fixed assets will be found in the fixed assets section.

A patent is an intangible asset. It is classed as one because it is owned by the company, can be sold, and is used to generate profit.

2.4.4
Suppliers will use published accounts to check on the liquidity of the business. They will want to see that enough assets are held in liquid form so they will get paid. This is important since businesses have problems due to liquidity more than due to low profits.

Shareholders will use published accounts to see how hard their money is working for them. They will be interested in the profitability of the business. They will want to see a good return on investment, a good profit margin, and will want to see that expenses (like paying suppliers) are kept as low as possible.

3.1.1
(a) Net realisable value
(b) Amplifier: £120 as the purchase price is lower than the net realisable value Guitar: £74 as the net realisable value is lower than the purchase price Snare drum: £49 as the purchase price is lower than the net realisable value
(c) Prudence

3.1.2
(a) £39
(b) £48.50
(c) 4 × £39 = £156
(d) 10 × 4.99 = £49.90, less £20 = 29.90

3.2.1 Shaun Wayne
(a) 27,000 × 25% × 3 = 20,250. 27,000 less 20,250 = 6,750. 5,999 less 6,750 = £751 loss. You must make clear that it's a loss.

(b) It is recorded as an expense in the profit and loss account.
(c) 5,999 less 5,832 = £167 profit.

3.2.2 Steve De'ath
(a) Straight-line: 14,000 × 30% = £4,200.
Reducing balance: 14,000 × 50% = £7,000.
(b) Depreciation affects profit, not cash flow.
(c) Depreciation is an expense and so reduces Net Profit. The straight line option gives the smaller expense in this case, and so higher Net Profit.
(d) The straight line option leaves the machinery worth more after one year in this case.
(e) Net Profit adds to capital. Straight line, since it gives higher Net Profit.
(f) Straight-line: 14,000 – (3 × 4,200) = £1,400.
Reducing balance: 14,000 × 50% × 50% × 50% = £1,750

3.2.3
(a)

Profit and Loss Account – Lee Noogan – 31 May 2009

	£	£
Gross Profit		74 700
Discounts received		1 500
Bad debts recovered		300
		76 500
Less Expenses		
Depreciation (machinery) (10,000 × 20%)	2 000	
Depreciation (vehicles) ((19,000 – 5,700) × 30%)	3 990	
Bad debts	100	
Provision for doubtful debt	500	
Discounts allowed	600	
Other expenses (30 200 + 4 000 – 1 500)	32 700	39 890
Net Profit		36 610

(b)

Balance Sheet Lee Noogan 31 May 2009

	£	£	£
Fixed Assets			
Building	230 000	0	230 000
Vehicles	19 000	9 690	9 310
Machinery	10 000	4 000	6 000
			245 310
Current Assets			
Stock	1 800		
Debtors	60 000		
Less provision for doubtful debt	(4 500)		
Prepayments	1 500	58 800	
Less Current Liabilities			
Creditors	41 000		
Accruals	4 000		
Bank	1 000	(46 000)	
Working Capital			12 800
			258 110
Financed by:			
Capital	240 000		
Add Net Profit	36 610		
	276 610		
Less Drawings	(18 500)		
	258 110		

3.2.8 (E) Vlasmin plc
+ 50 000; + 50 000; + 50 000; no change; no change.
no change; – 25 000; no change; no change; no change.
no change; –43 000; –43 000; no change; + 43 000.

3.2.9 (E) Abel Brown
(a) 278 400 less 152 500 = 125 900 gross profit.
Less 117 800 = 8 100 net profit.
(b) £11 100.

3.2.10 (E) Mary Khan
+ 190; no change; + 190; no change; no change.
+ 1 200; no change; + 1 200; no change; no change.

3.3.1 Lucia Walters
(a) Buying or improving fixed assets that are used to make money for the business.
(b) Spending on expenses or on stock, including repairs and maintenance.

(c)

Installing new sign	210
Extending the patio	950
New tables, chairs and parasols	720
	1 880

(d)

Repainting woodwork	150
Replacing broken glass	80
Extra labour	90
Hire of outdoor heaters	55
	375

3.4.2 (E) Cathy Yow

(a) Materials: 9 000 add 63 600 less 9 400 = 63 200.
Add 150 250 and 8 140 = 221 590.

(b) £100

(c) See notes in section 3.5 on concepts.

3.4.3 (E) Jacqui King plc

(a) Materials: 47 600 + 498 000 less 50900 = 494 700.
Add 639 600 + 17 000 = 1 151 300 Prime Cost.
Add (319 800 + 48 000 + 548 000 =) 915 800 = 2 067 100.
Add 23 000, less 24 100 = 2 066 000 Total production cost.

(b) Money you have to pay for patents / copyrights / ideas and designs.

3.5.1

(a) The prudence concept The accruals concept

(b) The prudence concept says you should not overstate the value of an asset like stock. This means you must use the net realisable value for an item if it is lower than the purchase cost.
The accruals concept says you should match revenues against expenses. This means you must add opening stock to the figure for purchases for the year, and deduct closing stock.

3.5.2

(a) The accruals concept states that revenues must be matched against the expenses incurred to generate them.
Accruals refers to the time period in which activity takes place. Credit transactions mean there's a time difference between the revenue being generated and cash being received, and also between expenses being incurred and cash being spent. Revenue, or income, is generated when a sale is made, not necessarily when it's paid for. Expense, meanwhile, is incurred when a purchase is made, not when it is paid for.
The accruals concept means that profit depends on revenue and expense, not the receipts and payments of cash.

(b) Since bad debts have to be matched against the sales they apply to, we make a provision – an estimate of which debts for this time period will be found to be bad in the next one.

An asset which is used in the business and lasts more than a year cannot be called an expense in one year. Its cost must be spread over the years when it is used to help generate revenue.

3.5.3

(i) The going concern concept states that the financial statements (e.g. Balance Sheet) should assume that the business will still be running next year. An asset like a vehicle may be depreciated over its useful life to the business. At any stage its value on the books may be greater than (or less than) the price that would be paid by another business. If the business will continue to operate then this difference is not critical.

(ii) The cost, or historical cost, concept, states that an asset should normally be recorded at its purchase price (unless it has been depreciated). If an asset like a building increases in value, it will still normally be recorded as being worth its purchase value.

3.5.4

An asset which is used in the business and lasts more than a year cannot be called an expense in one year. Its cost must be spread over the years when it is used to help generate revenue. This complies with the accruals concept.

If an asset has previously been depreciated using the straight line method, a business should not change to the reducing balance method, or vice versa. This complies with the consistency concept.

3.5.5

(i) The accurals concept: revenues must be matched against the expenses incurred to generate them. For example, since many transactions are made on credit, an accounting period looks at the sales and purchases, not the receipts and payments.

(ii) The prudence concept: profits should not be overstated (nor understated). For example, we should not list the value of stock at its purchase price if its net sale price would be lower.

(iii) If a sale is agreed in principle but has not actually been made, when the accounting period ends, it should not be counted as a sale. Accruals states that revenues should be matched against expenses, and this revenue belongs in next year's accounts. Prudence states that profits should not be overstated.
This example can also be applied to the realisation concept.
You could also have mentioned depreciation or doubtful debt.

3.5.6 Cliff's Theatricals

(ii) Concept: consistency
Reason: once a procedure has been adopted it should be continued.
Action: continue to use 15%.

(iii) Concept: prudence
Reason: figures should not be overstated, and some debtors may not pay.
Action: make a provision for doubtful debt.

(iv) Concept: historical cost
Reason: assets should be recorded at their cost price.
Action: leave it at its original value.

(v) Concept: prudence
Reason: values should not be overstated.
Action: use the net realisable value.

(vi) Concept: accruals (or realisation)
Reason: a transaction is recorded when it is made, not when money changes hands.
Action: record the purchase.

(vii) Concept: accruals
Reason: expenses should be matched against revenues.
Action: subtract the payment for October and account for it next year.

(viii) Concept: business entity
Reason: accounts measure the money of the business, not the owner.
Action: class the assets as goods taken for own use.

(ix) Concept: objectivity
Reason: an accountant should not allow subjective feelings to affect the neutrality of the accounts.
Action: record the value as £7.

(x) Concept: materiality
Reason: if a long-term asset is inexpensive enough to be of no material interest, it should be counted as an expense.
Action: allow it as an expense over one year of £9.90.

3.5.7 (E)

Lotte Betz: The business entity concept. Enter the whole £36,000 as drawings.
Harry Jones: The accruals or prudence or realisation concept. Don't include the sale in the year ending June 2001.

3.6.1 Zanchetta RDL

(a) Ordinary shares are rewarded with a variable dividend which depends on profit, whilst preference shares are rewarded with a fixed percentage. Ordinary shares have the advantage that the dividend will be low in an unprofitable year, but the disadvantage that the profit will need to be shared in a good year. Preference shares have the advantage that the pay-out is relatively low in a good year, but a burden in a poor year.
(b) Issued ordinary share capital.
(c) Buildings reserve, general reserve, retained profit (30.04.08).
(d) Profit adds to capital. All shareholders, including Carl, own this capital. Any undistributed profit is being used to support assets and activity in the business. Carl has not lost his money; his share of the profit has simply not been paid out.
(e) The value of shares has risen, and the extra 60p per share is a share premium. This money will be recorded as a share premium in the capital section of the balance sheet, with the regular entry for ordinary shares. The premium means that Carl's new shares entitle him to an equal claim on the company's assets.

3.6.2

See notes in this section.

3.6.6 (E) Grift Ltd

(a) Authorised or Nominal share capital is the maximum amount of capital a company can have. The company must state in its Memorandum of Association a figure for this. If they need more money than their maximum they have to vote for it at the AGM.

However, the directors may choose only to sell enough shares to raise the finance they need. These shares are issued, and the money raised is Issued Share Capital. It can issue more shares at a later date if it needs to raise more money.

(b) Fixed: 270 000 + 150 000 + 170 000 = 590 000.
Current: Add (27 000 less 24 000 =) 3 000 = 593 000.
Capital: 500 000 + 93 000 = 593 000.

(c) You can choose from: limiting liability to protect personal assets, losing control of business to other shareholders, ability to expand by attracting more capital, whether to issue shares or debentures. See notes in this section.

3.6.7 (E) Leroy McDade plc

(a) 546 000 less 180 000 = 366 000
less 50 000 = 316 000, less (40 000 + 160 000 =) 200 000 = 116 000.

(b) (i) Capital: 1 600 000 + 800 000 + 200 000 + 728 000 = 3 428 000.
(ii) Creditors: 78 200 + 180 000 + 160 000 + 7000 = 425 200.

(c) Debentures: predictable rate of return, low risk, first claim on assets if the company closes, investment will be reclaimed in the period 2020–2025 in this instance, might miss out on big dividends or growth in value of shares. Ordinary shares can sell at any time at current value which may be more or less than was paid for them. More risky investment. Value of shares can increase or fall. Dividend is variable, depending on performance of business. Right to vote at AGM.
See notes in this section. Try to identify the advantages and disadvantages of each clearly to gain points.

4.1.1

(a) Fixed costs don't change (or 'vary') with output. They stay fixed for a given period, and can be called 'period costs'. Examples include rent and interest payments variable costs, however, do change with output. Examples include raw material and labour.

(b) A semi-variable cost is part fixed and part variable.

(c) Marginal cost is the cost of making one more unit. It has the same meaning as variable cost.

(d) Variable, or marginal costs.

4.2.1 Madobie Ltd

(a) Price less variable costs per unit. 39 – 19 = £20

(b) Fixed costs divided by contribution. 3 000 / 20 = 190 units

(c) Break-even volume × price. 190 × 39 = £7 410

(d) Sales volume × contribution less fixed costs. 350 × 20 – 3 800 = £3 200

(e) Sales volume less break-even volume. 350 – 190 = 160 units

(f) £4.

4.2.2 Vicky Faversham Ltd

	£
Total fixed costs	2 200
Total variable costs	4 000
Variable costs per unit	80
Contribution per unit	110
Breakeven quantity	20
Expected profit	3 300

4.2.4 (E) Pinder Ltd

(a) Sale price per unit less variable costs per unit. Contribution pays off fixed costs and adds to profit.

(b) (i) 44 less 34 = 10, (ii) 44 less 31.50 = 12.50.

(c) Profit without machinery: 22 000 × 10 less 134 000 = 86 000.
Profit with machinery: 22 000 × 12.50 less 166 000 = 109 000.
There may be little benefit in the short term, with the cost of training and the depreciation of the new machinery. However, the increase in contribution will give a higher profit in the long term.

4.2.5 (E) Suddley Ltd

(a) (i) Formula: Sale price per unit less variable costs per unit.
Definition: Contribution is the money available after variable costs to pay off fixed costs and add to profit.
Calculation: 50 less 35 = 15

(ii) Formula: fixed costs ÷ contribution.
Definition: The minimum volume that must be produced and sold to cover all costs, or the revenue value of sales at this volume.
Calculation: 450 000 ÷ 15 = 30 000 units or £1 500 000

(b) Fixed costs = B, Revenue = D, Break-even = C, Margin of safety = A.

(c) 1 750 000 less approx 1 650 000 = 100 000

(d) Lower price means less contribution and higher break-even point. In this case 450 000 ÷ (47 – 35) = 37 500 units, which is the whole capacity. No extra capacity is available to make a profit. A lower price should mean higher demand, although, in effect, the margin of safety would be reduced to zero.

4.3.1 Sarah Brazil Films Ltd

(a) For each of the following, state the formula and calculate the figure for each year.
(i) Current assets / current liabilities: 1.17, 1.05
(ii) Current assets less stock / current liabilities: 0.67, 0.63
(iii) Creditors / purchases × 365: 60 days, 55 days
(iv) Debtors / sales × 365: 29 days, 25 days
(v) Average stock / cost of sales × 365: 17 / 218 × 365 = 28.5 days, 17.5 / 271 × 365 = 23.6 days

(vi) Net profit / capital: 12.6%, 16.7%
(vii) Net profit / sales: 8%, 10%
(viii) Gross profit / cost of sales: 82 / 218 – 37.6%, 109 / 271 – 40.2%

(b) The liquidity ratios are smaller in 2008 than in 2007. Liquidity is lean and getting leaner using the current ratio, but dangerously tight and getting tighter using the acid test ratio. Sarah could consider lengthening her creditor payment period and shortening her debtor collection period to correct this, although they are both very favourable already.
Sarah's efficiency ratios are all good. Creditor payment, debtor collection and stock turn are all getting shorter.
The profit ratios are all bigger in 2008 than in 2007. ROCE is good in 2007 and very healthy in 2008, and the mark-up looks good.

4.3.4 (E) Williamson Ltd

(a) Working capital is the money that is actively moving in the business, i.e. it is used for regular trading and expenses, not for fixed assets. It is the difference between current assets and current liabilities, and represents net liquid assets.

(b) (i) CA ÷ CL = 1.52 : 1
(ii) (CA – stock) ÷ CL = 0.86 : 1
(iii) Debtors ÷ sales × 365 = 44 days
(iv) Creditors ÷ purchases × 365 = 50 days

(c) (i) Reduces debtors, so reduces current assets and decreases the working capital ratio and the acid test ratio. This means worse liquidity. With the asset of this cash owing gone, Williamson has less liquid assets to operate with. The debtor collection period, however, has also decreased.
(ii) Stock is 50% higher at the end of the year. More stock means a higher working capital ratio, but has no effect on the acid test ratio. This means that liquidity is not decreased, unless slow stock movement means that creditors are getting paid without cash coming in.

4.4.3 (E) N Kayali, Strudwick Stationers Ltd

(a) May: receipts: 44 400, payments: 48 600.
Opening balance: 12 100, net cash flow = –4 200, closing balance = 7 900
June: receipts: 45 600, payments: 47 400.
Opening balance: 7 900, net cash flow = –1 800, closing balance = 6,100
July: receipts: 42 800, payments: 48 400.
Opening balance: 6,100, net cash flow = –5 600, closing balance = 500
August: receipts: 43 600, payments: 46 300.
Opening balance: 500, net cash flow = –2 700, closing balance = –2 200

(b) By making a plan the business can see problems before they become problems, and take action to deal with them in good time. In this case, it can act to reduce the net negative cash flow, or arrange a loan facility. It improves coordination and efficiency.

4.4.4 (E) Peversal Papers Ltd

(a) March: receipts: 88 451, payments: 83 200.
Opening balance: 6 000, net cash flow = 5 251, closing balance = 11 251
April: receipts: 99 440, payments: 95 200.

Opening balance: 11 251, net cash flow = 4 240, closing balance = 15 491
May: receipts: 110 429, payments 102 800
Opening balance: 15 491, net cash flow = 7 629, closing balance = 23 120

(b) Production: March: 4 600, April: 5 100, May: 5 400

(c) Planning: allows you to prepare for purchases, labour, storage etc. A purchases budget needs a production budget first. Aids coordination, decision making, target setting, cash flow etc.

4.4.5 (E) Sunshine Ltd

(a) July: receipts: 20 400, payments: 24 000
Opening balance: –7 200, net cash flow = –3 600, closing balance = –10 800
August: receipts: 25 200, payments: 26 000
Opening balance: –10 800, net cash flow = –800, closing balance = –11 600
September: receipts: 26 800, payments: 22 000
Opening balance: –11 600, net cash flow = 4 800, closing balance = –6 800
October: receipts: 24 000, payments: 16 000
Opening balance: –6 800, net cash flow = 8 000, closing balance = 1 200

(b) (i) The position improves dramatically for Sunshine Ltd. The cash coming in increases by several thousand over the period, from 20 400 to around 24 000. The cash going out decreases steadily by several thousand from 24 000 to 16 000. This changes a negative cash flow in July into a positive cash flow in October. This in turn changes the bank balance from a £7 200 overdraft to a £1 200 positive balance.

(ii) The large overdraft in August (£11 600) should be managed, for example by making an overdraft arrangement with the bank. Debtors could be encouraged to pay more quickly, perhaps by offering a larger cash discount. Creditors could be asked to reschedule payments until a positive balance is available. Sunshine could consider buying less stock in July and August.

4.5.1 Jesper Hansen

(a) (i) £1 200 000
(ii) £1 030 000
(iii) £780 000

(b) Option (i) is financially unsustainable as he makes a loss, which would result in closure of the facility in the long term and the loss of all jobs. Option (ii) is regrettable, since the lost jobs will cause stress and hardship and will have a knock-on economic effect in the local community. However, the remaining staff will benefit from the training and will not feel too insecure about their jobs. The money saved may be enough to sustain the business. Option (iii) offers the greatest profit, but would involve a lot of work and risk, and would result in a lot of hardship in the local community if the whole facility closes.

4.5.2 Abercrombie Davis and Briggs Ltd

(a) Write a report to the directors of Abercrombie Davis and Briggs Ltd, advising them of the consequences of these courses of action:

(i) For shareholders: all of the above measures would increase profits in the short term, but might lead to long-term reductions.

(ii) Employees: a reduction in quality control costs and waste management costs could affect morale, while a reduction in health and safety costs would almost certainly mean more accidents and days off work.

(iii) Customers: a reduction in quality control costs could mean that they use faulty or substandard medical equipment.

(iv) The environment: a reduction in waste management costs would probably lead to less recycling or pollution.

(b) A reduction in quality control costs could result in a lower quality product, lower sales, and lower profits in the long term. A reduction in health and safety costs could mean lower productivity in the long term, or that profits are reduced by fines or higher insurance premiums. A reduction in waste management costs could damage the firm's reputation, and affect sales. The company also needs to be sure that it doesn't break any laws governing the measures, which could have very serious consequences for profit.

4.5.3 Doug Green

If Doug sells on the seat covers, he could make a good profit from unusual merchandise in a country where there could be a market for such items. He would also be helping people in a struggling economy to make a living in a country where resources are limited. However, if the animals are endangered, he would be helping to make the species extinct by providing money for the poachers. He should also beware that the sale is probably illegal and he should be careful of being punished by the law. Bad publicity would be bad for business. Doug should investigate the facts thoroughly and consider his options.

Index